Issues of State Responsibility before International Judicial Institutions

This book contains papers presented at a high-level conference jointly organised by the Institute of Global Law, University College London and the Institute of International Law, Queen Mary, University of London. The chapters cover issues of State Responsibility before the following international judicial institutions: the International Court of Justice, International Tribunal for the Law of the Sea, World Trade Organization, United Nations Compensation Commission, International Centre for the Settlement of Investment Disputes, and International and Regional Human Rights Courts.

Issues of State Responsibility before International Judicial Institutions

Edited by

Malgosia Fitzmaurice
Queen Mary, University of London

and

Dan Sarooshi
The Queen's College, Oxford

The Clifford Chance Lectures
Volume 7

·HART·
PUBLISHING

OXFORD AND PORTLAND OREGON
2004

Published in North America (US and Canada) by
Hart Publishing
c/o International Specialized Book Services
5804 NE Hassalo Street
Portland, Oregon
97213-3644
USA

Hart Publishing is a specialist legal publisher based in Oxford, England.
To order further copies of this book or to request a list of other
publications please write to:

Hart Publishing, Salters Boatyard, Folly Bridge, Abingdon Rd, Oxford,
OX1 4LB Telephone: +44 (0)1865 245533 Fax: +44 (0)1865 794882
e-mail: mail@hartpub.co.uk
WEBSITE: http//:www.hartpub.co.uk

British Library Cataloguing in Publication Data
Data Available

ISBN 1-84113-389-2 (hardback)

Typeset by Olympus Infotech Pvt Ltd, India, Sabon 10/12pt
Printed and bound in Great Britain by
Lightning Source UK Ltd

Table of Contents

Preface

The contribution of the International Law Commission (ILC) to the codification and progressive development of international law in the period since its first session in 1949 has been nothing short of remarkable. The ILC's Articles on State Responsibility, although taking over 50 years to produce, can rightly be regarded as one of the ILC's most important contributions to the system of international law.[1] The ILC, however, is not the only body that makes such contributions. International courts and tribunals have increasingly played an important role in clarifying and developing a number of areas of international law, including the law of State responsibility. It is the purpose of this volume to examine the treatment by international courts and tribunals of the law of State responsibility. There is consideration of specific courts and tribunals including the International Court of Justice (chapters by Rosalyn Higgins, Ian Brownlie, Malcolm Shaw and Maurice Mendelson), the European Court of Human Rights (Benedetto Conforti and Malcolm Evans), the International Covenant on Civil and Political Rights (Dominic McGoldrick) and the UN Compensation Commission (Olufemi Elias); the chapters by Christopher Greenwood on State responsibility for the decisions of national courts, Guy Goodwin-Gill on asylum and refugees, Matthew Craven on human rights, and Gerhard Loibl on the environment are more thematic in their focus.

This volume would not have been produced without the generous support of Clifford Chance, the Institute of Global Law (and its Director Basil Markesinis), and the International Law Institute at Queen Mary College, University of London (and the Vice-Principal of Queen Mary College, Philip Ogden) to whom the editors wish to express their thanks.

[1] On the history of the topic of State responsibility in the ILC, see J Crawford, *The International Law Commission's Articles on State Responsibility: Introduction, Text and Commentaries* (Cambridge, 2002), p 1 *et seq*.

1

Issues of State Responsibility before the International Court of Justice

ROSALYN HIGGINS*

ISSUES OF STATE responsibility have engaged the attention of both the Permanent Court of International Justice and the International Court of Justice (the 'Court'). Every law student knows that the phrase 'State responsibility' in an exam question requires reference to the *Factory at Chorzów* case[1] in the answer. Issues of State responsibility before the Court may be said to have fallen into three broad categories. First, do the actions concerned actually engage the responsibility of the State concerned? Second, if the respondent State is responsible for an international wrong, what is the appropriate remedy? Third—and it is a more recent manifestation—what is the relationship between the law of State responsibility and other applicable substantive law in the particular case? On 10 October 2002, in the Court's judgment in the *Land and Maritime Boundary between Cameroon and Nigeria (Cameroon v Nigeria)* case,[2] a fourth aspect of the law of State responsibility was very much in focus, although the case principally concerned territorial title.

This paper touches very lightly on the first three categories, and focuses a little more on the last. Before doing so, there is a general observation to make: Since the early 1970's, the periodic findings on State responsibility that the Court has had occasion to make have been pronouncements handed down against the background of intermittent work by the International Law Commission on State responsibility,[3] recently culminating, of course, in the

* DBE, QC; Judge, International Court of Justice.

[1] *Factory at Chorzów* case, *Jurisdiction, 1927, PCIJ, Series A, No 9*; *Merits, 1928, PCIJ, Series A, No 17.*

[2] *Land and Maritime Boundary between Cameroon and Nigeria (Cameroon v Nigeria: Equatorial Guinea intervening), Judgment, 2002;* available at http://www.icj-cij.org/icjwww/idocket/icn/icnframe.htm.

[3] For the text of the articles and a commentary, see J Crawford, *The International Law Commission's Articles on State Responsibility: Introduction, Text and Commentaries*

final impressive and scholarly push to the articles which were the subject of a General Assembly Resolution adopted on 12 December 2001.[4] Whether there is a symbiotic relationship to be traced is for others to decide.

1. ATTRIBUTION OF CONDUCT TO THE STATE

Certain cases have focused on attribution of conduct to the State. On 4 November 1979, the United States Embassy in Tehran was occupied by what the Court termed 'militants'.[5] The United States alleged violations by Iran of both the Consular Convention[6] and the Treaty of Amity of 1955.[7] The Court found that although the attacks on the Embassy and on Consulates the following day 'cannot be considered as in itself imputable to the Iranian State', Iran was however in violation of its *own* obligations under the Diplomatic and Consular Conventions, in particular to take all appropriate steps to protect the premises.[8] In *Military and Paramilitary Activities in and against Nicaragua (Nicaragua v United States of America)*,[9] the Court had imposed the test of effective control to determine whether the activities of the *Contras* were attributable to the United States. (This is the test effectively not followed by the International Criminal Tribunal for the Former Yugoslavia in the *Tadic* case[10]). Another example of this first category of State responsibility issues in the jurisprudence of the Court is to be found in the *Cumaraswamy* case.[11] The Court cited the rule enunciated in the then draft articles of the ILC that 'the conduct of any organ of a State must be regarded as an act of that State', and categorised it as a customary rule of international law.[12] It applied the rule to the failure of the Malaysian courts to deal with the immunity issues *in limine litis*, that is, at the outset.

(Cambridge, 2002). See also the earlier work of S Rosenne, *The International Law Commission's Draft Articles on State Responsibility* (Dordrecht, 1991).

[4] Resolution adopted by the General Assembly, 85th plenary meeting, 12 Dec 2001. UN Doc: A/RES/56/83.

[5] *United States Diplomatic and Consular Staff in Tehran (United States of America v Iran)* case, *Judgment, ICJ Reports*, 1980, p 3 at p 12 (para 17).

[6] Vienna Convention on Consular Relations, done at Vienna on 24 April 1963, entered into force on 19 March 1967.

[7] The Treaty of Amity, Economic Relations, and Consular Rights between the United States of America and Iran, done at Tehran on 15 Aug 1955, entered into force on 16 June 1957.

[8] *United States of America v Iran* case, above n 5, pp 29–30 (especially para 61).

[9] *Military and Paramilitary Activities in and against Nicaragua (Nicaragua v United States of America)* case, *Merits, Judgment, ICJ Reports*, 1986, p 14 at p 65 (para 115), see also p 62 (para 109).

[10] *The Prosecutor v Dusko Tadic*, International Criminal Tribunal for the Former Yugoslavia, Appeals Chamber, 15 July 1999 (Case No IT–94–1–A), pp 47–92 (paras 115–145).

[11] *Difference Relating to Immunity from Legal Process of a Special Rapporteur of the Commission on Human Rights, Advisory Opinion, ICJ Reports*, 1999, p 62.

[12] *Ibid*, p 87 (para 62).

2. APPROPRIATE REMEDIES AND THE RELATIONSHIP OF STATE RESPONSIBILITY TO JURISDICTION

As to remedies, I have already referred to the *Factory at Chorzów* case. Everyone knows the celebrated *dictum* of the Permanent Court that 'it is a principle of international law, and even a general conception of law, that any breach of an engagement involves an obligation to make reparation'.[13] What is less well recalled is that in that case the Court also made observations alluded to in the following statement of *LaGrand*:

> where jurisdiction exists over a dispute on a particular matter, no separate basis for jurisdiction is required by the Court to consider the remedies a party has requested for the breach of the obligation.[14]

Nonetheless, the point was pleaded again by the United States in the *LaGrand* case,[15] where it contended that the Court's jurisdiction flowed only from the Consular Convention, whereas the guarantees and assurances of non-repetition sought by Germany lay in the law of State responsibility. The Court again confirmed that no separate basis of jurisdiction was required for it to consider the appropriate remedy for a particular breach of the Consular Convention.

Before leaving remedies I will also briefly recall that in neither the *LaGrand* case nor in the recent *Land and Maritime Boundary between Cameroon and Nigeria (Cameroon v Nigeria)* judgment did the Court show an inclination to order guarantees of non-repetition, different reasoning being given in each case.[16]

3. THE RELATIONSHIP OF STATE RESPONSIBILITY TO SUBSTANTIVE LAW

Our third category of case—the *substantive* (as opposed to jurisdictional) relationship between an applicable norm and the law of State responsibility—was

[13] *Factory at Chorzów* case, *Merits, 1928, PCIJ, Series A, No 17* at p 29.

[14] *LaGrand (Germany v United States of America)* case, *Merits, Judgment*, 2001, at para 48; available at: www.icj-cij.org/icjwww/idocket/igus/igusframe.htm; citing *Factory at Chorzów* case, *PCIJ, Series A, No 9*, p 22.

[15] *LaGrand* case, *ibid.*

[16] In both cases the Court found it unnecessary to order guarantees of non-repetition. In *Cameroon v Nigeria*, the Court held that while Cameroon's submissions in this regard were undoubtedly admissible: 'the judgment in itself specifies in definitive and mandatory terms the land and maritime boundary between the two States. With all uncertainty dispelled in this regard, the Court cannot envisage a situation where either Party, after withdrawing its military and police forces and administration from the other's territory, would fail to respect the territorial sovereignty of that Party. Hence Cameroon's submissions on this point cannot be upheld'. (*Cameroon v Nigeria*, above n 2, para 318.)

very much in play in the *Gabčíkovo-Nagymaros Project (Hungary/Slovakia)* case.[17] There the question arose as to whether a treaty may lawfully be terminated or suspended *only* through application of the substantive rules governing the law of treaties; or whether the State responsibility provisions on non-wrongfulness of conduct (for example, a state of necessity)[18] *also* excuse termination or suspension of a treaty. If these questions received no clear answer from the Court in that case, nor do they from the International Law Commission in its Final Articles. The matter is still open.[19]

4. A FOURTH CATEGORY: REQUESTS FOR SEPARATE FINDINGS OF STATE RESPONSIBILITY AS A CONSEQUENCE OF FINDINGS OF ILLEGAL CONDUCT

In the *Land and Maritime Boundary between Cameroon and Nigeria (Cameroon v Nigeria)* case, the Court was faced with requests that it should make findings in the field of State responsibility.[20] The foundation of these requests developed and changed through the Application, Additional Application and Final Submissions. And they were somewhat unusual requests, because they assumed particular findings that the Court was not in terms asked to make. Let me explain each of these observations.

At issue in the case was title to the Bakassi Peninsula in the south, the location of the international boundary in Lake Chad in the north and the correct line on the long land boundary in between.

In its Application, Cameroon did *not* ask the Court to adjudge and declare that Nigeria had invaded the Bakassi Peninsula and in so doing had

In *La Grand*, the Court was satisfied that actions taken by the United States to institute a programme of reviewing and improving its procedures under consular notification obligations were already sufficient to meet Germany's request for guarantees of non-repetition. The Court said: 'The Court considers that the commitment expressed by the United States to ensure implementation of the specific measures adopted in performance of its obligations under Article 36, paragraph 1 *(b)*, must be regarded as meeting Germany's request for a general assurance of non-repetition.' (*La Grand* case, above n 15, para 124.)

[17] *Gabčíkovo-Nagymaros Project (Hungary/Slovakia)* case, *Judgment, ICJ Reports*, 1997, p 7.
[18] See further, Ch V of the ILC Articles dealing with 'Circumstances precluding wrongfulness'.
[19] See the views of Crawford that 'Unless otherwise provided, they [the ILC non-wrongfulness of conduct provisions] apply to any internationally wrongful act whether it involves the breach by a State of an obligation arising under a rule of general international law, a treaty ... or from any other source. They do not annul or terminate the obligation; rather they provide a justification or excuse for non-performance while the circumstance in question subsists.' (Crawford, above n 3, p 160.) Crawford notes that this point was emphasised by the Court in the *Gabčíkovo-Nagymaros Project (Hungary/Slovakia)* case. (*Ibid.*)
[20] The Pleadings and the Applications are available at: www.icj-cij.org/icjwww/idocket/icn/icnframe.htm.

violated Article 2 (4) of the Charter. Rather, Cameroon asked the Court to adjudge and declare that Bakassi belonged to Cameroon. It did ask the Court to find that by the use of force and by military occupation, Nigeria was violating obligations incumbent on it.

Cameroon asked the Court to find that these 'internationally unlawful acts ... involve the responsibility of Nigeria'. (In fairness, the French text says that 'la responsibilité du Nigeria est engagée par ... ').[21]

Further grounds of Nigerian responsibility were invoked. The Court was also asked to find that Nigeria was in violation of the 'fundamental principle' of *uti possidetis juris*[22]—a principle that is usually advanced as a legal reason for an argued-for outcome, rather than characterised as an international obligation the violation of which 'involves' international legal responsibility. And in another clause the Court was asked to adjudge and declare that Nigeria must immediately and unconditionally withdraw from Nigeria—understandable as a *consequence* of a finding of title, but in Cameroon's Application this stated duty *itself* was among the numbered clauses characterised as 'an internationally unlawful act' that 'involved' the responsibility of Nigeria.[23]

In the Additional Application by Cameroon, comparable requests were made in respect of a disputed area on the bed of Lake Chad—namely, that sovereignty belonged to Cameroon,[24] that Nigeria had violated *uti possidetis juris*,[25] that occupation was illegal,[26] and that Nigeria had the duty to withdraw[27]—and that *all* these were internationally unlawful acts involving Nigerian responsibility.[28]

Finally, I must explain that the Court was asked to 'specify definitively' the frontier from Lake Chad to the sea because of 'repeated incursions of Nigerian groups and armed forces ... all along the frontier'.[29] Although no claim that Nigeria's responsibility was engaged was initially made in respect of this long land frontier, by the time of Cameroon's Reply these alleged incursions were included among the 'internationally wrongful acts ... [that] engage the Responsibility of Nigeria'.

So the formulation of the responsibility requests put to the Court were somewhat complex and decidedly unusual.

Nigeria entered Counter Claims, particularly as regards Bakassi and the land frontier, and in turn asked the Court to 'adjudge and declare that

[21] Application, para 20 (e), *Memorial*, p 670 (para 9.1(g)).
[22] Application, *Ibid*, para 20 (b).
[23] Application, *Ibid*, para 20 (e).
[24] Application Additional to the Application instituting proceedings brought by the Republic of Cameroon, above n 20, para 17(a).
[25] *Ibid*, para 17 (b).
[26] *Ibid*, para 17 (c).
[27] *Ibid*, para 17 (d).
[28] *Ibid*, para 17 (e).
[29] *Ibid*, para 17 (f).

Cameroon bears responsibility to Nigeria in respect of those claims'.[30] I should finally explain that both Cameroon and Nigeria, in respect of these claims, envisaged possible further hearings to determine the question of reparations due.

These claims and Counter Claims raised many questions for the Court. Let me start with the most fundamental.

4.1. Claims of State Responsibility in Territorial Disputes

What place do claims of international State responsibility have in cases brought to determine legal title to territory? Looking back over cases whose main object was to determine title to territory, one can see that separate and distinct findings of State responsibility are not usual. It has not been regarded as necessary, either by the parties concerned or indeed by the Court, to have a 'stepping stone' of formal findings that the respondent State's 'responsibility is engaged'. Generally, States have felt it sufficient to ask for findings of law and then to ask that the Court find, as a consequence of a finding of violation of legal obligation, that certain remedies must follow (whether compensation or otherwise). This is the clear practice in, for example, the following cases: *Gabčíkovo-Nagymaros Project (Hungary/Slovakia)*;[31] *Fisheries Jurisdiction (Federal Republic of Germany v Iceland)*;[32] *Minquiers and Echrehos*;[33] *Norwegian Fisheries*;[34] *Territorial Dispute (Libyan Arab Jamahiriya/Chad)*[35] (where Libya had been in occupation for 14 years); *Maritime Delimitation and Territorial Questions between Qatar and Bahrain (Qatar v Bahrain)*[36] (even though Qatar claimed that Bahrain had 'seized territory'); *Kasikili/Sedudu Island (Botswana/Namibia)*;[37] *Frontier Dispute (Burkina Faso/Republic of Mali)*[38] (although the provisional measures order had referred to 'grave incidents' having occurred); and also in *Sovereignty over Pulau Ligitan and Pulau*

[30] Counter-Memorial of Nigeria, pp 834–35, Submissions of Nigeria, para 7: above n 20.
[31] *Gabčíkovo* case, above n 17, p 7.
[32] *Fisheries Jurisdiction (Federal Republic of Germany v Iceland): Jurisdiction* case, *Judgment, ICJ Reports*, 1973, p 49, *Judgment, Merits, Judgment, ICJ* Reports, 1974, p 175.
[33] *The Minquiers and Ecrehos (France/United Kingdom)* case, *Judgment, ICJ Reports*, 1953, p 47.
[34] *Fisheries* case, *(United Kingdom v Norway)*, *Judgment, ICJ Reports*, 1951, p 116.
[35] *Territorial Dispute (Libyan Arab Jamahiriya/Chad)* case, *Judgment, ICJ Reports*, 1994, p 6.
[36] *Maritime Delimitation and Territorial Questions between Qatar and Bahrain* case, *Jurisdiction and Admissibility, Judgment, ICJ Reports*, 1994, p 112, *Jurisdiction and Admissibility, Judgment, ICJ Reports*, 1995, p 6; *Merits, Judgment of 16 March 2001, available at*: http://195.195.195.1/icjwww/idocket/iqb/iqbframe.htm.
[37] *Kasikili/Sedudu Island (Botswana/Namibia)* case, *Judgment, ICJ Reports*, 1999, p 1045.
[38] *Frontier Dispute (Burkina Faso/Republic of Mali)* case, *Judgment, ICJ Reports*, 1986, p 554.

Sipadan (Indonesia/Malaysia)[39] (though Indonesia regarded Malaysia as in illegal occupation of these islands).

All of this is consistent with what the Court said in the *Temple of Preah Vihear* case,[40] when explaining that no separate jurisdictional basis was needed for a finding of restitution. In the *Temple of Preah Vihear* case, the Court found that a request for an order of restitution is 'implicit in, and consequential on, the claim of sovereignty itself'.[41]

Neither a separate jurisdictional basis nor a separate finding of the engagement of responsibility is needed for the Court to order a remedy—once it has determined conduct to be illegal.

4.2. When *Should* a Distinct Finding on Responsibility be Requested?

In another recent case, *Arrest Warrant of 11 April 2000 (Democratic Republic of the Congo v Belgium)*,[42] the Court also declined to make a separate finding of 'responsibility'. No such finding was needed for the order that the arrest warrant be withdrawn. The determination that Belgium was not entitled to issue the international arrest warrant was enough.

When, then, *is* it more usual, and perhaps necessary, for a distinct finding on responsibility to be requested? The answer would seem to be in those cases where the violations of obligations are raised *as the central issue*—and sometimes in these cases the *attribution* of unlawful conduct to a government is also a key issue. The obvious example is the *Corfu Channel* case,[43] where attribution of the illegal mine laying was a key element. But even in *this* category of cases, often concerned with the use of force, the more usual pattern of practice has been to ask for a finding of a breach of a specific obligation and to couple that with a request for compensation or other remedy. The *LaGrand* case[44]; *Elettronica Sicula SpA (ELSI)* case[45]; *Military and Paramilitary Activities in and against Nicaragua* case[46]; the *Nuclear*

[39] *Sovereignty over Pulau Ligitan and Pulau Sipidan (Indonesia/Malaysia)* case, *Judgment*, 2002; *available at* www.icj-cij.org/icjwww/idocket/iinma/iinmaframe.htm.
[40] *Temple of Preah Vihear (Cambodia v Thailand)* case, *Merits, Judgment, ICJ Reports*, 1962, p 6.
[41] *Ibid*, p 36.
[42] *Arrest Warrant of 11 April 2000 (Democratic Republic of the Congo v Belgium)* case, *Judgment*, 2002, at para 75; available at: www.icj-cij.org/icjwww/idocket/iCOBE/iCOBEframe.htm.
[43] *Corfu Channel (United Kingdom v Albania)* case, *Merits, ICJ Reports*, 1949, p 4.
[44] *LaGrand* case, above n 14.
[45] *Elettronica Sicula SpA (ELSI) (United States of America v Italy)* case, *ICJ Reports*, 1989, p 15.
[46] *Military and Paramilitary Activities in and against Nicaragua (Nicaragua v United States of America)* case: *Jurisdiction and Admissibility, ICJ Reports*, 1984, p 392; *Merits, ICJ Reports*, 1986, p 14.

Tests cases[47]; and the pending *Genocide* cases[48]; *Kosovo* cases[49]; *Ahmadou Sadio Diallo* case[50]; and *Oil Platforms* case[51] are all examples. The focus in these cases is on the *substantive law*, and not on any free-standing finding that State responsibility is incurred as a consequence of such breach.

5. SUMMARY AND CONCLUSIONS

Let me summarise:

1. It is not unusual, in cases where the law of obligations is at the centre of things, to ask for findings of illegality and also to ask for compensation or other remedies (or to reserve the right to do so later);
2. Only rarely, even in this category of cases, is a separate finding on responsibility sought—it is usually treated as implicit.
3. The Court has *never yet made a finding* that a State's responsibility is engaged in a case whose main focus is territorial title.

Is a finding of illegal conduct really the *same* as a request for a finding of responsibility? The answer is yes, and no. Yes, in that findings of illegal conduct and the fashioning of remedies are all, in our modern way of looking at substantive obligations and remedies for breach, 'part of the law of responsibility'. No, in that no separate pleadings, with prolonged excursions into the law of responsibility and the work of the ILC, are needed on this issue. Given the heavy docket of the Court, and the absence of a need for a 'stepping stone' between illegality and remedy, this is not unimportant.

Let me return to *Land and Maritime Boundary between Cameroon and Nigeria (Cameroon v Nigeria)* and what the Court did with the responsibility claims.

[47] *Nuclear Tests (Australia v France)* case, *ICJ Reports*, 1974, p 253; *Nuclear Tests (New Zealand v France)* case, *ICJ Reports*, 1974, p 457.
[48] *Application of the Convention on the Prevention and Punishment of the Crime of Genocide (Bosnia-Herzegovina v Yugoslavia)*; pending. *Application of the Convention on the Prevention and Punishment of the Crime of Genocide (Croatia v Yugoslavia)*; pending.
[49] *Legality of Use of Force (Yugoslavia v Belgium); Legality of Use of Force (Yugoslavia v Canada); Legality of Use of Force (Yugoslavia v France); Legality of Use of Force (Yugoslavia v Germany); Legality of Use of Force (Yugoslavia v Italy); Legality of Use of Force (Yugoslavia v Netherlands); Legality of Use of Force (Yugoslavia v Portugal); Legality of Use of Force (Yugoslavia v United Kingdom)*; pending.
[50] *Ahmadou Sadio Diallo (Republic of Guinea v Democratic Republic of the Congo)*; pending.
[51] *Oil Platforms (Islamic Republic of Iran v United States of America); Preliminary Objection, ICJ Reports*, 1996, p 803; *Counter-Claim, ICJ Reports*, 1996, p 803; *Merits* pending (for oral and written pleadings, see the Court's web-site: http://www.icj-cij.org/icjwww/idocket/iop/iopframe.htm).

For the Court it was clear that title to Bakassi belonged to Cameroon. But the evidence presented by Cameroon, which bore the burden of proving the facts it had alleged, did not allow the Court to form 'a clear and precise picture' of the sequence of events on the ground in Bakassi.[52] Accordingly, the Court rejected Cameroon's claims on responsibility. The responsibility counter-claims by Nigeria in relation to Bakassi were rejected for comparable reasons.[53]

The specification of the long land frontier between Cameroon and Nigeria largely favoured the arguments that had been advanced by Nigeria. The Court was not prepared to deal with Cameroon's request for a responsibility finding in respect of incidents along the land boundary 'as a whole', Cameroon having decided not to deal with them incident by incident. The Court found again that it had not been presented with sufficient evidence to make such a global finding.

The Court found in favour of Cameroon over title to the disputed areas in Lake Chad,[54] but again made no separate responsibility finding. After these findings the Court immediately stated that the parties are under an obligation to withdraw with all expedition from the areas the Court has found not to belong to them; and rejected all other submissions of Cameroon regarding the State responsibility of Nigeria and rejected the Counter Claims of responsibility by Nigeria.

Counsel pondering the formulation of future Applications to the Court will no doubt notice that the voting on these provisions was unanimous.

[52] *Cameroon v Nigeria*, above n 2, para 322.
[53] *Ibid*, para 324.
[54] The maritime delimitation effected by the Court falls beyond the scope of the theme of this chapter.

2

State Responsibility and the International Court of Justice

IAN BROWNLIE*

BY WAY OF introduction it is necessary to place the subject-matter in context. The primary context is the role of the International Court of Justice (the 'Court') in the making of general international law. Sir Hersch Lauterpacht expressed the view that this was a major role of the Court when he published his book on the *Development of International Law by the Permanent Court of International Justice* (in 1934), which appeared in a revision published in 1958, referring to the work of both the pre-war and post-1946 Courts.

In the long-term the most important role of the Court is, no doubt, the peaceful settlement of disputes. But the role of law-making has been, and remains, significant. Whilst courts of arbitration may make a contribution, it is the Court which, as a mainstream interpreter of general international law, has produced the most important decisions on State responsibility. Such decisions include the *Factory at Chorzów* case,[1] the *Corfu Channel* case,[2] the *Nicaragua* case,[3] the *Nauru* case,[4] and the *Case concerning United States Diplomatic and Consular Staff in Tehran.*[5] A related issue concerns the relationship between the Court and the International Law Commission. This relationship does not involve any problems and there is a complementarity. In its work of codification and progressive development

* CBE, QC; Barrister, Blackstone Chambers, London; and Member, International Law Commission. The author has made use of previous publications of his relating to State responsibility and especially issues relating to the *Corfu Channel* case.

[1] *Factory at Chorzów (Indemnity)* case (1928), Series A, No 17.

[2] *Corfu Channel (United Kingdom v Albania)* case, *ICJ Reports*, 1949, p 4.

[3] *Military and Paramilitary Activities in and Against Nicaragua (Nicaragua v United States)* case, *ICJ Reports*, 1986, p 14.

[4] *Certain Phosphate Lands in Nauru (Nauru v Australia)* case, *ICJ Reports*, 1992, p 240.

[5] *United States Diplomatic and Consular Staff in Tehran (United States v Iran)* case, *ICJ Reports*, 1980, p 3.

the Commission pays careful attention to all the sources, and especially the jurisprudence of the Court. Conversely, as in the *Gabčíkovo-Nagymaros* case,[6] the Court will, when it sees fit, rely heavily upon the draft articles produced by the Commission, even if these were not yet at the stage of second reading in the Commission.

And there is one other question of context and relationship. State responsibility is sometimes seen as a special topic within public international law, and so of course, in some sense, it is. Yet it is a motor or foundation subject, and thus has a quasi-constitutional role. State responsibility, after all, provides the foundation of the law of treaties and constitutes the most basic part of general international law.

The question debated in the literature from time to time is whether the basis of State responsibility is fault *(faute, culpa)* or a concept of relatively strict liability normally referred to as 'objective responsibility'. Of course, no one doubts that either fault or intention *(dol, dolus),* when proved, are *sufficient* to generate responsibility. The question is whether responsibility can exist in the absence of proof of fault or intention to cause harm. The technically correct response is to point out that each individual rule or principle of international law contains a specific content. However, few rules include explicit guidance on the role of fault and, consequently, the relevance of the general principles remains.

As a matter of positive law the position is clear. Both the practice of States and the preponderance of the decisions of international tribunals adopt the concept of objective responsibility. The small number of jurists who favour fault tend to do so because they have misunderstood the reasoning of the Court in the *Corfu Channel* case (Merits).[7] This misunderstanding arises from the emphasis in the judgment upon the need to prove knowledge (or the means of knowledge) on the part of Albania of the existence of the mines in her territorial sea. In fact, in the light of the subject matter, knowledge was the prerequisite of the legal duty of the territorial sovereign to give warning of the existence of the mines. The Court was not deciding on the basis of an acceptance of some general theory of fault or otherwise.

In any case, considerations of sound legal policy militate against adoption of the fault approach. Governments act through agents. Like corporations, they are legal entities and therefore *can only* act through agents. The effectiveness of international duties would be much reduced if the complainant State had to prove some level of knowledge or intention at a high level of government in respect of the acts or omissions of subordinate officials.

[6] *Gabčíkovo-Nagymaros Project (Hungary/Slovakia)* case, *Judgment, ICJ Reports*, 1997, p 7.
[7] *Corfu Channel (United Kingdom v Albania)* case, *ICJ Reports*, 1949, p 4.

I shall now move to another aspect of the subject, which is the relationship of responsibility to other areas of international law. Many principles of international law are concerned with the allocation of powers and relationships which do not generate State responsibility. Thus, for example, a claim to title to a particular parcel of territory, or area of continental shelf or exclusive economic zone, may be contested but such a claim, even if it is proved to be well founded, does not entail State responsibility.

A different situation arises when a claim to territorial sovereignty or other jurisdictional rights results in the use of coercive measures. Thus in the *Anglo-Norwegian Fisheries* case,[8] the International Court was asked to give a declaration concerning the legal validity of a system of baselines of a fisheries zone. The United Kingdom, as the Applicant State, also asked for compensation in respect of arrests of British fishing vessels in the waters regarded as high seas by the United Kingdom. In the course of the oral hearings the issue was dropped.

However, it is of interest to recall that, in the context of the proceedings in the *Anglo-Norwegian Fisheries* case,[9] Norway reserved the right to make a claim for damages against the United Kingdom for the harm caused by a refusal to recognise Norwegian sovereignty and the resulting activity by British trawlers in the Norwegian fishing zone.

A particular constraint imposed by the International Court is the refusal to allow Applicant States to extend their original claims by amendment of the submissions. Amendment of submissions is a common practice and the distinction between permissible modification of a claim and the formulation of a different claim by amending submissions has led to differences of judicial opinion. In the *Temple of Preah Vihear* case (Merits),[10] Cambodia in its final submissions had asked the Court to order restitution of sculptures and other objects removed from the Temple by the Thai authorities since 1954. The International Court regarded this claim—which had not appeared in the Application—to be 'implicit in, and consequential on, the claim of sovereignty itself'.[11] In a Joint Declaration in that case Judges Tanaka and Morelli expressed a different view and stated that the claim relating to the objects removed from the Temple was one 'having a complete different subject' to the claim of sovereignty.[12] In the *Fisheries Jurisdiction (Federal Republic of Germany v Iceland)* case (Merits) the Court set aside the Applicant's claim to compensation for alleged acts of harassment by Icelandic patrol boats, but this refusal to accede to the request was not based on the view that the

[8] *Anglo-Norwegian Fisheries (United Kingdom v Norway)* case, *ICJ Reports*, 1951, p 131.
[9] *Ibid.*
[10] *Temple of Preah Vihear (Cambodia v Thailand)* case, *ICJ Reports*, 1962, p 6.
[11] *Ibid*, p 36.
[12] *Ibid*, pp 37–38.

issue was outside the dispute over which the Court had jurisdiction. The Court expressed itself as follows:

> The matter raised therein is part of the controversy between the Parties, and constitutes a dispute relating to Iceland's extension of its fisheries jurisdiction. The submission is one based on facts subsequent to the filing of the Application, but arising directly out of the question which is the subject matter of that Application. As such it falls within the scope of the Court's jurisdiction defined in the compromissory clause of the Exchange of Notes of 19 July 1961.[13]

It is obvious that the problem of innovative submissions is by no means procedural and that matters of substance are involved. This is true also of other issues arising from the way in which submissions are formulated. Thus in the *Nuclear Tests* cases the important Joint Dissenting Opinion of Judges Onyeama, Dillard, Jimenez de Arechaga and Waldock was much concerned to demonstrate that the essential character of the Australian claim was that of an action for a declaratory judgment and consequently it was impossible to reject the Applications on the ground that the cases had ceased to have any object in view of the French declaration of a cessation of atmospheric testing.[14]

At this stage it is necessary to return to the leading cases on State responsibility decided by the Court. I begin with the *Corfu Channel* case. This decision provides a very helpful demonstration of the necessary transition from the generalities of the literature to the particular problems of the marshalling of evidence, the standard of proof and the application of the relevant legal principles in particular situations.

As to the facts of the mining, the Court made the following determinations:

> The two ships were mined in Albanian territorial waters in a previously swept and check-swept channel just at the place where a newly laid minefield consisting of moored contact German GY mines was discovered three weeks later. The damage sustained by the ships was inconsistent with damage which could have been caused by floating mines, or German GR mines, but its nature and extent were such as would be caused by mines of the type found in the minefield. In such circumstances the Court arrives at the conclusion that the explosions were due to mines belonging to that minefield.[15]

The consequential findings were that there was no evidence that Albania had laid the mines and that Albania had no means of minelaying. There

[13] *Fisheries Jurisdiction (Federal Republic of Germany v Iceland)* case, *ICJ Reports*, 1974, p 175, at p 203 (para 72).
[14] *Nuclear Tests (Australia v France)* case, *ICJ Reports*, 1974, p 253, at pp 312–19.
[15] *Corfu Channel* case, above n 7, p 15.

was no reliable evidence that the mines had been laid by a third State. Furthermore, there was no evidence to establish that Albania had direct knowledge of the existence of the mines in the North Corfu Channel in a navigable channel previously swept for mines.

The final argument of the United Kingdom had been that the minelaying could not have been done without the knowledge of the Albanian Government. The Court first of all sought to establish the appropriate standard of proof. In the first instance, the Court determined that the existence of control exercised by a State over its territory and territorial waters neither involved prima facie responsibility nor shifted the burden of proof.[16]

The Court then continued:

> On the other hand, the fact of this exclusive territorial control exercised by a State within its frontiers has a bearing upon the methods of proof available to establish the knowledge of that State as to such events. By reason of this exclusive control, the other State, the victim of a breach of international law, is often unable to furnish direct proof of facts giving rise to responsibility. Such a State should be allowed a more liberal recourse to inferences of fact and circumstantial evidence. This indirect evidence is admitted in all systems of law, and its use is recognised by international decisions. It must be regarded as of special weight when it is based on a series of facts linked together and leading logically to a single conclusion.
>
> The Court must examine therefore whether it has been established by means of indirect evidence that Albania has knowledge of minelaying in her territorial waters independently of any connivance on her part in this operation. The proof may be drawn from inferences of fact, provided that they leave *no room* for reasonable doubt. The elements of fact on which these inferences can be based may differ from those which are relevant to the question of connivance.[17]

The Court then carefully analysed the *indirect* evidence of Albania's knowledge of minelaying in her territorial waters. Such evidence included the fact that Albania had kept close watch over the waters of the North Corfu Channel after the earlier incident of May 1946, and evidence—and observations made on site by Experts of the Court—to the effect that any minelaying would have been detectable by the Albanian coastguard.

In the result the Court held that Albania was responsible for the explosions that occurred on 22 October 1946 in Albanian waters. This decision was consequential upon the Court's conclusion on the law and the facts, which were as follows:

> From all the facts and observations mentioned above, the Court draws the conclusion that the laying of the minefield which caused the explosions

[16] *Ibid*, p 18.
[17] *Ibid*.

on October 22nd, 1946, could not have been accomplished without the knowledge of the Albanian Government. The obligations resulting for Albania from this knowledge are not disputed between the Parties. Counsel for the Albanian Government expressly recognised that *[translation]* 'if Albania had been informed of the operation before the incidents of October 22nd, and in time to warn the British vessels and shipping in general of the existence of mines in the Corfu Channel, her responsibility would be involved ….

The obligations incumbent upon the Albanian authorities consisted of notifying, for the benefit of shipping in general, the existence of a minefield in Albanian territorial waters and in warning the approaching British warships of the imminent danger to which the minefield exposed them. Such obligations are based, not on the Hague Convention of 1907, No. VIII, which is applicable in time of war, but on certain general and well-recognized principles, namely: elementary considerations of humanity, even more exacting in peace than in war; the principle of the freedom of maritime communication; and every State's obligation not to allow knowingly its territory to be used for acts contrary to the rights of other States.

In fact, Albania neither notified the existence of the minefield, nor warned the British warships of the danger they were approaching.[18]

The judgment of the Court provides a valuable reminder of the need to avoid generalising principles and simplistic polarities in the sphere of State responsibility.

The significance of focusing upon the precise character of the legal principles and causes of action involved in the individual case appears again in the *Case Concerning Military and Paramilitary Actions In and Against Nicaragua* (Merits).[19]

In this case also the basis of imputability was related to the nature of the particular cause of action, and to the type of evidence available. With respect to the direct attacks on ports and installations, and the laying of mines in Nicaraguan internal or territorial waters, these were carried out by United States nationals or by other agents of the United States. The planning, direction, support and execution of the operations involved United States nationals or foreign agents of the United States. On this basis the imputability of these acts to the United States was held to be established.[20] In respect of violations of Nicaraguan sovereignty by overflights, the evidence consisted for the most part of admissions in documents submitted to the Security Council,[21] and consequently the attribution of responsibility to the United States created no difficulties.

[18] *Ibid*, p 22.
[19] *Case Concerning Military and Paramilitary Actions In and Against Nicaragua (Nicaragua v United States)* case, *ICJ Reports*, 1986, p 14.
[20] *Ibid*, pp 45–51 (paras 75–86).
[21] *Ibid*, pp 51–53 (paras 87–91).

Responsibility for the paramilitary activities of the *Contras* directed against Nicaragua from bases in Honduras and Costa Rica involved the Court in significant distinctions. In particular, the degree of control exercised by the United States was critical. The Court recognised the partial dependency of the *Contras* upon the United States but concluded that the degree of control exercised by the latter did not have the implication that the acts committed by the *Contras* in and against Nicaragua were attributable to the United States.[22]

The result was that assistance to the *Contras* by the United States, in the form of training, arming and financing the *Contras,* constituted a breach by the United States of its obligations under customary international law not to intervene in the affairs of another State.[23] In the same way, assistance to the *Contras* constituted a breach of the principle of the prohibition of the use of force,[24] and infringements of the territorial sovereignty of Nicaragua.[25]

In contrast to these determinations, the Court held that the relationship of the United States to the *Contras* was not so close as to render the United States responsible for breaches of humanitarian law committed by members of the *Contras*.[26] It is to be recalled that in the *Tadic* case the UN International Criminal Tribunal for the former Yugoslavia, Trial Chamber II, carefully distinguished the *Nicaragua* case on the facts.[27]

In concluding, I must complete, in summary form, my review of the leading cases. The *Tehran Hostages* case[28] is important. It confirms the existence of responsibility on the basis of the approval and adoption of the harmful acts of individuals who are not, as such, agents of the Respondent State.[29] The case also involved the existence of a closed system of obligations relating to the Vienna Convention on Diplomatic Relations. And, finally there is the *Nauru* case,[30] which related to the complex case of multilateral disputes. This review has been curtailed in certain respects in order to avoid comment on certain very recent proceedings in the Court.

In conclusion, two general observations are called for. In the first place, the law of State responsibility grows on the basis of its application in concrete situations. In this respect the Court's jurisprudence has been of primary importance. Secondly, there is a nice question, which will no doubt remain unresolved, concerning the balance between the role of the Court,

[22] *Ibid,* pp 61–65 (paras 109–16).
[23] *Ibid,* pp 123–25 (paras 239–42).
[24] *Ibid,* pp 118–19, (paras 227–28), p 128 (para 251).
[25] *Ibid,* pp 127–28 (paras 250–52).
[26] *Ibid,* pp 62–65 (paras 109–16); pp 129–30 (paras 254–56).
[27] *Prosecutor v Tadic* case, *International Law Reports,* vol 112, p 2 at pp 188–200.
[28] *United States Diplomatic and Consular Staff in Tehran (United States v Iran)* case, *ICJ Reports,* 1980, p 3.
[29] *Ibid,* paras 73–76.
[30] *Certain Phosphate Lands in Nauru (Nauru v Australia)* case, *ICJ Reports,* 1992, p 240.

in the context of dispute settlement, as the author of declarations of rights, and the Court's role in the context of the implementation of judgments and crisis management. This difficult question of balance arises especially in the sphere of remedies.

3

The International Court, Responsibility and Remedies

MALCOLM SHAW*

THE INTERNATIONAL COURT of Justice (the 'Court') makes determinations as to the responsibility of States for violations of international law with regard to which it has jurisdiction, at least in the implicit sense of saying who violates the applicable rule. How the Court defines such responsibility and how it determines the consequences of the breaches in question are the subject of much current interest in the light not only of the ILC's Articles on State Responsibility,[1] but also in the light of the developing work of the Court in recent years. Violations of international law, State responsibility and remedies are closely interlinked. A finding that a rule of international law has been breached by a particular party constitutes the indispensable first stage in a remedial action; to put it another way, a remedy is contingent upon the determination and definition of responsibility, which in turn relies upon an earlier decision as to the existence of a breach of international law. Of course, the Court can also provide a remedy in determining a legal situation where no party is condemned for a violation as such, for example where a boundary line is made clear in circumstances of previous doubt and dispute. The provision of a remedy also constitutes the link between the judicial phase and the post-judicial resolution of the dispute and as such marks a critical contribution to the practical arrangements leading to peaceful settlement.

This chapter will make reference to an upward trend in the Court's consideration of remedies, by which is meant the perceived movement from studied caution to studied activism. The Court is in the course of reassessing

* QC; Sir Robert Jennings Professor of International Law, University of Leicester; and Barrister, Essex Court Chambers, London.

[1] Adopted by the International Law Commission on 9 August 2001, A/56/10, p 43 *et seq* and noted and commended to Governments by the General Assembly in Resolution 56/83 on 12 Dec 2001.

its approach to remedies as a critical element in the judicial process and this is deserving of careful consideration and analysis. Closely allied with questions of responsibility and remedies one finds issues of jurisdiction and of the accepted limits of judicial function. Recent cases have raised a number of interesting points. However, it should be noted that the question of provisional measures will not be covered,[2] other than to say that now that such measures are clearly accepted as binding, their profile in a remedial sense will surely rise. No doubt questions as to their implementation and supervision will assume greater importance now that the Court has held that where it has jurisdiction to decide a case, it also has jurisdiction to deal with submissions requesting it to determine that a relevant provisional measures Order has not been complied with.[3] However, the Court has drawn attention to the critical issue of evidence by emphasising that the litigant who seeks to establish a fact as a basis, for example, for a claim for provisional measures must prove it, and in the absence of such evidence being established, the submission in question may be rejected as unproved in the judgment.[4] Accordingly, the Court in considering Cameroon's argument that Nigeria had failed to comply with the provisional measures Order of 15 March 1996[5] concluded that just as it was unable to form any 'clear and precise' picture of the events taking place in Bakassi in February 1996,[6] so was it also unable to do so after the 1996 Order and that, since 'Cameroon has not established the facts which it bears the burden of proving', its submissions had to be rejected.[7] Further, nothing will be said about intervention by third States, other than to note their interesting role for the third States in question in allowing their interests to be raised in a case with variable effect, depending, of course, upon the situation.

As a general observation one can say that the issue of remedies available in the International Court is one that has received relatively little detailed analysis.[8] This is remarkable in the circumstances, and ever more so in the light of the increasing docket of the Court. It is difficult to consider at the moment that there is a Court-defined systematic international law of remedies.[9] The topic of remedies in this context, of course, has a wide initial compass. It covers areas beyond the actual remedial Order of

[2] On provisional measures ordered by the ICJ, see ch 4 by Maurice Mendelson in this volume.
[3] See the *LaGrand* case, *ICJ Reports,* 2001, para 45 and the *Avena* case, ICJ Reports, 2004.
[4] *Nicaragua v USA (Jurisdiction and Admissibility), ICJ Reports,* 1984, p 437.
[5] *ICJ Reports,* 1996, p 13.
[6] *Ibid,* p 22.
[7] *Cameroon v Nigeria (Merits), ICJ Reports,* 2002, para 322.
[8] See, for example, C Gray, *Judicial Remedies in International Law* (Oxford, 1987); I Brownlie, 'Remedies in the International Court of Justice', in V Lowe and M Fitzmaurice, eds, *Fifty Years of the International Court of Justice* (Cambridge, 1996), p 557; and R Higgins, 'Remedies and the International Court of Justice: An Introduction', in M Evans, ed, *Remedies in International Law* (Oxford, 1998), p 1.
[9] See eg Gray, *Ibid,* p 107.

the Court, since the terms of the jurisdictional instrument bringing the case before the Court or the provisions of the Special Agreement, if any, between the parties[10] will be of great significance and may be determinative, for example, where the Court is specifically requested by the parties to spell out the consequences of its principled decision.[11]

The reference in the Court's Statute to remedies is less than clear. Article 36 (2) (d) provides that States parties may in their optional declarations recognise the compulsory jurisdiction of the Court with regard to inter alia 'the nature or extent of the reparation to be made for the breach of an international obligation'. Nothing broader or more substantive is present in the Statute. Where the parties expressly provide for the Court to make a decision on specific requested remedies in the Special Agreement, then the issue is one for the exercise of the jurisdiction and discretion of the Court. Beyond this, the scope of the Court's power to Order remedies has not been well defined, whether one is considering damages, restitution, satisfaction or even the extent of a statement of the consequential legal situation for the parties.[12] Brownlie has noted in this context that the Court's 'creative process has been pragmatic, unselfconscious, and somewhat unreflective'.[13] Whatever the accuracy of this, it does appear that we may now be entering a period of increased activity, certainly increased creativity, with regard to remedies.

It is, of course, the duty of the Court in principle to declare the law in so far as the parties have made relevant submissions in the case in question.[14] Further, it is quite clear that, as stated by the Court in the *LaGrand* case,

> [w]here jurisdiction exists over a dispute over a particular matter, no separate basis for jurisdiction is required by the Court to consider the remedies a party has requested for the breach of the obligation.[15]

However, the question as to the nature and scope of pertinent remedies remains to be tackled.

That the Court has jurisdiction to give declaratory judgments is uncontentious.[16] The intention of a declaratory judgment was defined in the *Chorzów Factory* case, as being 'to ensure recognition of a situation at law, once and for all and with binding force as between the Parties'.[17] Such a

[10] A good example of this is the *Gabcikovo-Nagymaros* case, *ICJ Reports,* 1997, p 7 at p 81.
[11] See, for example, the *Tunisia/Libya* case, *ICJ Reports,* 1982, pp 18, 21.
[12] See Gray, above n 8, p 64. See also Brownlie, above n 8, p 558.
[13] Brownlie, *ibid.*
[14] See the *Asylum* case, *ICJ Reports,* 1950, pp 395, 402.
[15] *LaGrand* case, *ICJ Reports,* 2001, para 48 and the *Avena* case, *ICJ Reports,* 2004, para 34.
[16] See the *Northern Cameroons* case, *ICJ Reports,* 1963, pp 15, 37. See also S Rosenne, *The Law and Practice of the International Court, 1920–1996* (The Hague, 1997), vol III, p 1636.
[17] *Factory at Chorzów* case, Judgment, Merits, 1928, *PCIJ Series A,* No 17, p 20.

declaration would, if concerned with a customary rule or interpretation of a treaty in force, be of 'continuing applicability', as was noted in the *Northern Cameroons* case.[18] What is important to note is that the concept of a declaratory judgment is very flexible and over-arching in containing elements that would, in domestic tribunals, be separately provided.

This power, however, might be constrained in the light of the Court's examination of, and conclusion with regard to, the judicial function of the Court. This has two particular aspects; first, with regard to the jurisdictional issue and here the question will focus upon the precise extent to which the jurisdiction to award remedies as a consequence of the jurisdiction to decide may be implemented in the instant case. Secondly, where the issue between the parties centres upon the interpretation and application of a Treaty no longer in force so that for the Court to reach a decision would be rendered 'devoid of purpose'.[19] Then, quite irrespective of jurisdictional issues, the Court may have to consider whether for it 'to proceed further in the case would not, in its opinion, be a proper discharge of its duties'.[20] This statement by the Court in the *Northern Cameroons* case referred specifically to 'the duty to safeguard the judicial function'.[21] In his Separate Opinion, Judge Fitzmaurice noted that 'if the judgment neither would have nor could have any effective sphere of *legal* application', then even though there may be moral or political uses or consequences to such a judgment, the Court should not get involved.[22] However, the question of determining whether any particular judgment could have only political consequences and no legal application is not an easy one. Where the line is to be drawn is going to be exceptionally difficult since in principle any statement of law by the Court would invariably have legal consequences of some kind, if not in terms of altering the actual legal situation as between the parties themselves then as a guide to future conduct which may or may not be directly linked to the action brought.

How far the Court may go beyond an exposition of the relevant law is unclear. It may lay down the essential legal framework in the instant matter.[23] It may go a little further and expressly declare that the conduct or omission in question was either consistent with or contrary to law. The Court may go further and actually specify the consequences for the parties of the particular judgment and may render a formal Order. This in turn raises the question as to the line dividing declaratory judgments from

[18] *ICJ Reports*, 1963, pp 15, 37.
[19] *Ibid*, p 38.
[20] *Ibid.*
[21] *Ibid.*
[22] *Ibid*, p 107. Emphasis in original quotation.
[23] See, for example, the *Indonesia/Malaysia* case that simply states: 'Sovereignty over Pulau Ligitan and Pulau Sipadan belongs to Malaysia' (*ICJ Reports*, 2002, operative para 150).

formal Orders to the parties and the circumstances in which the latter may be formulated,[24] an issue implicitly raised in the *Iranian Hostages* case where the Court, after determining that particular violations of international law had taken place for which Iran bore responsibility, proceeded to spell out a series of steps that the respondent State had to take.[25] The move from simply establishing that a breach of international law had occurred to detailing the specific consequences for the relevant State—a matter considered below—is to be applauded as a move towards clarity and coherence and away from opaque mysticism.

A further point in this context concerns the addressees of such Orders. This issue was raised in the *LaGrand* case, where, in the rather carefully worded provisional measures Order of 3 March 1999, the Court accepted that 'implementation of the measures indicated in the present Order falls within the jurisdiction of the Governor of Arizona'. However, the Court emphasised that the international responsibility of a State was engaged by the action of the competent organs and authorities acting in that State whatever they may be and that the US government was under an obligation to transmit the Order to the Governor of Arizona. The Court moved beyond this, however, and stated that: 'the Governor of Arizona is under the obligation to act in conformity with the international undertakings of the United States'.[26] It may be, of course, that this statement is merely the logical conclusion of the two earlier propositions. It may be that the statement is merely one as to US constitutional law. However, both seem unlikely. First, because the comment as to the Governor is more than the sum of the earlier statements, and, secondly, because it is highly improbable that the International Court would wish or feel competent to make assertions as to US domestic law. It is more likely that the Court has taken a patent decision to make a subordinate organ of a sovereign State a direct addressee of a Court Order. What the consequences of this may be are unclear at this stage. Of course, the responsibility of the US in failing to 'take all measures at its disposal' to ensure that Walter LaGrand was not executed pending the International Court's final decision was asserted in the Court's judgment and it may be that the call for 'review and reconsideration of the conviction and sentence' by the US Government of other German nationals in similar circumstances required by the Court is a relevant reflection upon the earlier Order.[27] Nevertheless, the Court's action constitutes an interesting step and one that may be pregnant with possibilities.

[24] See, for example, Gray, above n 8, pp 65–66.
[25] *ICJ Reports*, 1980, p 3.
[26] *ICJ Reports*, 1999, pp 9, 16.
[27] *ICJ Reports*, 2001, operative para 128 (5) and (7). See also the Order of 5 February 2003 for Provisional Measures in *Mexico v United States of America*, available at: http://www.icj-cij.org/icjwww/idocket/imus/imusframe.htm.

Such issues are, however, also linked with questions as to fundamental effectiveness as well as consideration of the nature and limitations of the judicial function and the determination by the Court of the object of the application. In the *Haya de la Torre* case, for example, the Court noted that its decision in the preceding *Asylum* case entailed the obligation of compliance. It was not part of the judicial function of the Court to:

> make a choice amongst the various courses by which the asylum may be terminated, since such a choice was based not on legal considerations but only on considerations of practicability or of political expediency.[28]

The Court declared that having defined the legal relations between the parties in so far as relevant, it was 'unable to give any practical advice as to the various courses which might be followed ... since by doing so it would depart from its judicial function'.[29] Quite how the judicial function in such a situation might be understood is a matter for some interpretation, both cautious, as in the *Northern Cameroons* case[30] and otherwise.

Issues of subtle definition apart, the Court may in principle characterise a particular act or acts in question in the litigation as legal, as in the *Anglo-Norwegian Fisheries* case,[31] or illegal, as in the *Nicaragua* case,[32] and as such it acts entirely in accord with the judicial function. The extent to which the proposed declaratory judgment may be seen as having a 'continuing applicability' with regard to the international norm in question or be contrary to the judicial function as having no 'forward reach' is controversial and appears to be evolving. Indeed, it is entirely unclear what the absence of 'forward reach' actually means here. It may be that the particular Treaty provision or Treaty or custom has come to an end one way or another, but that does not necessarily mean that the legal consequences of that rule have also terminated.

In the *Northern Cameroons* case, the Court took the view that the request for the interpretation of a terminated treaty (here the trusteeship agreement) would not be in accord with the judicial function. The Court relied on the reason that: 'there can be no opportunity for a future act of interpretation or application of that treaty in accordance with any judgment the Court might render'.[33] But what if the provisions of the treaty in question were indeed to be in issue in subsequent legal proceedings? As indeed they were in the *Cameroon v Nigeria* case, where Cameroon

[28] *ICJ Reports,* 1951, pp 71, 79.
[29] *Ibid,* pp 71, 83.
[30] *ICJ Reports,* 1963, pp 15, 37 and see also the *Fisheries Jurisdiction* case *(Federal Republic of Germany v Iceland), ICJ Reports,* 1974, pp 175, 205.
[31] *ICJ Reports,* 1951, pp 116, 143.
[32] *ICJ Reports,* 1986, pp 14, 146–68.
[33] *ICJ Reports,* 1963, pp 15, 37.

argued inter alia that the trusteeship agreement and earlier mandate agreement were additional elements of proof in its territorial title.[34] The Court indeed accepted this and underlined the relevance of such agreements, noting for example, that: 'Bakassi was necessarily comprised within the mandate'.[35] Was the Court too cautious in the *Northern Cameroons* case? There are good reasons for thinking so.

Again, in the *Nuclear Tests* case, the Court examined the terms of the Application as a whole, the arguments of the Applicant, diplomatic exchanges and public statements before concluding that the 'original and ultimate objective of the Applicant was and has remained to obtain a termination' of French nuclear tests in the South Pacific, so that 'its claim cannot be regarded as being a claim for a declaratory judgment'.[36] This position has been much criticised, not least in a Joint Dissenting Opinion, which it would appear correctly pointed out that the termination of nuclear tests would not necessarily mark the end of the consequential legal path since claims could be made, or could have been made, with regard to nuclear tests held since the date of the application.[37]

The question reappeared in the *LaGrand* case in a different form. In its submissions, the US admitted the violation of international law in question (the breach of the Vienna Convention on Consular Relations), apologised for this and declared that it was 'taking substantial measures aimed at preventing any recurrence'.[38] Where, one might argue, was the 'dispute' in the light of the earlier case-law?[39] Might it not be seen as moot? In the event, the logic of this was not rigorously followed and the broader approach was accepted by the US and the Court that there was a dispute between the parties over the Convention provisions as they relate to Germany's rights as a State party and with regard to German nationals in terms of their own rights.

The issue came before the Court again in the *Democratic Republic of the Congo v Belgium* case (or the *Yerodia* case), where the Court took the view that its finding in the case—that the issue and circulation of the arrest warrant by Belgium violated the immunity from criminal jurisdiction and inviolability of 'the then Foreign Minister of the Congo'—constituted a form of satisfaction, making good the moral injury complained of by the Congo.[40] But this characterisation of the situation that had existed prior to Mr Yerodia's move from the post of Foreign Minister can only with effort

[34] *ICJ Reports*, 2002, para 210 *et seq*.
[35] *Ibid*, para 212.
[36] *ICJ Reports*, 1974, pp 253, 263.
[37] *Ibid*, pp 318–20.
[38] *ICJ Reports*, 2001, para 12.
[39] See the *Dissenting Opinion* of Judge S Oda, available at: http://www.icj-cij.org/icjwww/idocket/igus/igusframe.htm.
[40] *ICJ Reports*, 2002, para 75.

really be seen as one of 'continuing applicability'. After all, Mr Yerodia, the very focus of the *ad hominem* arrest warrant, had ceased to hold that governmental office. The Court noted that at the time of the application when Mr Yerodia was Foreign Minister there was a dispute, and that, accordingly, it had jurisdiction.[41] It held that the continuance in force of the international arrest warrant sufficed for concluding that the application of the Congo was not without object and thus not moot.[42] The Court was thus clearly prepared to make a declaratory judgment concerning a legal situation even where that situation no longer existed as a matter of fact or at least not in the same essential configuration. We have moved on from *Northern Cameroons* and *Nuclear Tests* and it can safely be concluded that the broader, more flexible approach to a declaratory judgment has, in this context, been accepted.

The next question is to determine to what extent the Court feels able to proceed from the characterisation of a situation as illegal to lay down the particular consequences in law and otherwise for the parties. It is clear that the interpretation of the *Haya de la Torre* judgment—according to which it was not for the Court to lay down the practical consequences for the parties once a determination of the legal situation has been made—is no longer applicable. Let us consider some examples of this approach. In the *Temple* case, the Court held that Thailand was under an obligation to withdraw its forces from the Temple area and further to restore to Cambodia any objects specified in the latter's submissions as having been removed since the commencement of the Thai occupation.[43] In the *Iranian Hostages* case, the Court listed a series of steps that Iran 'must immediately take' to redress the illegal situation, including terminating the unlawful detention of diplomatic staff and others and returning the occupied premises, property, archives and documents of the US Embassy and Consulates.[44] In *Cameroon v Nigeria,* the Court in its operative paragraph after determining the territorial and maritime boundary between the parties proceeded to state that each of the parties was under 'an obligation expeditiously and without condition to withdraw its administration and its military and police forces' from areas now deemed to belong to the other.[45]

In the process of implementing its findings, the Court may be assisted by experts (as in the *Corfu Channel* case[46]) or by the UN (as in the *Libya/Chad* case[47]). Additionally, subsequent proceedings may be needed in order

[41] *Ibid,* paras 23–28.
[42] *Ibid,* para 32.
[43] *ICJ Reports,* 1962, pp 6, 36–37.
[44] *ICJ Reports,* 1980, pp 3, 44–45 and see also Order of 12 May 1981, *ICJ Reports,* 1981, p 45. See also the *Nicaragua* case, *ICJ Reports,* 1986, pp 14, 149.
[45] *ICJ Reports,* 2002, para 325 (V) A and B.
[46] *ICJ Reports,* 1949, p 244.
[47] *ICJ Reports,* 1994, p 6 and Security Council Resolution 910 (1994).

to specify the resulting consequences of the Court's judgment.[48] The Court may also undertake at the request of the parties, an ongoing supervisory role.[49]

This trend of not refusing to spell out the consequences of decisions was reaffirmed in the *Yerodia* case, where the Court rejected the argument of Belgium based on the *Haya de la Torre* and *Northern Cameroons* cases that having defined the relevant legal relations of the parties, the Court should refrain from giving practical advice as to the ways in which its judgment should in practice be implemented by the parties.[50] Instead, the Court concluded that: 'Belgium must, by means of its own choosing, cancel the warrant in question and so inform the authorities to whom it was circulated'.[51] But it is in the *LaGrand* case that one finds the most interesting expression of the evolution in the Court's approach to spelling out the consequences of its legal findings. Germany's fourth submission asked the Court to adjudge and declare that the US provide Germany with an assurance that it would not repeat its unlawful acts and that it would ensure in law and practice the effective exercise of the rights provided for by Article 36 of the Vienna Convention on Consular Relations. It was argued, in particular, that in cases involving the death penalty this would require the US to provide effective review of and remedies for criminal convictions of the rights provided for by Article 36.[52] The US condemned this submission, contending that a requirement of assurances has no precedent in the jurisprudence of the Court and that it would in any event exceed the Court's jurisdiction and authority.[53]

The Court took the view that the US's apology to Germany was insufficient as a remedy. It referred to the 'substantial activities' that the US declared that it was carrying out in order to comply with the Convention in question and concluded, interestingly, that such behaviour 'expresses a commitment to follow through with the efforts in this regard' and must be regarded as meeting Germany's request for a general assurance of non-repetition.[54] Accordingly, one assumes that this would be treated by the Court as a binding unilateral declaration by the US and one that would be of consequence in any future litigation or negotiation.[55]

The Court turned to consider the remaining two legs of Germany's fourth submission and—repeating that an apology would not suffice should

[48] See eg the *Corfu Channel* case (above n 46) and *Nicaragua* case (above n 32).
[49] See, for example, Art 5 (3) of the Special Agreement between the parties of 7 April 1993 in the *Gabcikovo-Nagymaros* case, *ICJ Reports*, 1997, pp 7, 12.
[50] See, for example, CR 2001/9, pp 33–4 and ch 6 of the Counter-Memorial of the Kingdom of Belgium, 28 September 2001, paras 3.6.1–3.6.11.
[51] *ICJ Reports*, 2002, para 76.
[52] *ICJ Reports*, 2001, para 117.
[53] *Ibid*, para 119.
[54] *Ibid*, paras 123–4. See also para 125 and the *Avena* case, *ICJ Reports*, 2004, para 150.
[55] See the *Nuclear Tests* case, *ICJ Reports*, 1974, pp 253, 267.

the US fail in its obligations under the Consular Convention with regard to German nationals—stated that:

> In the case of such a conviction and sentence [ie death penalty], it would be incumbent upon the United States to allow the review and reconsideration of the conviction and sentence by taking account of the violation of the rights set forth in the Convention. This obligation can be carried out in various ways. The choice of means must be left to the United States.[56]

In the two succeeding paragraphs the Court referred again to this 'obligation ... to review' and the 'duty' of the US to address any future violations of the Convention.[57] In operative paragraph (7) of the dispositif, the Court, by a majority of 14 votes to one, finds that:

> should nationals of the Federal Republic of Germany nonetheless be sentenced to severe penalties, without their rights under Article 36, paragraph 1 (b), of the Convention having been respected, the United States of America, by means of its own choosing, *shall* allow the review and reconsideration of the conviction and sentence by taking account of the violation of the rights set forth in that Convention.[58]

The sole dissentient to this part of the judgment was Judge Oda, who declared that he was 'utterly at a loss as to what the Court intends to say in this subparagraph'.[59]

This requirement or recognition of an obligation upon the US in the circumstances marks a complete turn from the approach adopted in the *Haya de la Torre* case on this point. The Court not only in its decision draws practical conclusions from its legal finding, but it imposes upon the US an obligation to review and reconsider particular domestic judgments. This goes beyond the status of a declaratory judgment as traditionally understood to laying down one consequence of its legal decision in the form almost of an Order of contingent specific performance. It is potentially a very significant step in terms of the Court's remedial operations. Jennings has referred to this part of the decision as being 'quite remarkable' and one for which 'one would surely have to search long for any parallel in the history of international tribunals'.[60] This issue has been further raised in the current proceedings brought by Mexico against the US concerning 54 Mexican citizens on 'death row' in the US in circumstances allegedly where

[56] *ICJ Reports*, 2001, para 125. See also the *Avena* case, *ICJ Reports*, 2004, para 120 *et seq*.
[57] *Ibid*, paras 126 and 127.
[58] *Ibid*, para 128. Emphasis added.
[59] *Ibid*, para 37 of his dissenting opinion. See also the Declaration of Judge G Guillaume.
[60] R Jennings, '*The LaGrand* case', 1 *The Law and Practice of International Courts and Tribunals* (2002), pp 1, 40.

the US failed to comply with Article 36 (1)(b) of the Vienna Convention on Consular Relations.[61]

The Court has moved further in the direction of specifying the consequences of its rulings in terms of the future behaviour of the parties in the *Cameroon v Nigeria* case. Again, the Court shied away from requiring a guarantee of non-repetition of the conduct complained against by the applicant,[62] but again the Court drew attention to the comments of the respondent State and drew legal consequences from these. The Court referred, both in the text of its judgment[63] and significantly in the operative paragraph,[64] to the comment of the Cameroon Agent that 'Cameroon will continue to afford protection to Nigerians living in the [Bakassi] Peninsula and in the Lake Chad area' and concluded that it 'takes note with satisfaction of the *commitment* thus undertaken in respect of these areas where many Nigerian nationals reside'.[65] Whether the Cameroon Agent actually intended to lay down a legal obligation or whether his words could be so interpreted is not a matter to be considered here. What is crucial is that the Court determined to interpret the words as a 'commitment' and thus as a unilateral obligation from which legal rights and duties could flow. It is also of some significance that the Court moved further and sought to give some substantive content to this commitment. It observed that:

> the implementation of the present Judgment will afford the Parties a beneficial opportunity to co-operate in the interests of the population concerned, in order notably to enable it to *continue to have access to educational and health services comparable to those it currently enjoys*. Such co-operation will be especially helpful, with a view to the maintenance of security, during the withdrawal of the Nigerian administration and military and police forces.[66]

This phrase may be seen as establishing or recognising a special regime for Nigerian nationals living in the Bakassi Peninsula and Lake Chad area from which Nigerian troops and administrative structures are to withdraw. As such, it marks a distinctive and important move by the Court specifically within the remedial context.

Questions of remedial consequences, whether greater or lesser, will flow only from a finding as to responsibility, which in itself will be precedd by a finding of a violation of international law of one kind or another. In the

[61] See Provisional Measures Order of 5 February 2003, above n 27. See now the decision of the ICJ of 31 Mar 2004.
[62] *ICJ Reports*, 2002, para 318.
[63] *Ibid*, para 317.
[64] *Ibid*, para 325 (V) C.
[65] *Ibid*, para 317. Emphasis added.
[66] *Ibid*, para 316. Emphasis added.

Gabčíkovo-Nagymaros Project (Hungary/Slovakia) case, the Court was faced with the problem of an uncompleted dam complex where one party asked for inter alia a return to the *status quo ante* (and thus destruction of various constructions) and the other called for completion of the projected works.[67] As it happened, the Court rejected both options because of unlawful conduct by both sides. Having been asked further by the parties to determine the consequences of the judgment insofar as damages were concerned, the Court, declaring that both parties had committed internationally wrongful acts giving rise to damage, held that consequently both parties were under an obligation to pay compensation and thus to receive compensation. This conclusion was reflected in paragraph D of the dispositif.[68] However, the Court made an observation to the effect that in the light of the relevant 'intersecting wrongs', as the Court elegantly put it, the issue of compensation could be resolved satisfactorily by a mutual renunciation or cancellation of all financial claims and counter-claims.[69]

This case is thus interesting in demonstrating not only the obvious point that the Court will determine responsibility for breaches of international law, but that the Court is prepared to allocate responsibility as between States and that it is currently less tempted to enter into the complex issue of valuation of damages in a way typical of many arbitration proceedings. There may be other situations where the Court will not so easily be able to ascribe responsibility equally and thus set off one party's claim for damages against the other party's claim.

The Court is able to award damages not only to the applicant party in its own right, but also with respect to losses suffered by nationals of that party. This is clear from inter alia the *Corfu Channel*,[70] *Iranian Hostages*[71] and *Nicaragua*[72] cases. The Court may also interpret a relevant international legal provision so that individual rights as well as State's rights are recognised in a particular case, thus opening the door to a claim for damages on behalf of the former by the national State where there has been a breach of such rights.[73]

In principle, a State responsible for an internationally wrongful act is under an obligation to cease the act in question and to make full reparation for the injury caused.[74] And, as the Court noted in *Yerodia*,

[67] *ICJ Reports*, 1997, pp 7, 15–17.
[68] *Ibid*, pp 7, 83.
[69] *Ibid*, p 81.
[70] *ICJ Reports*, 1949, p 4.
[71] *ICJ Reports*, 1981, p 45.
[72] *ICJ Reports*, 1986, p 14.
[73] See the *LaGrand* case, *ICJ Reports*, 2001, at paras 3 and 4 of the dispositif contained in para 128 of the judgment.
[74] See Arts 30 and 31 of the International Law Commission's Draft Articles on State Responsibility, Report of the ILC, 2001, A/56/10, p 43 *et seq* and see Crawford, *The*

quoting from the Permanent Court's judgment in the *Chorzow Factory* case,

> reparation must, as far as possible, wipe out all the consequences of the illegal act and reestablish the situation which would, in all probability, have existed if that act had not been committed.[75]

In this context, the Court concluded that 'Belgium must, by means of its own choosing, cancel the warrant in question and so inform the authorities to whom it was circulated'.[76] This conclusion was reached by 10 votes to six, whereas the conclusions as to jurisdiction and admissibility were reached by 15 votes to one and on the violation of the immunity of the then Foreign Minister, by the issue and international circulation of the arrest warrant, by 13 votes to three.

In the *Yerodia* case, the Court's conclusion as to cancellation of the warrant was clearly premised upon the notion of a continuing violation, that violation being the continuing existence of the arrest warrant itself, and the need for *restitutio in integrum*. However this does not follow from the terms of its discussion and decision. The declaratory judgment of the Court as put in paragraph 2 of the *dispositif* was rather that the issue and international circulation of the arrest warrant failed to respect the immunity of Mr Yerodia, the then Foreign Minister.[77] From this, it is logical to conclude that it was not the warrant itself that was per se illegal, but rather its application to a particular person deemed immune and inviolable in the circumstance of the moment since that person was then Foreign Minister. There is no formal statement that the issue and international circulation of a warrant concerning Mr Yerodia after he had ceased to be Foreign Minister and thereby ceased to benefit from immunity *ratione personae* would have, as such, been illegal. However, in the section concerned with remedies, the Court declared rather baldly, and with surprising absence of legal argument, that the warrant 'is still extant, and remains unlawful, notwithstanding the fact that Mr Yerodia has ceased to be Minister for Foreign Affairs'.[78] It is hard to see the legal basis for this leap in logic since the judgment was primarily concerned with immunity issues. More persuasive is the Joint Separate Opinion of Judges Higgins, Kooijmans and Buergenthal, which expressed the view that: 'As soon as he ceased to be

International Law Commission's Articles on State Responsibility (Cambridge, Cambridge University Press, 2002).

[75] *ICJ Reports*, 2002, at para 76 and see *PCIJ, Series A, No* 17, p 47.
[76] *Ibid*, para 76.
[77] *Ibid*, paras 70–71.
[78] *Ibid*, para 76.

Minister for Foreign Affairs, the illegal consequences attaching to the warrant also ceased'.[79]

Further, the Court by its quotation from the *Chorzow Factory* case was expressly seeking to restore the *status quo ante*. That, of course, would only be possible if Mr Yerodia were to be reappointed Foreign Minister of the Congo. There was no suggestion that this must happen. There is clearly room for a careful analysis of the concept of restitution in so far as the Court is concerned. In addition, the logic of the Court's approach is such that it should have directly addressed the legal source of the arrest warrant itself, that is the Belgian legislation of 16 June 1993 as amended by the Law of 19 February 1999.[80]

Whether, and to what extent, the Court may grant a remedy will thus depend upon a determination by the Court of its judicial function in the circumstances coupled with its view of the nature, scope and object of the claims made by the parties. The loose constitutional framework for remedies serves to place more stress upon the subjective perception by the Court of such variables than might be the case for domestic tribunals. Further, it is clear that the concept of declaratory judgments is very wide, including elements familiar as separate remedial Orders in domestic courts. There is tremendous scope here for clarification and evolution.

One may conclude, therefore, that we are in a period marked by judicial confidence and activism. The Court has rightly rejected a restrictive approach to its judicial function in the context of the issuance of declaratory judgments and has rightly rejected a narrow view of the relationship between such declaratory judgments and statements of legal consequences for the parties. Accordingly, it is clear that such judgments constitute a rather wider category than would be the case for domestic courts. Further, one may point to the wide view of restitution adopted in the *Yerodia* case and the emphasis in that and in the *LaGrand* case for the appropriate action to be taken by the State concerned 'by means of its own choosing'. However, that expression may be seen as something of a gentle cover for the requirements imposed by the Court.

Insofar as remedies are concerned, one has the sense that the Court is feeling its way forward and seeking to expand from a very cautious historical base. Binding provisional measures—coupled with the possibility of redress at the merits stage should such measures not be implemented—taken together with the reference to the limits of apology as remedy and the call for a review procedure in *LaGrand* and a broad (perhaps too broad)

[79] Joint Separate Opinion, available at: *http://www.icj-cij.org/icjwww/idocket/iCOBE/iCOBEframe.htm*, at para 89. See also the Dissenting Opinion of Judge C Van den Wyngaert, available at http://www.icj-cij.org/icjwww/idocket/iCOBE/iCOBEframe.htm, at para 83.

[80] And further amended twice during 2003.

approach in *Yerodia*, coupled with the significant comments made in the *Cameroon v Nigeria* case as to the legal consequences for the population once the boundary line had been determined; these all mark clear stages in the Court's thinking and signal perhaps important days yet to come in the rather muddy waters of international remedies.

4

State Responsibility for Breach of Interim Protection Orders of the International Court of Justice

MAURICE MENDELSON*

THIS CHAPTER CONSIDERS the responsibility of States for breaches of provisional (also known as interim) measures of protection ordered by the International Court of Justice,[1] and certain connected questions.

Logically, the first question to be considered is whether interim measures are binding. Article 41 of the Statute of the International Court of Justice, which is for present purposes identical to Article 41 of the Statute of the Permanent Court of International Justice, provides:

> 1. The Court shall have the power to indicate, if it considers that circumstances so require, any provisional measures which ought to be taken to preserve the respective rights of either party.
> 2. Pending the final decision, notice of the measures suggested shall forthwith be given to the parties and to the Security Council.

'Ought to be taken' seems rather weaker than 'must' or 'shall' be taken; and 'suggested' in paragraph 2 seems to point clearly to a lack of binding force.[2]

*QC; Barrister, Blackstone Chambers, London; Emeritus Professor of International Law, University of London.

[1] This essay is not concerned with what might be the position in other international courts and tribunals.

[2] J Elkind, *Interim Protection: A Functional Approach* (The Hague, 1981), p 153 is mistaken when he says that the reference to 'the respective rights of the parties' necessarily implies a correlative duty to observe *interim measures*: the phrase plainly relates to the substantive rights and duties of the parties, and in itself implies nothing about the 'incidental jurisdiction', as it has been called. He also seems mistaken when he says, 'The word 'ought' is normally used in

However, matters are not so simple. The equally authentic French text provides:

1. *La Cour a le pouvoir d'indiquer, si elle estime que les circonstances l'exigent, quelles measures conservatoires du droit de chacun doivent être prises à titre provisoire.*
2. *En attendant l'arrêt definitif, l'indication de ces mesures est immédiatement notifiée aux parties et au Conseil de sécurité.*

There is no mention here of 'suggestion'; and that being so, the expression '*doivent être prises*' is perhaps stronger than the English equivalent. On the other hand, the term '*indiquer*' is a little weak, and at best neutral.[3] At the end of the day, the French text is not conclusive either. The Chinese, Russian and Spanish texts of 1945 (there were no earlier versions in these languages) were apparently based on the English or French, and cast no more light.[4]

The drafting history is not entirely clear either. In the Advisory Committee of Jurists appointed by the League of Nations to draft the Statute of the Permanent Court of International Justice,[5] the original proposal of Raoul Fernandes used the word 'order', and he also wanted the measures to be supported by 'effective remedies'. Although, logically, the issue of binding force is different from that of enforcement, if a decision of the Court does have binding force, the question of how to enforce it naturally arises.[6] The Committee was very anxious to avoid getting into the deep waters of enforcement and accordingly, after some argument over 'order' and 'suggest', settled on the word '*indiquer*' in French, which was translated into English as 'to suggest'. It is interesting that, in his report on the draft Article (39) adopted by the Committee, Albert de La Pradelle nevertheless repeatedly referred to the Court making a '*suggestion*' and observed that the provision did not involve '*un arrêt, même interlocutoire, immédiament exécutoire*'.[7] He said that great care must be

law to describe a legal duty, not merely a moral one': the word would be equally appropriate on the hypothesis that the measures were not legally, but only morally, binding.

[3] The use by the Court of the term 'order' to describe its interim decisions does not assist in this context.
[4] I am grateful for the assistance of Professor Bin Cheng in relation to the Chinese version.
[5] See League of Nations, *Procès verbaux of the Proceedings of the Advisory Committee of Jurists, 1920*, I (Doc LN V 1920.2), pp 567–68, 588, 608–9, 637–38, 735–36. The text was originally drafted in French: the English translation came later.
[6] Hence the provision in Art 94(2) of the United Nations Charter about the enforcement of *judgments*.
[7] Above n 5, p 735. The English translation is perhaps misleading in rendering what he said as 'There is no question of a definite order, even of a temporary nature, which must be carried out at once': it looks as if the translator did not know what was an interlocutory judgment. De La Pradelle's observations were not referred to by the ICJ in the *LaGrand case*, discussed below.

taken in any exercise involving the limitation of sovereignty, and pointed to the difficulty in ensuring compliance with a definitive decision, let alone a temporary one. In the League Assembly, the choice of the precise verb was again a matter of discussion, but at the initiative of Max Huber, the word 'indicate' was retained; it was felt to be stronger than 'suggest', but not to give rise to problems of execution.[8] It seems that it was by an oversight that the word 'suggested' was left in paragraph 2 in the English, but not the French, text. The drafters of the UN Charter and the new Statute of the Court at Dumbarton Oaks and San Francisco did not change this wording and apparently regarded the whole subject of interim measures as uncontroversial. Adopting Article 94 of the Charter did not alter the position.[9] The subsequent practice of States and of the ICJ itself tended to support the conclusion that interim measures were not binding.[10] The opinion of writers, however, was more divided, though the preponderance of opinion was probably that they were not binding.[11]

Nevertheless, in its final judgment of 27 June 2001 in the *LaGrand case*[12] the Court, to the surprise of many,[13] clearly held that interim measures *are* binding and decided—by 13 votes to two (Judges Oda and Parra-Aranguren)—that:

> by failing to take all measures at its disposal to ensure that Walter LaGrand was not executed pending the final decision of the International Court of Justice in the case, the United States of America breached the obligation

[8] *LNOJ*, Records of 1st Assembly (1920), Meetings of Committees, I, 3rd Committee, Minutes of Meetings of Sub-Committee, 5th meeting, pp 368–69.

[9] Art 94 provides: '1. Each Member of the United Nations undertakes to comply with the decision of the International Court of Justice in any case to which it is a party. 2. If any party to a case fails to perform the obligations incumbent upon it under a judgment rendered by the Court, the other party may have recourse to the Security Council, which may, if it deems necessary, make recommendations or decide upon measures to be taken to give effect to the judgment.' An interim order of protection is not a 'judgment' within the meaning of para 2. See further, below n 25.

[10] A particularly good analysis is J Sztucki, *Interim Measures in the Hague Court* (Deventer 1983), pp 260–302, even if I would quibble with some specific parts of the discussion of the case-law.

[11] For my own part, I attempted to analyse the problem briefly in an essay in 1983 in 'Interim Measures of Protection and the Use of Force by States', in A Cassese, ed, *The Current Regulation of the Use of Force* (Dordrecht, 1986), p 339. I there suggested that, although the drafting history and subsequent practice of the PCIJ and ICJ, as well as States, did not in themselves warrant the conclusion that interim measures were binding, the position was more complicated than that. As well as the fact that certain treaties in force made such orders obligatory, there were circumstances—perhaps particularly if force were used contrary to the Court's order—where the State concerned could be said to be acting illegally, or at any rate at its peril if the judgment on the merits went against it.

[12] Not yet printed, but available on the internet at www.icj-cij.org/icjwww/idocket.

[13] See eg R Jennings, 'The *LaGrand* case', 1 *Law & Practice of International Courts & Tribunals* (2002), pp 13, 29–36; and H Thirlway, 'The Law & Procedure of the International Court of Justice 1960–1989, Part XII', 72 *BYIL* (2001), pp 32, 110–26.

> incumbent upon it under the Order indicating provisional measures issued by the Court on 3 March 1999.[14]

The majority relied principally on Article 33(4) of the Vienna Convention on the Law of Treaties 1969—which it held to reflect customary international law. This paragraph states in pertinent part that:

> ... when a comparison of the authentic texts discloses a difference of meaning which the application of Articles 31 and 32 does not remove, the meaning which best reconciles the texts, having regard to the object and purpose of the treaty, shall be adopted.

The Court found that it would be more consistent with Article 41's object and purpose of protecting the rights of the parties if provisional measures had binding force. It did not consider that the drafting history of the Statute or the wording of Article 94(1) of the Charter—requiring a party to a case to comply with the Court's 'decision'—contradicted this conclusion.[15] Although it has been suggested to the author, informally but from a very authoritative source, that such measures might bind in only some circumstances, there is nothing in the Judgment to qualify that holding or confine it to certain classes of case.[16] The Court seems unlikely to depart from, or even distinguish, this precedent in the foreseeable future. Indeed, in its judgment of 10 October 2002 in the *Case concerning the Land and Maritime Boundary between Cameroon and Nigeria*—to which I shall return very shortly—the Court referred, with apparent approval, to its earlier finding in the *LaGrand case* that interim measures are binding.[17]

The old debate about whether interim measures of the ICJ are binding must, therefore, be treated as having been authoritatively and definitively resolved. What I want to consider in this essay is: what are the consequences of this binding force in terms of State responsibility? I shall also consider the related, but wider, question of how, if a breach of interim measures is proved, the Court should respond. In examining these questions, we must bear in mind that the claim may ultimately fail, either for lack of jurisdiction and/or admissibility, or on the merits. There has been little consideration of these issues previously,[18] and I cannot claim to offer

[14] Above n 12, paras 92–116 & *dispositif*, sub-para 5.

[15] Amongst the separate and dissenting opinions and declarations, only the dissenting opinion of Judge Oda expressly questioned the majority's reasoning. A critical analysis of the Court's reasoning is to be found in the articles by Jennings and Thirlway, respectively, above n 13.

[16] Though, as Jennings points out, it is presumably open to the Court in some future case to couch some of the provisional measures it indicates in terms that are not legally binding.

[17] *LaGrand* case, above n 12, para 321. The *Case concerning the Land and Maritime Boundary between Cameroon and Nigeria* is not yet printed, but is available on the internet at www.icj-cij.org/icjwww/docket.

[18] Though I allude to them in my 1983 essay, above n 11. The article by Thirlway referred to, above n 13 (published after the present paper was given, though obviously written before),

definitive answers. Rather, I shall pose some questions and suggest some possible approaches.

The Court chose not to take the opportunity to provide some enlightenment in its recent final judgment in the *Cameroon v Nigeria case*.[19] In its Order of 15 March 1996[20] the Court had indicated that 'Both Parties should ensure that no action of any kind, and particularly no action by their armed forces, is taken which might prejudice the rights of the other in respect of whatever judgment the Court may render in the case, or which might aggravate or extend the dispute before it'; that an agreement of the previous month for a ceasefire in the Bakassi Peninsula should be respected; that both sides should ensure that there were none of their armed forces in the Peninsula beyond the positions that they held on 3 February 1996; that they should 'take all necessary steps to conserve evidence relevant to the present case within the disputed area'; and that they should lend every assistance to the UN Secretary-General's proposed fact-finding mission to the Peninsula. In its formal submissions on the merits, as well as claiming sovereignty over the Bakassi Peninsula and certain parcels of territory in the area of Lake Chad (together with contested areas along the long land boundary), Cameroon put forward a claim of State responsibility for the internationally wrongful acts done by Nigeria in occupying its territory, and sought reparation. (Nigeria put forward a similar counter-claim.) Cameroon specifically asked the Court to find that 'in failing to comply with the Order ... of 15 March 1996 the Federal Republic of Nigeria has been in breach of its international obligations'. In the event, though the Court upheld Cameroon's claims over the Bakassi Peninsula and the relevant part of the Lake Chad area[21] and ordered Nigeria to withdraw from those territories, it decided (without much in the way of supporting reasoning) that this decision was a sufficient remedy and declined to order any further redress.[22] On the specific issue of the breach of the provisional measures, it unanimously held that Cameroon had failed to discharge its burden of proving precisely what had occurred in Bakassi, either prior to the provisional measures Order or subsequently.[23] Likewise, neither party had discharged its burden of proving who was responsible for which of the many alleged incidents along the border or at sea.[24] Accordingly, the

also touches on some of these issues, but only briefly and in the context of his attack on the Court's finding in *La Grand* that interim measures are binding.

[19] In the interests of full disclosure I should mention that I was counsel for Cameroon in this case.
[20] *ICJ Reports*, 1996, p 13.
[21] As well as over some, but not all, of the contested frontier points.
[22] Above n 17, paras 308–19.
[23] *Ibid*, paras 320–22.
[24] *Ibid*, paras 323–24.

implications of the fact that interim measures are now to be regarded as binding have still to be worked out.

My present focus on the extent to which a State can be held responsible for breach of an order of interim protection does not mean, however, that I consider this as the main purpose of such measures. On the contrary: their object is to preserve rights that may be endangered and to prevent escalation of the dispute. The aim is preventive, not restitutionary; and one does not judge the efficacy of a watchdog by the number of people it bites. Furthermore, it would be a mistake to imagine that the obligation to comply, on the one hand, and the availability of remedies, on the other, are coterminous. Despite some progress, it is still the case that most of international law is not backed up by a system of compulsory adjudication, let alone enforcement of judgments; but we international lawyers have long resisted the claims of the ignorant (and the not-so-ignorant) that lack of enforceability prevents our system from being law. Nonetheless, as lawyers we are not likely to content ourselves with the mere notion that interim measures are binding: we want to know what this means *in practical terms*. The party that has committed, or is contemplating committing, the breach, wants to know what is likely to happen to it in consequence; and the victim of the breach likewise wants to know what redress it can expect.

In considering the practicalities, it may be useful to distinguish between the 'public order' aspect on the one hand, and, on the other hand, the interest of a particular litigant in seeking redress for a breach of an order. Let us consider, first, the 'public order' aspect.

In domestic law, courts have the means to ensure compliance with their interim orders. In common-law systems, for instance, either party can be fined or imprisoned for 'contempt of court'. The ICJ does not have these instruments available to it.[25] Another possibility might be to impose procedural sanctions, such as dismissing the claim or handing down a judgment in default. However, there is nothing in the Statute or Rules of the

[25] I shall not deal here in any detail with the question of enforcement by the Security Council of an order of provisional measures made by the ICJ; but some brief remarks may be appropriate. In *LaGrand* (para 108), the Court thought that no light was shed on the binding force of orders of interim protection by Article 94 (1) of the UN Charter (which requires States to comply with the Court's 'decision' in a case to which they are a party), since it was not clear whether such an order was a 'decision' for this purpose. (The terms of Article 94 are set out above, n 9.) In the course of its reasoning, it seems to have accepted that an order of interim protection is not a 'judgment' within the meaning of Article 94(2). It appears, therefore, that para 2 cannot be relied upon by a party who complains to the Security Council that an order of interim measures has not been complied with by its opponent. However, presumably (and notwithstanding the maxim *expressio unius, exclusio alterius)* this would not preclude the Council, in an appropriate case, from determining under Article 39 of the Charter that the resulting situation is a 'threat to the peace, breach of the peace or act of aggression', and taking such enforcement action as it deems appropriate under Chapter VII. Indeed, Article 40 of the Charter gives the Security Council the right to order its *own* provisional measures, irrespective of whether or not the Court has been seised.

Court that seems to authorise either course of action. Indeed, Article 53 expressly states that, even where a party does not appear or does not defend its case, the Court still cannot give a default judgment, but must satisfy itself that it has jurisdiction and that the case is well founded in fact and law. Given this general approach to default, it seems unlikely that a failure to comply with provisional measures will be treated differently. And if this is so, there would be a lack of congruity if the respondent could not lose its case merely through breach of an order, but the claimant could be non-suited for similar behaviour.

Another weapon in the armoury of public order in domestic law is the award of punitive damages: though the money goes to the private claimant, from the viewpoint of the party ordered to pay such damages it is equivalent to a fine.[26] Once again, it is questionable whether the International Court has an equivalent power. Certainly there is nothing in the Charter, Statute, or Rules of the Court authorising it to impose punitive damages, although this is not in itself conclusive since these instruments do not deal with remedies as such. However, it is by no means clear that punitive or exemplary damages, as opposed to compensation for 'moral damage' to nationals, are available in general international law—leaving aside, as irrelevant for our purposes, international criminal law.[27]

Of course, the public interest in compliance does not necessarily require punishment or the award of punitive damages. The whole system of international (non-criminal) adjudication is, after all, premised on the fact that in many cases it will be sufficient for the court to pronounce a declaratory judgment or order that the losing party perform certain acts (or refrain from performing them, as the case may be). As has often been noted, the pronouncements of the ICJ are more like those of a municipal constitutional court than those of a criminal court: there is an expectation of compliance by the authorities without the need for sanctions.

On the other hand, it could be argued that a breach of binding interim measures is not the same as other breaches of international law, precisely because the law has already been formally laid down in an order of the court. Take a case where two States claim sovereignty over an island, and no provisional measures are sought. Whatever the parties and outside observers may think about the strengths and weaknesses of one side's claims as compared to the other's, the fact remains that there has not yet

[26] The extent to which this type of remedy is available varies considerably from country to country.

[27] A useful recent survey is n Jørgensen, 'A Reappraisal of Punitive Damages in International Law', 68 *British Yearbook of International Law* (1997), p 247. See also Articles 36 & 37 of the International Law Commission's Articles on State Responsibility, and especially paras 4 & 16 of the Commentary on Article 36 in *Report of the International Law Commission on the Work of its 53rd session*. General Assembly Official Records, 56th Session, Supp. No. 10 (A/56/10).

been an authoritative pronouncement. But it is otherwise where interim measures are ordered in such a case. I do not assert that these measures would represent a finding on territorial sovereignty: the Court is careful to frame its orders in such a way as to make it clear that its interlocutory orders are without prejudice to the merits; and in a case like the one under consideration, the Court is most unlikely to make even a provisional finding that one State has sovereignty rather than the other. Rather, the law which is authoritatively laid down in the order is that neither party may do anything which would prejudice the rights of the other or aggravate or extend the dispute, that the use of force should be avoided, and/or that certain concrete steps should be taken (or avoided, as the case may be). To this extent, the law *has* been laid down: it is not merely conjectural. Logically, therefore, there is an argument for treating a breach of interim measures as a special case requiring a vindication of the public interest.

It might also be argued that a vindication of the 'private' interest of the injured party is—at least in most cases—a sufficient vindication of the public interest. But this assumes that the Court will be in a position to vindicate that private interest. As we are about to see, this is not necessarily the case. In particular, the victim of the breach may, for one reason or another, fail to obtain a remedy on the merits. In analysing the possibilities for vindicating the 'private' rights of the victim of a breach of interim measures, a variety of situations have to be envisaged. In doing so, it will be useful to recall that the claimant in the action on the merits[28] may not be the party who sought interim measures. Indeed, there may not be any claimant for interim measures at all: under Article 75 of the Rules of Court, the Court can order interim measures of its own motion, as well as ordering measures other than those requested.

1. Let us begin with a seemingly simple case. The State alleging that there has been a breach of an order of interim measures is also the successful claimant in the action on the merits. Let us suppose, further, that the case concerns sovereignty over an island and that, notwithstanding an order by the Court to maintain the *status quo*, the respondent State has built tourist hotels on the island. In that case, it might be thought, a judgment on the merits and an order to the respondent to withdraw from the island is remedy enough: the respondent has built the hotels at its peril, and has duly suffered financially through its non-compliance with the interlocutory order. But is the matter indeed so simple? The result would have been the same even if there had been no order for interim measures, or if there had been an order, but the Court had previously held that such measures are *not* binding. From the claimant's point of view, this may not matter: it has

[28] I deal with ancillary claims and counter-claims in cases 2–4 below, and cases where there is no formal 'claimant' or 'respondent' in case 6 below.

got its island, and some hotels besides. But from the standpoint of the public interest, the respondent is no worse off for having disobeyed the Court's order than if there had been no order.

2. Again, suppose the facts to be similar, save that oil has been extracted from the island, in violation of an order made under Article 41 of the Statute. The claimant has therefore suffered loss prior to the final judgment. Judging by the perfunctory treatment of Cameroon's State responsibility claims (and the counter-claims of Nigeria), it seems that the ICJ is not keen, in cases of disputed sovereignty or boundary delimitation, to have to go into questions of State responsibility for what was done, prior to judgment, by the State in fact controlling the territory.[29] In that case, the principal claims and counter-claims of State responsibility were sufficiently dealt with, in the Court's view, by its holding that, where it adjudged a particular piece of territory to belong to one State (mostly Cameroon), the other party was obliged expeditiously and unconditionally to withdraw its administration and/or any military or police forces.[30] And, as we have seen, on the particular issue of responsibility for breach of the provisional measures Order, the Court rejected the damages claims of both parties for lack of proof. Nevertheless, it did not rule that State responsibility is completely excluded in similar cases, and we may surmise that, if proper proof were forthcoming in a subsequent case, the Court might well feel constrained to deal with the issue. Some support for this view can be found in the *Case Concerning the Temple of Preah Vihear*.[31] There Cambodia had asked that the final judgment include an order that Thailand restore certain artefacts removed from the temple or the area around it. In holding that the claimant had sovereignty, the Court also decided that Thailand was obliged to restore any artefacts *of the kind specified* which *might have* been removed since the date of occupation of the temple by Thailand in 1954. The only reason it did not go further was that Cambodia had not sufficiently identified the objects or proved that they had been removed.

But the *Temple case* is instructive for another reason, too, for in that case there had been no request for, or order of, interim measures. Suppose that there had been, and that Thailand had violated the order by removing artefacts. Assume also that Cambodia was in a position to prove this. Presumably, the result would have been exactly the same, whether or not interim measures had been ordered. Once again, then, the fact that binding interim measures have been ordered in our hypothetical case of oil extraction from the disputed island makes no difference: there is no 'added value'.

3. Let us now suppose that the claimant is successful in its claim on the merits, but *it*—the claimant—is the party that has disobeyed the interim

[29] On this, see chapter 1 by Judge Rosalyn Higgins in this volume.
[30] Above n 17, paras 308–19.
[31] *ICJ Reports* 1962, pp 6, 36.

measures order. It is of course rather unlikely that, in the case of an order simply concerned with preserving the respective *rights* of the parties, the *claimant* will be in a position to violate the interim measures. For example, if its opponent is in possession of a piece of territory which the applicant claims, the applicant will not be in a position to exercise jurisdiction in that territory and, for instance, dispose of an artefact whose ownership is contested. But suppose that the order disobeyed was to refrain from using force. The applicant has invaded the island, contrary to this order, and has killed and injured civilians and members of the respondent's armed forces. This would be a breach of the substantive law regarding the use of force,[32] independent of the interim order of the Court. Provided that the jurisdictional title is broad enough to cover a counter-claim by the respondent,[33] and that the breach is properly pleaded and properly proved, there is no reason of principle why the Court should refuse it redress.[34] But if redress is given on *this* basis (breach of general law), what difference does it make that an interim measures order has been disregarded? And if the disobedience does not result in punitive damages, what difference does it make that a binding order has been flouted?

4. Up till now, we have been considering cases where the applicant is successful on the merits. Let us now consider the situation where the respondent has violated the interim measures of protection ordered by the Court, but it succeeds on the merits. For instance, it occupies a disputed island, but the island is subsequently held to belong to it. It might be argued that, if the respondent is successful on the merits, no damage has been done to the claimant by the respondent's breach of the interim measures. But even if that were so, damage has been done to the international legal order, inasmuch as the Court's order—*ex hypothesi* a binding order—has been ignored. Also, international peace has been disturbed. Moreover, it is not necessarily the case that the claimant itself has suffered no harm. For example, the claimant's nationals, living on the island, might have been killed or injured, or their property destroyed or damaged, during the invasion. It is

[32] An illustration of this proposition is the general refusal of the United Nations to accept the lawfulness of Argentina's invasion of the Falkland Islands, even though it claimed that it was simply recapturing its own territory and some UN Members supported its claim to sovereignty. See also Mendelson, above n 11.

[33] For instance, if both parties had made Optional Clause declarations with no limitation as to the subject matter—always supposing, of course, that the claim in question is 'directly connected with the subject-matter of the claim of the other party' within the meaning of Article 80 of the Rules of Court. I shall deal, in the context of case 4 below, with the question whether Article 41 of the Statute itself gives the Court jurisdiction to rule on such claims.

[34] Having said that, it should also be noted that it may not always be good tactics to make an elaborate ancillary claim for, eg, loss and damage. The Court is not particularly well equipped to establish who did what to whom, when, and with what consequences, and it lacks the time, and possibly the inclination, to enter into the detail of numerous incidents. I elaborate on the question of ancillary claims, this time by the *claimant*, in case 4 below.

an interesting question whether the Court would have jurisdiction to award damages to the claimant for breach of the order of interim protection.

It seems clear that the authority of the Court in respect of interim measures is distinct—at least to some extent—from its competence over the merits. In the context of the question whether the Court has jurisdiction to grant interim measures before it has definitively established that it has jurisdiction over the merits, the generally accepted view is that competence in respect of interim measures is part of the 'incidental jurisdiction' conferred by the Statute and, technically, independent of the Court's competence over the substance. Accordingly, the Court has repeatedly held that jurisdiction over the merits does not have to be definitively established before an order can be made under Article 41: it suffices that prima facie there seems to be such jurisdiction.[35] Still less is it inclined expressly to determine, at the interim measures stage, whether there is prima facie a good case on the merits themselves.[36] Building on this idea of an independent incidental jurisdiction, it might perhaps be argued that it is sufficient to empower the Court to grant a remedy, in the final judgment, even against a respondent who is successful on the main claim.

As against this, it may be pointed out that the incidental jurisdiction is a jurisdiction to *make* orders, not to 'enforce' them. It could also be observed that the measures are, after all, *provisional*. The language of Article 41 itself bears this out: paragraph 1 speaks of '*provisional* measures that ought to be taken to *preserve* the respective *rights* of either party', and paragraph 2 says that notice of the measures shall be given to the parties and to the Security Council '*pending the final decision*'. Furthermore, the form that orders tend to take is that they are preceded by words such as: 'The Court indicates, *pending a decision in the proceedings instituted as aforesaid*, the following provisional measures' (emphasis added). The better view therefore seems to be that the judgment on the merits puts an end to the interim measures.[37]

But is this the whole story? Certainly the measures are no longer in force once a judgment on the merits has been given. But does this preclude the

[35] See eg M Mendelson, 'Interim Measures of Protection in Cases of Contested Jurisdiction', 46 *British Yearbook of International Law* (1972–73), p 259; J Sztucki, above, n 10, pp 221–60; S Rosenne, 'Provisional Measures and Prima Facie Jurisdiction Revisited', in N Ando, E McWhinney & R Wolfrum, eds, *Liber Amicorum Judge Shigeru Oda* (The Hague, 2002), p 515; C Dominicé, 'La compétence *prima facie* de la Cour internationale de justice aux fins d'indication de mesures conservatoires', *ibid*, p 383; K Obata, 'The Relevance of Jurisdiction to Deal with the Merits to the Power to Indicate Interim Measures: A Critique of the Recent Practice of the International Court of Justice' *ibid*, p 451.

[36] Though see Thirlway, above n 13, pp 87–91.

[37] In the *Case concerning the Arbitral Award of 31 July 1989 (Guinea-Bissau v Senegal) (Provisional Measures)*, *ICJ Reports* 1990, pp 64, 70 (para 26), the Court refused to order certain measures which Guinea-Bissau had requested, because they were not the subject of the current proceedings and so 'any such measures could not be *subsumed* by the Court's judgment on the merits'. Emphasis added.

Court from taking into account the breach of interim measures *in framing its final judgment*? If, for instance, the (ultimately successful) respondent has violated interim measures of protection in invading the contested island, and has killed and wounded civilians of the claimant State, this is after a breach of the law relating to the use of force that is separate from the question of sovereignty. Could it perhaps be argued here (as in the converse case 3 above) that the Court has the power to award damages to the claimant, either because it has 'merits' jurisdiction over the (ancillary) claim for damages for injury to its personnel and nationals, etc, or because the competence to give relief is part of the 'incidental jurisdiction'?

If the answer is affirmative, but the sole reason is that the Court has jurisdiction over the ancillary claims on the merits, once again it makes no difference whether interim measures were ordered or not. The fact that the measures are binding would only make a difference if *their* breach was the basis on which the damages were awarded. However, my guess is that the Court will be unwilling to make a finding of this sort in the foreseeable future. It will probably think that it has been bold enough already in holding interim measures to be binding, without wanting to take the further step of 'punishing' their breach. It can avoid the issue, if it wishes, by stressing the provisional character of provisional measures, and that they have performed their role and cease to apply once judgment on the merits is given. But the implication of such a finding seems to be that the order was only conditionally binding—that is, binding subject to being rendered null and void as soon as the Court reaches the stage of handing down its final judgment. In other words, the order was only 'sort of' binding.[38]

5. Until now, we have been considering cases where the Court actually gives a judgment on the merits. But as we know, many cases in the ICJ fail because the Court holds that it does not have jurisdiction or that the case is inadmissible. Since interim measures can be (and often are) ordered prior to a decision on jurisdiction and admissibility, the question arises whether, in such a case, redress can be given for breach of the interim order, even if the Court has to remove the case from its list once it has given its judgment on jurisdiction and/or admissibility. There are three considerations that might be thought to support the view that redress should be given. First, as we have already seen, the 'incidental jurisdiction' is distinct from jurisdiction over the merits. Secondly, *ex hypothesi* a wrong has been committed: a party has violated binding provisional measures. Thirdly, it

[38] The lesson for litigators appears to be that it is unsafe to rely simply on the breach of interim measures as a 'cause of action'. The facts giving rise to the breach should be separately pleaded and properly proved. Since a judgment need not be entirely for one party or the other, this will enable the Court to uphold the ancillary claims on the merits even if it rejects the principal one—provided that the legal inferences to be drawn in respect of the ancillary claims do not logically depend on the claimant's being successful in its principal claim. Similarly, *mutatis mutandis*, for counterclaims. But see the caveat in n 33 above.

would of course be incorrect to assume that, just because the Court lacks jurisdiction, the victim of the breach of interim measures had no substantive rights. It might, for example, have had sovereignty over our hypothetical disputed island, even if the Court had no jurisdiction so to determine; and even if it did not have sovereignty, the invasion could well have been illegal. But against this, one could repeat the argument already made in connection with case 4 above, that provisional measures are just that, and in the present instance the 'final decision' referred to in Article 41(2) of the Statute is the judgment on jurisdiction (and/or admissibility) whereby the claim is dismissed.[39] My instinct is that, for the foreseeable future, the Court is going to be very reluctant to give redress for breach of interim measures where it dismisses the claim for lack of jurisdiction or admissibility. Perhaps less because it considers the legal arguments for refraining to be conclusive than because it will think that it has been bold enough already. But if so, once again the consequence is that a breach of 'binding' interim measures can go unredressed. Moreover, a respondent which considers that it has a strong case on lack of jurisdiction or admissibility, or indeed on the merits, may be tempted to disregard the interim measures ordered, knowing that, if its opinion turns out to be correct, it will suffer no adverse consequences from its disobedience.[40]

6. Up till now, I have assumed for the sake of clarity of exposition that there is a claimant and a respondent. But in a case brought by special agreement, this will not, strictly, be the case. This does not seem to affect our analysis significantly, but it does complicate it a little. Likewise if there are more than two parties. I have, moreover, so far assumed that only one party is guilty of a breach of interim measures. It is, of course, possible that both parties have disobeyed them. They may both have disobeyed the same injunction—for instance, they may both have invaded different parts of the same contested island. Or they may have committed different breaches. In principle, the reasoning set out above should still apply, *mutatis mutandis*; but here, the *mutanda* may be numerous and the complications multiplied. Moreover, if the parties are more or less equally at fault, the Court will probably be even less inclined to penalise disobedience or award compensation for it.

7. As we have already seen, the Court can order interim measures of its own motion or at the request of either (or both) of the parties. And when it does so, it can order measures different from, or additional to, those

[39] I appreciate of course that, despite the 1978 amendments to the Rules of the Court, objections to jurisdiction or admissibility can and are still sometimes joined to the merits. But this does not fundamentally affect the argument in the text.

[40] The Court is unlikely to be well-disposed to a party which disobeys it; but if it does not have the right to try the merits, there is, on the present hypothesis, little that it can do about it.

requested. So up till now, though I have considered whether the violator of the interim measures is the claimant or the respondent *in the main action*, I have not gone into the issue of who requested the *interim measures*. But suppose, now, that the party who violated the interim measures was the same one as had requested them in the first place. Is there not something particularly shocking about this case? And, if the transgressor cannot be punished either by being non-suited or by damages, how significant is it that interim measures are now to be regarded as binding? I think that perhaps it could make *some* difference, but very possibly not to the extent of additional relief being given. In the *Hostages case*, the United States of America had sought interim orders for the release of the US nationals who were being held hostage in Tehran; restoration of control over its embassy, chancery and consular premises; and general respect for diplomatic and consular immunities and privileges.[41] But in addition, the Court, widening the scope of a further measure requested by the claimant, ordered that *both* parties (not just Iran):

> should not take any action and should ensure that no action is taken which may aggravate the tension between the two countries or render the existing dispute more difficult of solution.

Nevertheless, whilst the case was pending—and, indeed, after hearings had been concluded and the Court was preparing its judgment on the merits—the United States made a military incursion (unsuccessfully, as it turned out) aimed at rescuing the hostages. The Court recognised the US Government's concern about the well-being of its nationals and its understandable frustration at Iran's long detention of them in defiance of two Security Council resolutions as well as of the Court's own interim order. Nevertheless, it reprimanded the United States in the following terms:

> The Court therefore feels bound to observe that an operation undertaken in those circumstances, from whatever motive, is of a kind calculated to undermine respect for the judicial process in international relations; and to recall that in paragraph 47.1.B. of its Order of 15 December 1979 the Court had indicated that no action was to be taken by either party which might aggravate the tension between the two countries.

It went on to say, however, that questions of the legality of the United States, action, or of responsibility for it, were not before the Court; furthermore, the action could have no bearing on the evaluation of the

[41] *United States Diplomatic and Consular Staff in Tehran (Provisional Measures), ICJ Reports* 1979, pp 7, 20–21.

actions of the Iranian Government some six months earlier.[42] At the time of this Judgment, it had not been settled that interim measures are binding. Now that it has, one might surmise that the condemnation for a breach of interim measures by the country that seeks them would be somewhat stronger. But it is questionable whether any action beyond strong condemnation would be taken.

8. So far, we have been considering redress for the harm done by a State's failure to comply with provisional measures. But for the sake of completeness, I should also mention the potential harm done if a State *does* comply. Suppose, for instance, that State A wants to build a dam which will cause great (and quantifiable) benefit to its nationals as soon as the project is completed. State B submits to the ICJ that interim measures are necessary in order to protect its own rights and interests, and the Court orders them. Ultimately, the Court dismisses the claim, either through want of jurisdiction or on the merits. So the measures are discharged. But it may well have taken years to reach this point. In the meantime, the respondent will have suffered significant economic loss through having to refrain from inaugurating the project. Arguably, even if the provisional measures had not been binding, the State would have refrained out of respect for the Court: but now that they are definitely obligatory, it has no choice, legally speaking. Should it be compensated for that loss? In English law, for instance, the problem is dealt with by what are called 'undertakings in damages'. If A applies for an interim injunction, compliance with which may cause B economic loss, it will normally be a pre-condition that A undertakes to compensate B for any loss if, ultimately, the main claim fails.[43] But this solution may not be suitable for the International Court. For one thing, the Court's power to order provisional measures of its own motion, or measures other than those that the applicant for them sought, could make the requirement of an undertaking difficult to administer. Secondly, whilst the issue of an interim injunction is discretionary in English law, and so can be subjected to conditions, it is questionable whether it is discretionary in the ICJ. Questions of judgment may be involved, certainly; but probably not discretion as such. Thirdly, there are great differences in context between the powers of domestic courts in relation to interlocutory injunctions and those of the ICJ: the former have compulsory jurisdiction (not to mention means of enforcement), while the latter does not. Fourthly, giving effect to the undertaking could involve the Court in detailed investigations of a technical and financial character which it is ill-suited, and probably disinclined, to conduct. In any case, there is no mention of undertakings in damages in the Statute or Rules of the Court.

[42] *ICJ Reports*, 1980, pp 3, 43–44 (paras 93–94).
[43] Civil Procedure Rules 1998, Part 25, Practice Direction 5.1 (1). This is separate from the issue of security for costs.

In the *Case concerning Passage through the Great Belt*, Denmark claimed that if the Court were disposed to grant Finland's request for interim measures of protection enjoining Denmark from proceeding with its plan to build a bridge, then the applicant should also be required to give an undertaking that it would compensate Denmark for all losses incurred in complying with the measures, should the application fail on the merits. Counsel for Finland (Sinclair) submitted that such a request at this stage was unfounded in international law: reparation was designed to compensate for an internationally wrongful act, and there was nothing wrongful in Finland's seeking relief from the Court. This appears to beg the question whether what is being sought is reparation. He also argued, more convincingly, that it was questionable whether the Court's powers under Article 41 extended so far, and that to require an undertaking in damages would, as a matter of policy, deter States from seeking the protection of the Court.[44] For Denmark, its Agent (Magid) asserted that it was a 'general principle of law recognised by civilised nations' that a party requesting an injunction is liable for damages suffered by the other party as a result of such injunction, if the court later decides that the actions in question were legal; and he 'suggested' that the principle should be applied by the ICJ. In support of his assertion about domestic law, he cited the laws of the Scandinavian States (other than Iceland), Germany, Italy, France, England and the United States of America.[45] Counsel for Finland (Treves), as well as repeating Sinclair's arguments, responded that Article 38(1)(c) of the Statute was not an appropriate basis on which to found the powers of the Court; that the selection of legal systems was too narrow; that there were differences between them; and that, bearing in mind that the object of interim measures was to preserve the rights to be adjudged on the merits, it could not be said that the payment of an indemnity had anything to do with free passage through the Great Belt.[46] The response of the Danish Agent added little to what had already been said.[47] In the event, the Court decided unanimously that the circumstances did not warrant the indication of interim measures, so the question of an undertaking did not need to be decided. However, it is plain from the above account that the question of undertakings in damages would be fraught with difficulties, and it seems unlikely that the ICJ will be prepared to require them in the foreseeable future, under its existing powers. It also seems doubtful that there would be the political will to seek an amendment to the Statute in this respect; in any case, such an amendment is subject to the same daunting obstacles that face amendment of the UN Charter itself.[48]

[44] *Pleadings, Oral Arguments, Documents*, pp 111–12.
[45] *Ibid*, pp 169–74.
[46] *Ibid*, pp 198–201.
[47] *Ibid*, pp 217–18.
[48] See Art 108 & 109.

SUMMARY AND CONCLUSIONS

The link between the binding force of interim measures and their enforceability was perceived as far back as 1920, when what became the substance of Article 41 of the Statute was drafted. However, the Advisory Committee of Jurists and the League of Nations hoped to avoid the problem by using wording which was at best weak, was certainly unclear, and was widely thought to mean that the measures were not binding. For some 80 years this remained the position, until the Court in *LaGrand* held—to the surprise of many—that provisional measures were binding, and that the United States was responsible for having disregarded them.

Many who favour the progress of international law will applaud this outcome (if not necessarily the reasoning). The uncertainty of the previous situation was not satisfactory, and it is probably more appropriate for all orders of a court in contentious matters to be binding. Certainly, this was the lesson drawn by those who established the International Tribunal for the Law of the Sea, for example.[49]

Nevertheless, the new-found obligatory character of provisional measures in the ICJ does throw up the question of the practical significance of their binding force. Enforceability, even in a broad sense, is of course not the only—or probably even the main—issue: the pull towards compliance will naturally be greater if obedience is not perceived to be a matter of choice. Nevertheless, it is appropriate to ask oneself what the consequences would be if—as is alas likely—some addressees of the Court's orders fail to comply.

Detailed analysis of the role of the Security Council in such a case is beyond the scope of this paper. However, on a brief examination it appears that the measures do not fall within Article 94 of the UN Charter. I suggest, however, that this does not exhaust the Council's powers, and that if it holds that there is a threat to the peace, breach of the peace or act of aggression under Article 39, then it would be entitled to take appropriate coercive measures under Chapter VII.

So far as the Court itself is concerned, it seems clear that it does not have the authority to fine States who do not comply, and still less to punish the individuals who acted on behalf of the State. It is also unlikely that the Court can impose procedural sanctions on the disobedient party, either by non-suiting the claimant or by giving a default judgment against the respondent. Certainly, nothing in the Statute or Rules of the Court expressly authorises the imposition of procedural penalties in such a case.

Whilst the Court may possibly have the power to offer redress for *dommage morale* in appropriate circumstances, it is questionable whether it has the right to award punitive or exemplary damages. If it has not, then this weapon is not available to ensure compliance with interim measures.

[49] See Law of the Sea Convention 1982, Art 290(6).

In that event, the only concrete sanction (as opposed to declaratory relief) in the public interest is for the Court to award simple damages to the victim of a failure to comply with binding interim measures. From the victim's point of view, this remedy is simply compensatory; but from the perpetrator's viewpoint, it might theoretically be a sanction. There are, however, difficulties with this approach.

First, where damages are awarded (or other relief given), it is difficult to identify what difference it makes that interim measures have been disregarded. Where the victim is entitled to relief in the main action, it will normally be entitled to a remedy for the particular conduct complained of, *whether or not provisional measures had been ordered.*

Secondly, if the victim of the breach is unable to obtain a remedy on the merits—either for reasons of jurisdiction or admissibility, or perhaps even because it is not seeking any substantive relief, but simply defending the action—it seems questionable that the Court's incidental jurisdiction will be sufficient to entitle it (the victim) to a remedy. It might be otherwise if the victim, whilst unsuccessful as to the main claim on the merits, has other claims (or counterclaims) of its own which the Court upholds. But in such a case the relief is given on the merits, and the fact that there has been a breach of interim measures is unlikely to make a difference to the level of damages awarded.

It seems to make no difference to this analysis even if the party who disobeys the order of interim measures is the one who requested it. So, if a potential transgressor were to ask its legal advisers 'What practical consequences will there be if we do not comply with interim measures?', the answer might well be:

> You will be declared a miscreant by the Court, but apart from that there are unlikely to be any different consequences from what would have happened if no interim measures had been ordered, or if they had not been binding.

Essentially similar considerations apply if both parties have disobeyed the interim measures or if there are more than two; but the analysis naturally becomes more complicated.

Most of my analysis has been concerned with the remedy for the prejudice suffered by a victim of a breach of interim measures. But I briefly examined the position where a party has suffered loss because it has *complied* with the interim measures, in a case where ultimately it succeeds on jurisdiction, admissibility or the merits. I could not find any existing mechanism by which relief could be granted.

I think it unlikely, for a variety of reasons, that the Court will add 'teeth' to binding interim orders in the near future. More probably, having taken a bold step, it will want to proceed with caution.

It makes sense for the interim injunctions of domestic courts to be binding, because they have compulsory jurisdiction and the means of enforcing their decisions. The International Court of Justice is not in that happy position. This is not necessarily to say that the decision in *LaGrand* was a mistake, but just that it has thrown up a new set of problems. In this paper I have sought to identify what practical difference the new dispensation is likely to make in terms of remedies for breach, and to identify the problem areas. In time, no doubt, the lineaments of the problems, and perhaps even their solutions, will become clearer. Meanwhile, I hope it has been of some use to focus attention on the issues.

5

State Responsibility for the Decisions of National Courts

CHRISTOPHER GREENWOOD*

STATE RESPONSIBILITY IS a subject much considered by courts—both national and international—as the essays in this collection demonstrate. Less frequently discussed, however, is the question of when a State can be held responsible for a violation of international law incurred as a result of a decision of a national court. There can be no doubting the principle that a State can be held responsible for the acts of its courts. The national courts are as much organs of the State as are its parliament, executive government and armed forces and their decisions are thus imputable to the State. Moreover, the concept of denial of justice as a wrongful act in international law has been well established for over a 150 years. Nevertheless, the circumstances in which the actions of a State's courts amount to a denial of justice for which the State can be held responsible in international law are not as clearly defined as might be expected.

In particular, there has long been a lack of clarity on whether a State can be held responsible for a denial of justice on the basis of the decision of a lower court or whether denial of justice requires a failure of the system of justice in a State, so that only if that system fails to correct, through its appeal mechanism, deficiencies in the proceedings in a lower court can there be said to be a denial of justice for the purposes of international law.

Discussion of this subject has been bedevilled by two problems. First, most of the cases in which this question has arisen are comparatively old—the standards which they apply, and the language on which they are couched, often sits oddly with modern notions of State responsibility.

* CMG, QC; Professor of International Law, London School of Economics and Political Science; and Barrister, Essex Court Chambers, London.

Secondly, much of the discussion—both in the jurisprudence and the literature on the subject—confuses the substantive law on denial of justice with the application of the local remedies rule, which is now recognised as a procedural matter but has not always been seen as such even in recent times.

The purpose of the present paper is, therefore, to explore the question of whether the decision of a lower court can constitute a denial of justice irrespective of the possibility of appeal or whether only a failure of the judicial system as a whole (either through the lack of an available appeal mechanism or the failure of that mechanism to correct a flawed decision of a lower court) is required.

Particular attention will be paid to the recent arbitral award in *Loewen v United States of America,*[1] which contains a detailed discussion of this question. The *Loewen* claim was brought under Chapter 11 of NAFTA and arose out of an award by a Mississippi State court of US$500 million in punitive and compensatory damages against the Loewen Group, a Canadian company with investments in the United States, in a civil action brought against Loewen by a Mississippi businessman and his family. The Tribunal concluded that 'the whole trial and its resultant verdict were clearly improper and discreditable and cannot be squared with minimum standards of international law and fair and equitable treatment'.[2] The Tribunal nevertheless rejected Loewen's argument that it had been the victim of a violation of Chapter 11 for which the United States could be held responsible in international proceedings. One of the reasons for reaching this conclusion was that Loewen had failed to demonstrate that it had not had available to it opportunities for correcting the decision of the Mississippi court on appeal.[3]

[1] The Final Award of 13 June 2003 appears at www.state.gov/documents/organization/22094.pdf. The Tribunal's earlier decision on the Respondent's objections to competence and jurisdiction ('the Preliminary Award') was given on 5 January 2001 and appears at www.state.gov/documents/organization/3921.pdf. The Tribunal, which was constituted under the Additional Facility of ICSID, comprised Sir Anthony Mason (Chairman), Judge Abner Mikva and Lord Mustill. Lord Mustill was appointed to replace Yves Fortier QC, who was party to the Preliminary Award but resigned in September 2001. Both awards will be reported in volume 126 of the *International Law Reports (ILR)*. The present writer was an expert witness called by the United States in these proceedings. The United States also filed an opinion by Professor Bilder, while the Claimant filed opinions from Sir Robert Jennings and Sir Ian Sinclair. All the opinions are available at www.naftalaw.org and www.state.gov/s/l/c3755.htm.

[2] Final Award, *ibid*, para 137.

[3] Space does not permit consideration of the other issues discussed in the two awards, in particular, the decision (in paras 220–239 of the Final Award, *ibid*) concerning the application of the continuing nationality principle, which was a separate ground for rejecting Loewen's claims.

1. THE CONCEPT OF DENIAL OF JUSTICE AND THE DECISIONS OF LOWER COURTS

Where a national of one State invokes international law (or where the State of his nationality claims on his behalf) against another State, there are usually three separate issues to be considered:

(a) whether there is an act which is imputable to the respondent State;
(b) whether that act is contrary to international law; and
(c) whether the respondent State can be held responsible for that act in international proceedings before local remedies have been exhausted.

The first issue presents no problems in this context. The decisions of a court—at whatever level in the judicial hierarchy—are plainly imputable to the State. As Article 4(1) of the International Law Commission's Articles on State Responsibility makes clear:

> The conduct of any State organ shall be considered an act of that State under international law, whether the organ exercises legislative, executive, judicial or any other functions, whatever position it holds in the organization of the State and whatever its character as an organ of the central government or of a territorial unit of the State.[4]

It should, however, be noted that not all of the earlier commentators accepted that the decisions of lower courts were imputable to the State. Thus, Borchard, in an influential work published in 1915,[5] doubted whether a State could be held responsible for the decisions of a lower court. In addition, Freeman, writing in 1938, commented that the 'responsibility [of a State] is engaged as the result of a definitive judicial decision *by a court of last resort* which violates an international obligation of the State'.[6]

To the extent that these writers were suggesting that the decisions of lower courts are not imputable to the State, contemporary international law has plainly disavowed that thesis. It is important to remember, however, that the rigid distinction between the primary (or substantive) rules of law for the violation of which the State could be held responsible

[4] J Crawford, *The International Law Commission's Articles on State Responsibility* (Cambridge, 2002), p 94. See also the *Salvador Commercial Company* case, *RIAA*, Vol XV, (1902), p 455, at p 477.

[5] E Borchard, *Diplomatic Protection of Citizens Abroad* (New York, 1915), p 198.

[6] A Freeman, *International Responsibility of States for Denial of Justice* (London, 1938), pp 311–12. Emphasis added.

and the secondary (or general) rules which governed the establishment of that responsibility—that has been the hallmark of discussion of the subject in the last 40 years[7]—was not so clearly understood (or, at least, was not regarded as so important) before that time. Even if the reservations which Borchard and Freeman expressed would not now be accepted as limitations within the secondary rules regarding imputability, they may nevertheless be important when one comes to consider the primary rules that define the scope of denial of justice.

It is harder to disentangle discussion of the second and third issues outlined above. The second issue concerns the content of the primary rule that prohibits the denial of justice to aliens, while the third appears to be concerned only with the conditions in which there may be an international claim for the violation of the primary norm. In practice, however, the two have been almost inextricably linked.

So far as the content of the primary norm is concerned, international tribunals are understandably cautious in concluding that the judicial system of a State has fallen so far short of international standards that it has perpetrated a denial of justice. Only if there is clear evidence of discrimination against a foreign litigant or an outrageous failure of the judicial system is there a denial of justice in international law. The point is very clearly put by O'Connell, who states that:

> When one comes to examine failure of the courts themselves 'palpable deviations' from the accepted standards of judicial practice are not so readily ascertained. For one thing, there is a presumption in favour of the judicial process. For another, defects in procedure may be of significance only internally, and not work an international injustice. For a third, wide discretion must be allowed a court in the reception and rejection of evidence, in adjournment, and in admission of documents, and it cannot be said that deviations even from the municipal law rules of evidence are deviations from an international standard. The first thing that must be ascertained is whether as a result of court manoeuvrings substantial injustice has been done the claimant; the second is whether these manoeuvrings really amount to obstruction of the judicial process, and are extrinsic to the merits of his claim. Bad faith and not judicial error seems to be the heart of the matter, and bad faith may be indicated by an unreasonable departure from the rules of evidence and procedure.[8]

[7] In particular since the late Roberto Ago took over work on the State Responsibility project within the ILC; see Crawford, above n 4, pp 1–4 and 74.

[8] D O'Connell, *International Law,* 2nd edn (Oxford, 1970), p 948. See also the authorities cited by D O'Connell, in particular, *Chattin v United Mexican States, RIAA*, Vol IV, (1927), p 282 and *Garcia and Garza v USA, RIAA*, Vol IV (1926), p 119; J Brierly and H Waldock, *The Law of Nations* 6th edn (Oxford, 1963), p 287; and Article 9, 'Harvard Research', (1929) 23 *American Journals of International Law* Supp P 173.

Other writers have taken a similar view. Thus, Garner thought that what was required was 'manifest injustice' or 'gross unfairness'.[9] Jimenez de Arechaga spoke of 'flagrant and inexcusable violation'.[10] As Baxter and Sohn put it (in the Commentary to their Draft Convention on the International Responsibility of States for Injuries to Aliens) 'the alien must sustain a heavy burden of proving that there was an undoubted mistake of substantive or procedural law operating to his prejudice.'[11]

The remarks of the Arbitration Tribunal in the NAFTA case of *SD Myers v Canada* that 'a Chapter 11 tribunal does not have an open-ended mandate to second-guess government decision-making'[12] and its reference to 'the high measure of deference that international law generally extends to the right of domestic authorities to regulate matters within their own borders'[13] are particularly apposite where a case is based on an allegation of denial of justice by a municipal court.

Let us suppose, however, that a decision of a court of first instance plainly falls short of the standards laid down by international law, even applying the strict test enunciated by O'Connell. Does that decision amount to a denial of justice under international law if there exists a reasonable possibility that it might be corrected by an appeal or other form of challenge within the national court system or is there a denial of justice only if no such possibility exists or once all avenues of appeal or challenge have proved fruitless? Properly understood, this question lies at the heart of the substantive rule, for it concerns what constitutes a denial of justice in international law—the flawed decision of a court or the failure of the judicial system as a whole. Unfortunately, consideration of this question has tended to be confused with discussion of the application of the local remedies rule.

Since the normal rule is that an alien must exhaust all available domestic remedies before his case can be taken up on the international plane, consideration of whether there is a remedy in the courts of the respondent State is usually necessary whatever was the original cause of harm to the alien. As a general rule, that is the case irrespective of whether the original cause of the harm is (1) an act that is plainly imputable to the State and contrary to international law—for example a discriminatory and uncompensated expropriation, carried out either by legislative decree or

[9] J Garner, 'International Responsibility of States for Judgments of Courts and Verdicts of Juries amounting to Denial of Justice', 10 *British Yearbook of International Law* (1929), p 181, at p 183.

[10] J de Arechaga, 'International Law in the Past Third of a Century', 159 *Recueil des Cours* (1978), p 282.

[11] F Garcia-Amador, L Sohn and R Baxter, *Recent Codification of the Law of State responsibility for Injury to Aliens* (Leiden, 1974), p 198 (commentary to Art 8; the text was prepared in 1961).

[12] 121 *International Law Reports* 72 (para 261).

[13] *Ibid*, para 262.

executive action—or (2) the act of a private party which is not imputable to the State.

Nevertheless, the significance of recourse to the courts of the respondent State in these two cases is quite different. In the first case, it is the expropriation that is the violation of international law. The function of recourse to the local courts here is properly regarded as procedural; it gives the respondent State the opportunity to rectify the original wrong in its own courts before calling it to account at the international level.[14] In the second case, the original cause of harm is not imputable to the respondent State and cannot, therefore, constitute a cause of action against that State in international law. If there is to be a cause of action at all it can only be denial of justice, arising either because the respondent State denies the alien access to the courts or because those courts behave in a way which is discriminatory or manifestly contrary to international standards of behaviour. In this case it is only the action of the courts (or of those organs of the State who deny access to the courts) which is imputable to the respondent State.

The second case is not really an instance of the application of the local remedies rule at all. Unlike the first case, where the question is whether the respondent State's courts have provided a remedy for that State's wrongful act, in the second case it is the behaviour of those courts which is itself said to constitute the wrongful act.

This distinction is clearly established. Nevertheless, discussion of it in the literature and the case law has often been confused and the second category of case has frequently been discussed as though it were an application of the local remedies rule, sometimes with the qualification that the local remedies rule is described in such a case as being 'substantive', whereas in the first category of cases it is regarded as procedural. Unless there has been a waiver of the local remedies rule, this confusion matters little, since the practical effect of the local remedies rule and the principle at issue in the second category of case is the same. Nevertheless, there is an important difference of principle between the two and once there is an agreement waiving the local remedies rule the distinction becomes critical. A waiver of the local remedies rule will affect the first case but not the second. In the second case, until the alien attempts to secure redress in a local court, there is nothing which could form the substance of an international claim, because there is nothing which is imputable to the respondent State.

Once, however, a court of the respondent State has taken a decision, then there is an act imputable to that State. Nevertheless, it is still necessary to

[14] Although some governments and commentators have sought to argue that it is the failure to provide a remedy, rather than the expropriation, that is the international wrong, this approach makes denial of justice the only cause of action in international law in cases of mistreatment of aliens. That is not the practice of most States and has not been the approach taken in the majority of judicial and arbitral decisions.

ask whether that act constitutes a violation of international law. As has been seen, it is well established that a mistake on the part of a court or an irregularity in procedure is not in itself sufficient to amount to a violation of international law; there must be a denial of justice.

The term denial of justice has been given different meanings by different commentators. 'Justice', however, refers to more than just the decision of an individual court. It is clear, for example, that the term denial of justice embraces a denial of access to the courts. There can also be a denial of justice because of a systematic bias or other failing on the part of the courts which would make recourse to those courts for the alien pointless or ineffective, even though there may be no decision of a court in the particular case.

While allegations of a denial of justice may turn upon decisions of the courts, what constitutes a denial of justice is a failure of the *system* of justice within a State. To put it another way, the obligation which the State owes the foreign national in this context (whether under general international law or under the specific provisions of a treaty like NAFTA or a bilateral investment treaty) is to provide a system of justice which affords fair, equitable and non-discriminatory treatment. So long as the system itself provides a sufficient guarantee of such treatment, the State will not be in violation of its international obligation merely because a trial court gives a defective decision which can be corrected on appeal. While legal systems strive for perfection at all levels, they also recognise that such a result is unlikely to be attainable. It is precisely for that reason that legal systems today make extensive provision for appeal and that many also contain other provisions for challenging decisions of the lower courts for violations of constitutional safeguards which are frequently very similar to the standards of international law. The duty of a State towards foreign nationals is to provide a *system* of justice which ensures fairness and compliance with other standards of international law in all cases. That system includes the appellate and review procedures for which it provides.

It follows that the responsibility of the State for a denial of justice arises only if the system as a whole produces a denial of justice. Where there is a manifestly defective judgment by a lower court, this will not amount to a denial of justice—and thus will not constitute a violation of international law by the State—if there is available to the foreign national an effective means of challenging the judgment.

That consequence is not always made clear in discussion of denial of justice and, as stated above, it is frequently (and, perhaps, understandably) confused with discussion of the local remedies rule. Nevertheless, it is recognised in a number of important texts. Thus, the ninth edition of *Oppenheim's International Law* states that:

> If the courts or other appropriate tribunals of a State refuse to entertain proceedings for the redress of injury suffered by an alien, or if the proceedings

are subject to undue delay, or if there are serious inadequacies in the administration of justice, or if there occurs an obvious and malicious act of misapplication of the law by the courts which is injurious to a foreign State or its nationals, there will be a 'denial of justice' for which the State is responsible (quite apart from the effect which such circumstances might have for the application of the local remedies rule). *The State's responsibility will at least require it to take the necessary action to secure proper conduct on the part of the court*... .[15]

This last sentence suggests a standard which would be met by the State ensuring that a manifestly deficient judgment was reversed on appeal or that judicial review were available to compel the lower court to adopt a proper decision. *Oppenheim* continues:

Where, however, a court observes its own proper forms of justice and nevertheless pronounces a materially unjust judgment, it is controversial whether a denial of justice is thereby occasioned for which a State is internationally responsible. The judgment giving rise to the material injustice (itself a relative concept) may be the result of the proper application by the court of a law which provides for such a result (in which case it is the law which should properly be the object of complaint), or of an erroneous application by the court of a law which is itself unexceptional. In this latter case, *if the error is not remedied on appeal*, there is probably no international responsibility for a denial of justice unless the error led to a breach of a treaty obligation resting on the State or, possibly, the result is so manifestly unjust as to offend against the standards of justice recognized by civilized nations.[16]

It is axiomatic in this passage that if an error is remedied on appeal there can normally be no violation.

It has already been seen that Freeman considered that only the decision of a court of last resort could constitute a denial of justice. Elsewhere, in discussing denial of justice resulting from manifest defects in the procedure followed by the national court, he stated:

Ample protection against arbitrary violations of the local law will normally be afforded within the State itself by the conventional means of appeal to a superior court. Ruling improperly on evidence, erroneously charging a jury, exceeding the decorous limits of judicial restraint with prejudicial effects for one of the parties, (such as openly insulting the claimant's attorney before the jury), emotionally addressing the jurymen with the aim of kindling their hostility, and the like will usually find rectification in the wisdom of the reviewing bench. *Where this does not happen*, there is still left the question of

[15] R Jennings and A Watts, eds, *Oppenheim's International Law*, 9th edn (London, 1992), vol I, pp 543–44. Emphasis added.
[16] *Ibid*, pp 544–45.

> whether these various deviations from regular judicial activity are sufficiently flagrant to embroil the State.[17]

It is true that, later in this work, Freeman refers to the principle that 'no claim based upon a denial of justice may be predicated upon the decision of a lower court'[18] as bound up with the local remedies rule but this confusion is common in the literature. The better view is that Freeman was commenting on the content of the international law standard of denial of justice.

The same approach to the State's duties to provide a fair and effective system of justice is taken by the late Judge Jimenez de Arechaga (who also carefully distinguishes between this issue and the local remedies rule, dealing with the latter in a different section of his work). Although he adopted a narrow definition of denial of justice, confining it to cases of denial of access to a court and distinguishing it from cases where a court perpetrated an injustice, he concluded that in the latter case:

> There have been cases ... in which a State was held responsible as a result of a judicial decision in breach of municipal law. Such exceptional findings have been justified on the basis of three cumulative requirements which must be satisfied for a State to be held responsible on this account:
>
> (a) the decision must constitute a flagrant and inexcusable violation of municipal law;
> (b) it must be a decision of a court of last resort, all remedies available having been exhausted;
> (c) a subjective factor of bad faith and discriminatory intention on the part of the court must have been present.
>
> ...
>
> The reason for the second requirement is that States provide in their judicial organization remedies designed to correct the natural fallibility of its judges. A corollary of this requirement is that a State cannot base the charges made before an international tribunal or organ on objections or grounds which were not previously raised before the municipal courts.[19]

The practical importance of distinguishing between the content of the substantive norm and the local remedies rule has become greater in modern times as instances of the waiver of the local remedies rule have become more common. If the principle that, in Freeman's words, 'no claim based upon denial of justice may be predicated upon the decision of a lower court' is treated as nothing more than an application of the local remedies rule, the effect of a general waiver of the rule would be that any judgment of a

[17] Above n 6, pp 291–92. Emphasis added.
[18] Above n 6, p 415.
[19] J de Arechaga, 'International Law in the Past Third of a Century', 159 *Recueil des Cours* (1978), p 282.

court at any level in the judicial hierarchy which was alleged to constitute a denial of justice could be the subject of a challenge in international proceedings, notwithstanding that there was an avenue of appeal open to the foreign national.

The effects of such an approach are potentially very far-reaching. That would be the case even with interlocutory decisions. If any decision of a court which failed to meet international standards constitutes a denial of justice and, in the event of a waiver of the local remedies rule, is actionable on the international plane, then a decision granting interlocutory relief could give rise to a cause of action in international law. For example, an English court issues freezing orders (formerly known as *Mareva* injunctions) on the basis of an application without notice to the other party (formerly known as an *ex parte* application). The order can, of course, be challenged by the defendant at a subsequent *inter partes* hearing. Yet the act of granting the original *ex parte* order is an act imputable to the State and, if the local remedies rule has been waived, then an alien defendant (or his State of nationality) could bring an international claim alleging that the granting of the order was a denial of justice, notwithstanding that he had not exercised his undoubted right to contest the order at the *inter partes* hearing.

It is inherently implausible that States would intend to produce such a result, the effect of which would be to give the foreign litigant the opportunity to engage in some quite extraordinary forum shopping and to set aside the entire system of checks and balances within the national judicial system. In the opinion of this writer, international law does not produce such a bizarre result. That is because what constitutes a denial of justice in international law is not the isolated decision to grant a freezing order on an *ex parte* application but only a failure of the system of justice, if that system either does not correct that decision where the decision was manifestly unjust or does not offer any effective means of challenging the decision.

To say that a decision of a lower court cannot constitute a denial of justice if the means exists for an effective recourse to correct the deficiencies in that decision is not the same as saying that a foreign national must always challenge any act of government before the courts. In the case of a denial of justice based on the actions of the courts, what is involved is not a challenge to one branch of government before another (as was the case, eg, in the *Interhandel* case)[20] but a challenge to the mechanisms that exist within the judicial system for correcting errors made within that same system. These methods generally exist as of right and recourse to them is largely in the hands of the parties to the proceedings.

[20] *ICJ Reports*, 1959, p 6.

There has been very little consideration by international tribunals of the distinction between the local remedies rule and the principle that a court decision which can be challenged through the judicial process does not amount to a denial of justice. The lack of discussion is scarcely surprising in view of the similar effects of the two principles and the fact that, until recently, the local remedies rule was seldom waived. Nevertheless, the distinction is clearly recognised by the Iran-United States Claims Tribunal in its decision in *Oil Field of Texas*.[21] The Iran-US Claims Tribunal there held that a judicial decision was capable of amounting to a measure of expropriation. The decision in question was that of the Islamic Court of Ahwaz, which appears to have been a lower court. The Tribunal held that:

> The Court order did not only have temporary effect, but, as evidenced by NIOC's continued retention of the equipment, amounted to a permanent deprivation of its use. In these circumstances, *and taking into account the Claimant's impossibility to challenge the Court order in Iran,* there was a taking of the three blowout preventers for which the Government is responsible.[22]

Since the Iran-US Tribunal operates on the basis of a waiver of the local remedies rule,[23] this passage is not referring to the need to exhaust local remedies. It is clear, therefore, that the Tribunal considered that, if there had been a means by which the Claimant could have challenged the decision of the Islamic court within the Iranian judicial system, the decision of the Islamic court would not have amounted to a violation of international law. Amongst older authorities, the decision of Umpire Thornton in *Jennings, Laughland and Co v Mexico*[24] also takes this view:

> The Umpire does not conceive that any government can thus be made responsible for the misconduct of an inferior judicial officer when no attempt has been made to obtain justice from a higher court.[25]

Most of the other decisions and awards say little, if anything, on the relationship between recourse to appeal as a requirement of the substantive law of denial of justice and recourse to appeal as part of the exhaustion of local

[21] 12 *Iran-US CTR*, p 308, at pp 318–19.
[22] *Ibid*, p 319.
[23] See Principle B of the General Declaration, G Aldrich, *The Jurisprudence of the Iran-United States Claims Tribunal* (Oxford, 1996), pp 129–31.
[24] Case No 374, J Moore, 3 *International Arbitrations* (Washington D C, 1898), p 3135.
[25] *Ibid*, p 3136. Umpire Thornton reached the same conclusion in *Green v Mexico* (*ibid*, p 3139), *Burn v Mexico* (*ibid*, p 3140), *The Ada* (*ibid*, p 3143), *Smith v Mexico* (*ibid*, p 3146) and *Blumhardt v Mexico* (*ibid*, p 3146). The decision of Umpire Little in *The Mechanic* (*Corwin v Venezuela*) (*ibid*, p 3210, at p 3218) is to the same effect.

remedies. For example, the famous award in the *Finnish Ships* case[26] does not address this question, because the issue before the arbitrator was specifically confined to whether or not local remedies had been exhausted; the arbitrator was not asked to address the merits of the shipowners' claim. Moreover, it was the original requisition of the ships, not the decision of the English tribunal, which had given rise to those claims.

Although the International Law Commission's work on State responsibility was concerned with the secondary rules, rather than the content of primary norms such as that on denial of justice, the discussion of the various drafts by the Commission and those States which commented thereon also sheds some light on the content of the relevant primary norms.

The earlier Draft Articles drawn up by Ago included, in Draft Articles 20 and 21, a complex distinction between 'obligations of conduct' and 'obligations of result':

> *Article 20*
>
> There is a breach by a State of an international obligation requiring it to adopt a particular course of conduct when the conduct of that State is not in conformity with that required of it by that obligation.
>
> *Article 21*
>
> 1. There is a breach by a State of an international obligation requiring it to achieve, by means of its own choice, a specified result if, by the conduct adopted, the State does not achieve the result required of it by that obligation.
> 2. When the conduct of the State has created a situation not in conformity with the result required of it by an international obligation, but the obligation allows that this or an equivalent result may nevertheless be achieved by subsequent conduct of the State, there is a breach of the obligation only if the State also fails by its subsequent conduct to achieve the result required of it by that obligation.[27]

In commenting on these provisions in 1998, the United Kingdom observed that:

> ... in a case where international law requires only that a certain result be achieved, the situation falls under draft article 21(2). *The duty to provide a fair and efficient system of justice is an example. Corruption in an inferior court would not violate that obligation if redress were speedily available in a higher court.* In the case of such obligations, no breach occurs until the State

[26] *RIAA*, Vol III, (1937), p 1497.
[27] Crawford, above n 4, p 353.

> has failed to take any of the opportunities available to it to produce the required result.[28]

The italicised passage is directly in point. It constitutes recent State practice, which clearly indicates that the substantive obligation imposed upon the State is to provide a fair and efficient *system* of justice and that the decision of a lower court (even if it is not merely wrong but 'corrupt') does not put the State in breach of that obligation if the State has provided the means within that system whereby that decision can be corrected.

This approach to the duty to provide a system of justice was accepted by the new ILC rapporteur, Professor James Crawford SC. After quoting the United Kingdom comments set out in the preceding paragraph, he observed that:-

> There are also cases where the obligation is to have a *system* of a certain kind, e.g. the obligation to provide a fair and efficient system of justice. There, systematic considerations enter into the question of breach, and an aberrant decision by an official lower in the hierarchy, which is capable of being reconsidered, does not of itself amount to an unlawful act.[29]

The International Law Commission subsequently discarded the provisions on obligations of conduct and obligations of result. It did so because the distinction was not considered useful in a set of general articles dealing with the secondary rules of State responsibility (ie the legal framework of responsibility rather than the specific rules—the 'primary rules'—for the breach of which the State would incur responsibility). The decision to drop the distinction from the Final Articles did not suggest that there was any doubt about the fact that certain obligations are plainly obligations of result, nor that there was any dissent regarding the statements quoted above.[30]

In light of the above discussion, it is suggested that the concept of denial of justice is systemic, ie, as Professor Crawford puts it, the obligation of the State is to provide a fair and efficient system of justice. That obligation is only violated by an unfair decision of a lower court if two requirements are met. First, the unfairness must be of such an extreme character that it

[28] UN Doc A/CN.4/488, p 68. Emphasis added.

[29] UN Doc A/CN.4/498, para 75. Original emphasis.

[30] The Commission's original approach to the local remedies rule was closely bound up with the distinction between obligations of conduct and obligations of result. Draft Art 22 on the application of the local remedies rule took the position that, in the case of an obligation of result, the local remedies rule took on a substantive character. This approach, of course, serves further to confuse the requirement of recourse to appeal as a part of the definition of denial of justice with the requirement of exhaustion of local remedies. It was heavily criticised and was not adopted in the Final Articles. Art 44 of the Final Articles (Crawford, above n 4, p 264) treats the local remedies rule as procedural in character.

satisfies the stringent criteria identified by O'Connell. While bad faith may not be necessary, what is required is something which goes far beyond mere error. Secondly, the decision of a national court, however badly flawed, will not amount to a denial of justice engaging the international responsibility of the State unless the system of appeals and other challenges which exists in that State either does not correct the deficiencies of the lower court's decision or is such that it does not afford a prospect of correcting those deficiencies which is reasonably available to the alien who has suffered from that decision.

2. THE *LOEWEN* CASE

These tentative conclusions receive considerable support from the Final Award in the *Loewen* case. The claimants in that case alleged that the conduct of the trial in the Mississippi court and the award of $500 million in damages amounted to a violation of Article 1105 of the NAFTA Treaty. Article 1105, which is headed 'Minimum Standard of Treatment', provides:

> 1. Each party shall accord to investments of investors of another party treatment in accordance with international law, including fair and equitable treatment and full protection and security.

This provision was the subject of an interpretation by the Free Trade Commission, a body comprising the representatives of the three NAFTA States (Canada, Mexico and the United States of America), in the following terms:

> (1) Article 1105(1) prescribes the customary international law minimum standard of treatment of aliens as the minimum standard of treatment to be afforded to investments of investors of another Party.
> (2) The concepts of 'fair and equitable treatment' and 'full protection and security' do not require treatment in addition to or beyond that which is required by the customary international law minimum standard of treatment of aliens.
> (3) A determination that there has been a breach of another provision of the NAFTA, or of a separate international agreement, does not establish that there has been a breach of Article 1105(1).[31]

The Tribunal accepted that this interpretation was binding upon it, notwithstanding that other tribunals had earlier taken a different view of

[31] 122 *ILR* 681.

Article 1105.[32] It considered, however, that the relevant international law standards were those of the present day and not those applied in the 1920's.

On the question of what constitutes unfair and inequitable treatment by a court (which appears, in the light of the interpretation given by the Free Trade Commission, to be the same as the concept of a denial of justice) today, the Tribunal followed the approach taken by an earlier NAFTA Tribunal in *Mondev International Ltd v United States of America,* which held that:

> ... the question is whether, at an international level and having regard to generally accepted standards of the administration of justice, a tribunal can conclude in the light of all the facts that the impugned decision was clearly improper and discreditable, with the result that the investment has been subjected to 'unfair and inequitable' treatment.[33]

The *Loewen* Tribunal considered that bad faith was not required but what had to be shown was 'manifest injustice in the sense of a lack of due process leading to an outcome which offends a sense of judicial propriety'.[34]

Applying this standard, the Tribunal held that the proceedings in the Mississippi court had been unfair and inequitable. It then went on, however, to state that:

> because the trial court proceedings are only part of the judicial process that is available to the parties, the rest of the process, and its availability to Loewen, must be examined before a violation of Article 1105 is established.[35]

There was no doubt that Loewen had a right of appeal against the decision and, in the view of the Tribunal, a good prospect of success in that appeal, at least as regards the amount of damages awarded (which was the largest ever awarded in a Mississippi court). The problem was that Mississippi law did not permit a stay of execution pending appeal unless the appellant posted a bond for 125 per cent of the amount of the damages within a short period of time. Although Mississippi law permitted either the trial judge or the Mississippi Supreme Court to relax the bond requirement, neither agreed to do so in this case. Loewen maintained that it could not afford the bond of $625 million. Rather than pursuing the appeal while allowing the

[32] Cf the Award on Damages in *Pope and Talbot v Canada*, 31 May 2002; available at www.naftalaw.org.

[33] 125 *ILR* 90.

[34] Final Award, above n 1, para 132.

[35] *Ibid*, para 137. Loewen also complained of violations of Art 1102 (discriminatory treatment) and Art 1110 (expropriation), but the Tribunal dismissed its claims under the former and held that the latter added nothing to Art 1105 in the present case.

judgment to be enforced, Loewen settled the case out of court for a sum estimated at $175 million.

The United States maintained that Loewen had failed to exhaust the avenues open to it within the United States and Mississippi court systems. In particular, the United States argued that Loewen could have challenged the bond requirement and its application in this case before the United States Supreme Court or filed for bankruptcy under Chapter 11 of the US Bankruptcy Code (which allows a form of protective bankruptcy and would have precluded enforcement of the judgment). Loewen denied that there was any realistic prospect of success in the Federal courts and rejected the Chapter 11 route as a viable option.

Two separate questions thus arose. First, assuming that there was an avenue—reasonably available to Loewen and offering some prospect of success—within the United States or Mississippi judicial systems by which it could challenge the judgment of the Mississippi court and that Loewen had failed to take advantage of that avenue, could the decision of the Mississippi court nevertheless amount to a violation of Article 1105 of NAFTA? Secondly, if that question was answered in the negative, was there, in fact, such an avenue reasonably available to Loewen? The first question is obviously the one which is of interest for the purposes of the present paper, although brief comment will be made on the second.

The Tribunal held that the decision of the Mississippi court, flawed though the Tribunal held it to be, could not constitute a violation of Article 1105 (and therefore of the customary law on denial of justice) if United States or Mississippi law offered Loewen a reasonably available means of challenging that decision. The Tribunal was impressed by the fact that:

> No instance has been drawn to our attention in which an international tribunal has held a State responsible for a breach of international law constituted by a lower court decision when there was available an effective and adequate appeal within the State's legal system.[36]

It held that:

> The purpose of the requirement that a decision of a lower court be challenged through the judicial process before the State is responsible for a breach of international law constituted by judicial decision is to afford the State the opportunity of redressing through its legal system the inchoate breach of international law occasioned by the lower court decision. The requirement has application to breaches of Articles 1102 and 1110 as well as Article 1105.[37]

[36] Final Award, above n 1, para 154.
[37] *Ibid*, para 156.

The Tribunal then considered the application of the local remedies rule in the context of a NAFTA claim. It started from the premise that the local remedies rule was an important part of international law, not a mere technical requirement, and that, as the International Court had held in the *Elettronica Sicula* case,[38] clear language in a Treaty was required before the rule would be held to have been waived. The Tribunal also rejected Loewen's submission that the rule was applicable only to cases of diplomatic protection, where a State brought a claim on behalf of one of its nationals. The local remedies rule was, therefore, applicable to a claim under NAFTA Chapter 11 unless Article 1121 of NAFTA[39] operated to waive the rule. The Tribunal held that the precise purpose of Article 1121(1) was not altogether clear but added that:

> One thing, however, is reasonably clear about Article 1121 and that is that it says nothing expressly about the requirement that, in the context of a judicial violation of international law, the judicial process be continued to the highest level.
>
> Nor is there any basis for implying any dispensation of that requirement. It would be strange indeed if *sub silentio* the international rule were to be swept away. And it would be very strange if a State were to be confronted with liability for a breach of international law committed by its magistrate or low-ranking judicial officer when domestic avenues of appeal are not pursued, let alone exhausted. If Article 1121 were to have that effect, it would encourage resort to NAFTA tribunals rather than resort to the appellate courts and review processes of the host State, an outcome which would seem surprising, having regard to the sophisticated legal systems of the NAFTA Parties. Such an outcome would have the effect of making a State potentially liable for NAFTA violations when domestic appeal or review, if pursued, might have avoided any liability on the part of the State. Further, it is unlikely that the Parties to NAFTA would have wished to encourage recourse to NAFTA arbitration at the expense of domestic appeal or review when, in the general run of cases, domestic appeal or review would offer

[38] *United States of America v Italy*, *ICJ Reports*, 1989, p 15, at p 42.
[39] Art 1121 (which is entitled 'Conditions Precedent to Submission of a Claim to Arbitration') provides that: '1. A disputing investor may submit a claim under Art 1116 to arbitration only if:

(a) the investor consents to arbitration in accordance with the provisions of this Subchapter; and
(b) both the investor and an enterprise of another Party that is a juridical person that the investor owns or controls directly or indirectly, waive their right to initiate or continue before any administrative tribunal or court under the domestic law of any Party any proceedings with respect to the measure of the disputing Party that is alleged to be a breach of Subchapter A of this Chapter, Art 1502(3)(a) (Monopolies and State Enterprises) or Art 1503(2) (State Enterprises), except for proceedings for injunctive, declaratory or other extraordinary relief, not involving the payment of damages, before an administrative tribunal or court under the domestic law of the disputing Party.'

> more wide-ranging review as they are not confined to breaches of international law.[40]

While this passage appears to elide the requirements of the local remedies rule with those of the substantive law on denial of justice, it seems that the Tribunal found against Loewen on both counts. The reasoning in this part of the award supports the following conclusions:

(1) that the substantive law on denial of justice (and other wrongs by a court) is such that a State does not incur responsibility for a flawed decision of a court if its legal system provides adequate and effective means for challenging that decision which are reasonably available to the foreign national and that foreign national does not take advantage of those means of challenge;
(2) that the local remedies rule is applicable in principle in claims brought directly by a foreign investor against a State;
(3) that NAFTA Article 1121 does not waive the application of the local remedies rule 'in its application to a breach of international law constituted by a judicial act'.[41]

Accordingly, if there was an adequate and effective remedy within the US or Mississippi court system, which was reasonably available to Loewen, then there was no violation of NAFTA unless Loewen had taken sufficient steps to pursue that remedy. That leads to the second question posed above, whether there were such remedies reasonably available to Loewen or whether Loewen had had no choice but to enter into the settlement agreement. On this aspect of the case, the Tribunal held that the onus was on Loewen to show why the various remedies that it might have pursued, noticeably the challenge to the bonding requirement in the United States Supreme Court, were not in fact reasonably available to it and found that Lowen had failed to discharge this burden. The Tribunal was 'simply left to speculate on the reasons which led to the decision to [conclude the settlement] rather than to pursue other options' and 'it is not a case in which it can be said that it was the only course which Loewen could reasonably be expected to take'.[42]

3. CONCLUSION

The award in *Loewen* is welcome confirmation of the principle, set out in Part 1, above, that the responsibility of a State for the decisions of its courts

[40] Final Award, above n 1, paras 161–62.
[41] *Ibid*, para 164.
[42] *Ibid*, para 216.

arises only when all adequate and effective means of challenge to a decision which exist within the national court system and which are reasonably available to the alien complaining of the decision have been exhausted. The contrary view would have allowed foreign investors who were covered by NAFTA to choose freely, and at will, between using the appellate system of the host State and resorting to NAFTA arbitration. The latter choice would inevitably have meant substituting a claim against the host State (in *Loewen*, the United States of America) for whatever redress might have been available against the other party to the proceedings before the national courts. Such a consequence is unlikely to have been what was intended by the parties to NAFTA and had the potential to wreak havoc with the orderly conduct of claims. While the *Loewen* award is not, of course, binding on other tribunals and, in so far as it addresses the question of waiver, is confined to the NAFTA framework, its careful analysis of the nature of a State's obligations with regard to the provision of a fair system of justice is likely to be highly influential not only with other NAFTA tribunals but in a broader investment context.

6

State Responsibility and the 'Good Faith' Obligation in International Law

GUY S GOODWIN-GILL*

THE ADOPTION OF the ILC's Articles on the Responsibility of States for Internationally Wrongful Acts makes a significant and substantial contribution to clarifying the obligations of States and the consequences of breach. And yet, as several commentators and the Special Rapporteur himself have already indicated, the picture is not complete. In particular, the legal dimensions remain uncertain in instances where the obligation alleged to have been violated is not clearly owed to one or another State (no injured State), where the beneficiaries or 'rights-holders' are individuals or non-State entities (such as international organisations), or where the very nature of the obligation itself makes it difficult to identify the elements which constitute the wrongful act.

Part One of the ILC Articles ('The Internationally Wrongful Act of the State') applies to all cases in which an internationally wrongful act may be committed. Article 1 'covers all international obligations *of* the State and not only those owed *to* other States',[1] while Article 12 emphasises that breach may occur, when an act of [the] State is not in conformity with what is required of it by [the] obligation, regardless of its origin or character.[2] Part One is thus broader than Part Two ('Content of the International Responsibility of a State'), which:

> does not apply to obligations of reparation to the extent that these arise towards or are invoked by a person or entity other than a State. In other

* Senior Research Fellow, All Souls College, Oxford; and Barrister, Blackstone Chambers, London.

[1] J Crawford, *The International Law Commission's Articles on State Responsibility: Introduction, Text and Commentaries* (Cambridge, 2002), pp 192–93, Art 28, Commentary, §3.

[2] On the Commentary to Art 12, see Crawford, *ibid*, pp 125–30.

> words, the provisions of Part Two are without prejudice to any right, arising from the international responsibility of a State, which may accrue directly to any person or entity other than a State, and article 33 makes this clear.[3]

The Articles leave open, and are even equivocal on, the issue of the consequences of breach where the primary beneficiary of the obligations is not a State, for example in human rights cases, or where a State is unable or unwilling to invoke rights on behalf of individual persons.[4] The problematic issues that can arise in such situations are illustrated by recent litigation in the United Kingdom, in which actual or potential applicants for asylum, among others, challenged the legality of controls exercised over them prior to departure from their country of origin.[5]

A procedure known as 'pre-entry clearance' was introduced in Prague because of what the Home Office called 'asylum overload'.[6] 'Asylum overload', in turn, was described as occurring when:

> a substantial number of those who seek asylum outside of entry, or of those who seek and obtain leave to enter on a different basis and then subsequently make their application for asylum, is found not to be entitled to asylum.[7]

The purpose of pre-entry clearance, according to the Home Office, is to deter people from 'abusing' UK asylum and immigration procedures.[8]

The principal claimant, the European Roma Rights Center ('ERRC'), was established in 1996 to monitor the human rights situation of Roma in Europe. The ERRC challenged the pre-clearance process on behalf of six claimants, referred to by their initials for reasons of confidentiality. The main grounds for challenge were that the practice of pre-clearance as implemented in Prague disclosed discrimination on racial grounds, contrary to

[3] Crawford, *ibid*, Art 28, Commentary, §3, pp 192–93.
[4] See Crawford, *ibid*, Art 1, Commentary, §7, p 80; see also *ibid*, pp 209–10, Art 33, Commentary, §§3–4, contrasting the situation in *LaGrand (Germany v United States of America), Merits, ICJ Reports*, 2001, para 77 (where the State of nationality could invoke the rights of its detained citizens), and other situations where, it is tentatively, perhaps hopefully opined, 'it may be that some procedure is available whereby [a non-State] entity can invoke the responsibility on its own account and without the intermediation of any State.'
[5] *European Roma Rights Center v Immigration Officer, Prague Airport and Secretary of State for the Home Department* [2003] EWCA Civ 666 (Court of Appeal); [2002] EWHC 1989 (Admin) (Burton J).
[6] *European Roma Rights Center & Others v Immigration Officer at Prague Airport and Secretary of State for the Home Department* [2002] EWHC 1989 (paras 11, 15).
[7] *Ibid*, para 19. Following agreement with the Czech Government, the pre-clearance procedure was operated by United Kingdom immigration officers placed at Charles Airport, Prague, from 18 July 2001, and thereafter continued irregularly.
[8] *Ibid*. In fact, numbers of Czech Roma have been determined to be refugees; see, for example, *Harakel v SSHD* [2001] EWCA 884 (Court of Appeal); and the following Immigration Adjudicator decisions: *Nanar v SSHD*, CC150587101, 3 April 2002; *Bily v SSHD*, HN5460312001, 2 April 2002; *Bihari & Rafaelova v SSHD*, HN43414101, 8 Feb 2002.

United Kingdom law; and that it was contrary to the obligations of the United Kingdom under the 1951 Convention and 1967 Protocol relating to the Status of Refugees. The claims were rejected at first instance, and by a majority in the Court of Appeal; leave to appeal to the House of Lords was granted by the Court of Appeal on the discrimination and 1951 Convention grounds, and was pending at the time of writing.

The domestic nature of the proceedings and the local rules governing the 'admissibility' of international law necessarily defined and limited the scope of review, in which the question whether the measures were based on racial discrimination contrary to UK law was a central feature. In the Court of Appeal, nevertheless, a number of international legal issues were presented, both by the Appellants and by the Office of the United Nations High Commissioner for Refugees ('UNHCR');[9] these included the scope of the obligation of *non-refoulement* accepted by States party both to the 1951 Convention and 1967 Protocol relating to the Status of Refugees,[10] and the duty of States generally to implement their treaty and other international obligations in good faith.[11] The nature of the proceedings meant that other relevant international legal issues, such as the identification of an injured State or other State having a legal interest in compliance, did not arise.

1. INTERNATIONAL OBLIGATIONS AND NATIONAL ACTIONS AND OMISSIONS

The ILC's final Articles abandon the distinction previously drawn between obligations of conduct, obligations of result, and obligations to prevent a particular occurrence. Many commentators have observed that, while these distinctions may serve a useful analytical purpose and in determining when a breach has occurred (provided always that they are

[9] UNHCR intervened in the case with the permission of the parties and of the Court. This chapter draws on the research undertaken for the purposes of this litigation by the author, who acted as Counsel *pro bono* for UNHCR. The views expressed are the author's alone, and are not necessarily shared by UNHCR or the United Nations.

[10] Art 33 of the 1951 Convention relating to the Status of Refugees ('CSR51') provides: '1. No Contracting State shall expel or return ('refouler') a refugee in any manner whatsoever to the frontiers of territories where his life or freedom would be threatened on account of his race, religion, nationality, membership of a particular social group or political opinion'. (189 *UNTS*, p 150.) At 1 Feburary 2004, the Convention had been ratified by 142 States. Under the 1967 Protocol, States parties agree to apply CSR51 without certain temporal and geographical limitations; 141 States have ratified the Protocol.

[11] The facts of the case disclose a potential incompatibility between UK legislation and the UK's obligations under the 1966 International Convention for the Elimination of All Forms of Racial Discrimination, and also raise the issue of the possible joint responsibility of the Czech Republic and the United Kingdom in relation to the former's obligations under Article 2, Fourth Protocol, European Convention on Human Rights. See further text corresponding to below nn 18–22.

used correctly), they do not have either specific or direct consequences for responsibility.[12] Dupuy and others pointed out that in Ago's original typology, the conduct/result distinction was back to front; in civil law, an obligation of *conduct* is 'une obligation de s'efforcer', that is, to endeavour or to strive to realise a certain goal or to prevent a certain occurrence.[13] An obligation of *result,* by contrast, is precisely that—an obligation, to borrow Crawford's words, which involves,

> in some measure a guarantee of the outcome, whereas obligations of conduct are in the nature of best efforts obligations to do all in one's power to achieve a result, but without ultimate commitment.[14]

In the one case, the fact that the result is not achieved is both necessary and sufficient to generate responsibility; in the other, 'what counts is the violation of the best effort obligation, not the end result generally achieved'.[15] In each case, it is the primary rule which determines the relevant standard of performance. As Crawford states:

> Some obligations of conduct or means may only be breached if the ultimate event occurs (i.e. damage to the protected interest); others may be breached by a failure to act even without eventual damage. International law neither has, nor needs to have, a presumption or rule either way. It depends on the context, and on all the factors relevant to the interpretation of treaties or the articulation of custom.[16]

At the level of analysis, the result/conduct distinction can nevertheless play a helpful role, not least in the human rights field, where *process* (and the adequacy, effectiveness and ultimately legality thereof) is also relevant. Conduct and result overlap; torture, ill-treatment, arbitrary deprivation of life, and *refoulement*, are all examples of forbidden conduct; but due process and accountability mechanisms are necessary, linked, but still separate bases for determining whether 'protection' is available or effective.

The particular nature of treaties for the protection of individuals and of human rights obligations illustrates the variety of what is required to avoid responsibility.[17] Thus, under the 1966 International Convention for the

[12] Crawford, above n 1, Article 12, Commentary, §11, pp 129–30.

[13] P-M Dupuy, 'Reviewing the difficulties of codification: On Ago's classification of obligations of means and obligations of result in relation to State responsibility', 10 *European Journal of International Law* (1999), p 371, at p 375.

[14] Crawford, 'Second Report on State Responsibility', UN doc A/CN.4/498, 17 March 1999, §57, cited by Dupuy, *ibid*, p 378.

[15] Dupuy, above n 13, p 379.

[16] Crawford, above n 1, p 22.

[17] See also the discussion in Crawford, above n 14, paras 69–76.

Elimination of All Forms of Racial Discrimination ('ICERD66'),[18] the United Kingdom has accepted that 'racial discrimination' means:

> any distinction, exclusion, restriction or preference based on race, colour, descent, or national or ethnic origin which has the purpose or effect of nullifying or impairing the recognition, enjoyment or exercise, on an equal footing, of human rights and fundamental freedoms in the political, economic, social, cultural or any other field of public life.

The Convention does not apply to 'distinctions, exclusions, restrictions or preferences made by a State Party ... between citizens and non-citizens' (Article 1(2)), but does not otherwise permit distinctions among non-citizens on racial grounds. Article 5(d)(ii) ICERD66 obliges all States parties to:

> undertake to prohibit and to eliminate racial discrimination in all its forms and to guarantee the right of everyone, without distinction as to race, colour, or national or ethnic origin, to equality before the law, notably in the enjoyment of ... [t]he right to leave any country, including one's own, and to return to one's country ....

The Race Relations Act 2000, however, expressly authorises racial discrimination in immigration and nationality matters.[19] Given the 'social importance'[20] of the prohibition of racial discrimination in general,[21] as well as the specific obligation accepted by the United Kingdom to prohibit and to eliminate racial discrimination in all its forms, the mere fact of keeping in force or passing the legislation may be considered an internationally wrongful act.[22]

[18] The United Kingdom ratified the 1966 International Convention for the Elimination of All Forms of Racial Discrimination ('ICERD66') (660 *UNTS*, p 276) on 7 March 1969 with the following interpretative statement: '... the United Kingdom does not regard the Commonwealth Immigrants Acts, 1962 and 1968, or their application, as involving any racial discrimination within the meaning of paragraph 1 of article 1, or any other provision of the Convention, and fully reserves its right to continue to apply those Acts.' The Acts in question are no longer in force.

[19] S 1(1)(a) of the Race Relations Act 1976 defines direct racial discrimination as treating a person less favourably on racial grounds than a person treats or would treat other persons. The Race Relations (Amendment) Act 2000 amended the 1976 Act by making it unlawful for a public authority to do any act which constitutes racial discrimination (section 19B). However, it also introduced section 19D, which provides that it is *not* contrary to section 19B for a person who is acting 'in accordance with a relevant authorisation' to discriminate against another person on grounds of nationality or ethnic or national origins in carrying out immigration and nationality functions. On 23 April 2001, two months before the Prague operation commenced, the Secretary of State made an authorisation pursuant to section 19D which permitted immigration officers to discriminate against members of various ethnic groups, including Roma, by refusing leave to enter the United Kingdom; it was revoked on 11 June 2002. See Crawford, above n 1, Art 12, Commentary, §12, p 130.

[20] Dupuy, above n 13, 364.

[21] Cf *Barcelona Traction Case, ICJ Reports*, 1970, p 3, at p 32.

[22] Cf the case of *Prosecutor v Anto Furundzija* before the International Criminal Tribunal for Former Yugoslavia (ICTY) (*Prosecutor v Anto Furundzija*, Trial Chamber, 10 Dec 1998,

In like manner, legislation expressly authorising *refoulement* contrary to the terms of Article 33 of the 1951 Convention relating to the Status of Refugees ('CSR51') would also constitute an internationally wrongful act.[23] The facts in the case under discussion did not include such explicit legislation, however, but rather a series of measures ('pre-clearance' at Prague Airport) intended to forestall the arrival of asylum seekers in the United Kingdom, thereby ensuring that the obligation of *non-refoulement* was not triggered by the presence in fact in the UK of individuals who might be entitled to the protection of the 1951 Convention.[24]

The question is whether, on the proper interpretation of the particular treaty obligation, it is the occurrence of the injury alone (*refoulement*) which triggers responsibility, or whether the treaty and the treaty regime as a whole require States parties to undertake or refrain from certain measures, in application of the obligation of good faith. In short, the issue may be whether the 1951 Convention and 1967 Protocol are about protecting refugees and asylum seekers generally; or are merely a series of disparate obligations due to individuals if, but only if, they have been recognised as refugees.

1.1. Invoking the Responsibility of the State: The Limitations of the Injured State Phenomenon

At the international level, invoking the responsibility of the State in the refugee and *refoulement* context is made more problematic by the fact that

§§149–50). In certain circumstances, responsibility for legislation contrary to a State's international obligations results only when the legislation is applied in a concrete case. However, as the ICTY Trial Chamber stated: 'By contrast, in the case of torture, the mere fact of keeping in force or passing legislation contrary to the international prohibition of torture generates international State responsibility. The value of freedom from torture is so great that it becomes imperative to preclude any national legislative act authorizing or condoning torture or at any rate capable of bringing about this effect.' (Judgment of the ICTY quoted in Crawford, above n 14, §78.)

23 Cf Crawford, above n 14, §73.

24 The 1951 Convention provides for refugee status in relation to those who are *outside* their country of origin by reason of a well-founded fear of persecution, and who in consequence are entitled to protection against *refoulement* (return in any manner whatsoever) to a country in which their lives or freedom would be threatened. The principle of *non-refoulement* is widely considered also to prohibit neighbouring States from rejecting refugees at the frontiers of their country of origin. As long ago as 1933, Article 3 of the Convention relating to the International Status of Refugees contained a provision under which States expressly accepted not to remove resident refugees or keep them from their territory, 'by application of police measures such as expulsions or non-admittance at the frontier (*refoulement*)', and 'in any case not to refuse entry to refugees at the frontiers of their countries of origin' (159 *LNTS* No 3663.) See also 1936 Provisional Arrangement concerning the Status of Refugees coming from Germany (171 *LNTS* No 3952); 1938 Convention concerning the Status of Refugees coming from Germany (192 *LNTS* No 4461); G S Goodwin-Gill, *The Refugee in International Law,* 2nd edn (Oxford,1996), pp 121–24.

individuals who have been returned to persecution are unlikely to have a State competent, able or willing to defend their interests. The notion of obligations *erga omnes partes* offers little more than theoretical redress in today's world of forced migration, and the dispute settlement mechanism provided by Article 38 CSR51 has never been employed.[25] States do differ on the interpretation of the Convention, but even where such differences actually or potentially increase the responsibilities of other parties, each State appears content to allow each other party to apply the Convention in its own way.[26]

In an oft-cited quotation, Crawford has argued that:

> [W]e cannot make progress in developing the idea of a public international law ... unless we distinguish between the primary beneficiaries, the right holders, and those States with a legal interest in compliance.[27]

Indeed, the notion of a 'strict bilateral relationship' between responsible State and injured State, or of an 'exact' correlation between breach and injury, simply does not fit the majority of legal relationships established in multilateral treaties for the protection of human rights.[28]

Sicilianos, commenting on the deficiencies of the 'old' version of Article 40 (injured State), notes several instances where the beneficiaries are not States but individuals, peoples or entities:

> [I]f no distinction is drawn between the rights of the victims and the response of states, then 'human rights' ... have *ipso facto* been transformed into

[25] Art 38 provides: 'Any dispute between parties to this Convention relating to its interpretation or application, which cannot be settled by other means, shall be referred to the International Court of Justice at the request of any one of the parties to the dispute.'

[26] In *R v Secretary of State for the Home Department, ex parte Adan* [1999] 4 All ER, p 774, involving a question of interpretation of the Convention refugee definition, the Court of Appeal said it would afford due respect to the system and practice of another country, but that it had to apply the 1951 Convention. If the State took a position which departed from the Convention's 'true interpretation', it could not be regarded as safe. In the view of the Court, the refugee definition did extend to persons who feared persecution at the hands of non-State agents, in circumstances in which the State itself was not complicit. In consequence, the appellants could not lawfully be returned to a country (in this case, Germany) that adopted an interpretation at variance with this view.

[27] J Crawford, 'Responsibility to the International Community as a Whole', Fourth Annual Snyder Lecture, April 2000, Bloomington School of Law, Indiana University (quoted in P-M Dupuy, 'A general stocktaking of the connections between the multilateral dimension of obligations and codification of the law of responsibility', 13 *European Journal of International Law* (2002), p 1053, at p 1074; and I Scobbie, 'The invocation of responsibility for the breach of "obligations under peremptory norms of general international law",' 13 *European Journal of International Law* (2002), p 1201, at 1205.)

[28] Cf L-A Sicilianos, 'The classification of obligations and the multilateral dimension of the relations of international responsibility', 13 *European Journal of International Law* (2002), p 1127, at p 1132. See also Dupuy, above n 27, pp 1169–70, noting that human rights are primarily *not* about reciprocity, bilateral relations, or even nationality. Historically, there

'states' rights', something that does not seem justifiable from a normative or conceptual viewpoint.[29]

The notion of 'injured State' seems especially unsuited to a theory of responsibility in matters of human rights generally, or refugee protection specifically.[30] There is consequently something attractive in the proposal for a category of States, not directly affected, which may nevertheless invoke responsibility; Sicilianos suggests that this would include,

> ... first and foremost those which, without being specially affected by the breach, participate in a specific legal regime from which obligations *erga omnes partes* derive. Furthermore, even if they are not specifically injured, all states are affected by the breach of obligations *erga omnes*; and *a fortiori* by a breach of obligations resulting from peremptory norms of general international law.[31]

As a practical matter, however, the beneficiaries or right-holders will remain confronted with the traditional reluctance of States to take up the case of non-nationals who are mistreated or at risk in another State.[32] Article 33 of the Refugee Convention, although central to the regime of international protection, is not of the category of integral obligations, such that it operates in an all or nothing fashion, conditioning each State party's performance on that of each other State party.[33] Nor is the obligation one, breach of which would equate to an 'ordinary wrongful act' giving rise to a 'responsibility relationship' exclusively with some or other directly injured State.[34]

are certainly instances in which States have protested against the conduct of other States in their treatment of refugees and asylum seekers. However, there are few such instances and they have tended to be reactions against egregious actions, such as mass expulsion or *refoulement:* Goodwin-Gill, above n 24, pp 132–33.

[29] Sicilianos, above n 28 p 1132 and n 23.
[30] As Crawford has remarked, this is not in fact how Courts and tribunals treat human rights obligations; Crawford, above n 14, §§69–76.
[31] Sicilianos, above n 28, p 1139.
[32] Moreover, it may be that the invocation of responsibility is expressly excluded through the operation of ILC Art 44 and 45, unless the nationality of claims rule is satisfied or the injured State (if any) has validly waived its entitlement, or acquiesced in its role being assumed by another State; see Scobbie, above n 27, pp 1215–17.
[33] Crawford, above n 1, Introduction, p 41.
[34] Cf M Spinedi, 'From one codification to another: Bilateralism and multilateralism in the genesis of the codification of the law of treaties and the law of State responsibility', 13 *European Journal of International Law* (2002), p 1099, at p 1120. The situation is thus readily distinguishable from that before the International Court of Justice in the *LaGrand Case (Germany v United States of America), Merits, ICJ Reports*, 2001. The Court accepted that Article 36 of the Vienna Convention on Consular Relations protected individual rights, which were indeed expressly referred to (see in particular para 77 of the judgment); and that the USA had violated not only the rights of Germany as a party to the Convention, but also the individual rights of the LaGrand brothers. In its view, the objective of 'effective implementation' had

The results are hardly satisfactory, and the objectives of protection and compliance are unlikely to be effectively fulfilled through the notions of 'concern'[35] or 'indirect injury'[36] alone. In such circumstances, the only way to the invocation of responsibility may be by finding an international organisation having a legal interest in compliance.

1.2. A Legal Interest in Compliance and the Nature of the Good Faith Obligation

In the absence of a State injured individually or specially affected under ILC Article 42, or of a State acting in the collective interest under ILC Article 48, the entitlement to invoke the responsibility of a State acting in violation of its obligations under the Refugee Convention falls prima facie to UNHCR, the organisation specifically charged by the General Assembly with providing 'international protection' to refugees,[37] and which States parties recognise as having the duty to supervise its application.[38]

But if UNHCR is the answer to the question, who has a legal interest in compliance, there remains the further question, what obligation (or provision of the Convention, to draw on the words of Article 35 CSR51) has

not been met, because US courts were prevented (by reason of the local 'procedural default' rule) from attaching any legal significance to the violation of Article 36 (para 91 of the judgment). Although it is tempting to transpose this reasoning to the practice of pre-clearance and Article 33 CSR51, the definitional problem remains, however, that CSR51 is a treaty regime which appears to be triggered only by the occurrence of certain events, among which crossing an international frontier is the *sine qua non.*

[35] C Dominicé, 'The international responsibility of states for breach of multilateral obligations', 10 *European Journal* of *International Law* (1999), p 353, at p 357.
[36] Cf E Brown Weiss, 'Invoking state responsibility in the twenty-first century', 96 *American Journal of International Law* (2002), p 798, at p 816.
[37] UN General Assembly Resolution 428 (V), 14 December 1950, Annex, UNHCR Statute, para 1. The High Commissioner is also instructed to 'provide for the protection of refugees falling under the competence of his Office by: (a) Promoting the conclusion and ratification of international conventions for the protection of refugees, supervising their application and proposing amendments thereto ... '. (UNHCR Statute, *ibid*, para 8. UNHCR's international status is that of a subsidiary organ of the General Assembly, created under Art 22 of the UN Charter.
[38] As Art 35 CSR51 provides: '1. The Contracting States undertake to co-operate with the Office of the United Nations High Commissioner for Refugees ... in the exercise of its functions, and shall in particular facilitate its duty of supervising the application of the provisions of this Convention.' The further question of a forum remains. In principle, the High Commissioner might request the General Assembly to seek an advisory opinion from the International Court of Justice, but this is unlikely in practice. Some national jurisdictions, such as the UK, allow UNHCR to intervene in proceedings, but this is necessarily subject to prevailing domestic law rules on the reception of international law. 'Protest' therefore remains important, but particularly as 'invocation of responsibility'; cf Crawford, above n 1, Article 42, Commentary, §2, p 256.

been breached? UNHCR's responsibility extends to refugees within the scope of the Statute.[39] Like the Refugee Convention, which was intended to complement it, the Statute defines a refugee as someone who, above all, is outside his or her country of nationality or, if stateless, of former habitual residence.

For this reason and from the compliance perspective, State practices, laws and procedures, which together effectively prevent the occurrence of the very events which would otherwise trigger breaches of international obligations are especially problematic. It is one thing to remove the necessity for flight;[40] quite another, to prevent the flight of those with a claim to protection. The United Kingdom's pre-clearance procedure in Prague Airport is intended to prevent anyone travelling to the UK from the Czech Republic, who is ineligible for entry, or who is seeking to enter for a purpose other than those laid down in the Immigration Rules and irrespective of whether they have a well-founded fear of persecution. As asylum is not a 'recognized purpose' under the Immigration Rules, there is effectively no 'lawful' way in which an individual may travel to the United Kingdom to seek refuge.[41] At the international level, the question is how far a State may go to avoid the incidence of obligations and responsibility; and whose legal interest in compliance is sufficient to allow that responsibility to be invoked.

No international frontier having been crossed, no Convention obligation appears to have been breached, and no prohibited event, such as *refoulement,* appears to have taken place. In the absence of actual injury, the answer may be to invoke the responsibility of the State party to implement its treaty obligations in good faith. This obligation is not one which obviously requires actual damage. Instead, its violation may be demonstrated by acts and failures to act which, taken together, render the fulfilment of specific treaty obligations remote or impossible, or which defeat the object and purpose of the treaty. In this sense, the Refugee Convention can be viewed as comprising a bundle of specific undertakings towards refugees, and also as possessing a 'steps' or programmatic dimension.[42] This may be characterised, not as a series of

[39] UNHCR Statute, above n 37, paras 1, 6.

[40] Arguably, this is what was achieved through the intervention and creation of a 'security zone' in northern Iraq in 1991: Goodwin-Gill, above n 24, pp 130, 133, 141.

[41] This initially curious position flows 'logically' from the UK's view that its obligations under CSR51 are limited essentially to not taking any immigration enforcement action which would result in an individual being removed from the UK in breach of its obligations under the Convention. See Home Office, Statement of Immigration Rules, §§327–352.

[42] Cf Art 2(2), 1966 International Covenant on Civil and Political Rights (999 *UNTS*, p 171) which states: 'When not already provided for by existing legislative or other measures, each State Party to the present Covenant undertakes to take the necessary steps ... to adopt such legislative or other measures as may be necessary to give effect to the rights recognized ... .' On 'effective implementation', see the *LaGrand Case,* above n 34.

actual or putative bilateral relationships, but rather as a general legal standard against which performance can be reviewed in the context of the regime of international protection as a whole.

2. THE PRINCIPLE OF GOOD FAITH IN INTERNATIONAL LAW

2.1. Background and Authority

The principle of good faith, as a legal principle, is not only an integral part of the rule *pacta sunt servanda,* but also applies generally throughout international law. As the International Court of Justice stated in the *Nuclear Tests* Case:

> One of the basic principles governing the creation and performance of legal obligations, *whatever their source*, is the principle of good faith . . . .[43]

The extent to which the principle of good faith pervades international relations has also been remarked on by the International Court of Justice in the following terms:

> The Court observes that the principle of good faith is a well-established principle of international law. It is set forth in Article 2, paragraph 2, of the Charter of the United Nations; it is also embodied in Article 26 of the Vienna Convention on the Law of Treaties of 23 May 1969. It was mentioned as early as the beginning of this century in the Arbitral Award of 7 September 1910 in the *North Atlantic Fisheries case* (*United Nations, Reports of International Arbitral Awards*, Vol XI, p 188). It was moreover upheld in several judgments of the Permanent Court of International Justice (*Factory at Chorzów, Merits, Judgment No 13, 1928, PCIJ, Series A*, No 17, p 30; *Free Zones of Upper Savoy and the District of Gex, Order of 6 December 1930, PCIJ, Series A*, No 24, p 12 and 1932, *PCIJ, Series A/B*, No 46, p 167). Finally, it was applied by this Court as early as 1952 in the case concerning *Rights of Nationals of the United States of America in Morocco* (*Judgment, ICJ Reports*, 1952, p 212), then in the case concerning *Fisheries Jurisdiction (Federal Republic of Germany v Iceland)*, (*Jurisdiction of the Court, Judgment, ICJ Reports*, 1973, p 18), the *Nuclear Tests* cases (*ICJ Reports*, 1974, pp 268 and 473), and the case concerning *Border and Transborder Armed Actions (Nicaragua v Honduras)* (*Jurisdiction and Admissibility, Judgment, ICJ Reports*, 1988, p 105).[44]

[43] *Nuclear Tests (Australia v France) Case, ICJ Reports*, 1974, pp 253, 268 (para 46); see also *Case Concerning Border and Transborder Armed Actions, ICJ Reports*, 1988, p 105 (para 94).

[44] *Cameroon v Nigeria, Preliminary Objections Judgment, ICJ Reports*, 1998, para 38. The municipal law origins of the principle of good faith in international law are generally and

Article 2(2) of the United Nations Charter, referred to by the Court, places the principle in the forefront of those which are to govern the conduct of Members:

> The Organization and its Members, in pursuit of the Purposes stated in Article 1, shall act in accordance with the following Principles …
>
> 2. All Members, in order to ensure to all of them the rights and benefits resulting from membership, shall fulfil in good faith the obligations assumed by them in accordance with the Charter.

In the words of the US delegate to the San Francisco conference, the principle, '… had the meaning that we are all to observe those obligations, not merely the letter of them, but the spirit of them.'[45] Consequently, Article 2(2) does not apply merely to obligations assumed under the Charter, but to all obligations that are in accordance with the Charter. This interpretation was confirmed in the 1970 Declaration on Principles of International Law Concerning Friendly Relations which provides as follows:[46]

> *The principle that States shall fulfil in good faith the obligations assumed by them in accordance with the Charter*
>
> Every State has the duty to fulfil in good faith the obligations assumed by it in accordance with the Charter of the United Nations.
>
> Every State has the duty to fulfil in good faith its obligations under the generally recognized principles and rules of international law.
>
> Every State has the duty to fulfil in good faith its obligations under international agreements valid under the generally recognised principles and rules of international law.

The principle of good faith is thus among the 'basic principles of international law'.[47] As Virally states, 'It is not a simple ethical principle, when

widely recognised amongst the proponents of natural law and in the writings of other commentators such as Suarez, Gentili, Grotius, and as such do not require detailed consideration here. The background is set out in J F O'Connor, *Good Faith in International Law,* (Aldershot, 1991). O'Connor notes: 'The elaboration of the concept of *bona fides* in Roman law as involving a *legal* obligation to do what a decent, fair and conscientious man would do in particular circumstances contributed very largely to the association of good faith, in a wider ethical sense, with *pacta sunt servanda.* In relation to keeping promises and agreements, good faith acquired the meaning of not only the obligation to observe literally the undertakings given, but also the advertence to the real intentions of the parties or to the "spirit" of the agreement.' (*Ibid*, p 39.)

[45] *United Nations Conference on International Organization (UNCIO)*, vol VI, p 71. The wording of Art 2(2) was adopted unanimously by Committee I. Cited in B Simma, *The United Nations Charter: A Commentary,* 2nd edn (Oxford, 2002), pp 91–101.

[46] The 1970 Declaration on Principles of International Law Concerning Friendly Relations and Co-operation among States in accordance with the Charter of the United Nations was adopted by consensus in UN General Assembly resolution 2625 (XXV), 24 October 1970.

[47] See *ibid*, para 3.

applied to law, even though it is *also* an ethical principle and was borrowed by law from the ethical realm.'[48] The essentially *legal* character of good faith in international law has also been recognized by the International Law Commission and by modern commentators. Hersch Lauterpacht, when dealing with the related issue of 'abuse of rights', noted in 1958:

> ... it is possible to see an indirect approach [by the international court] to the principle prohibiting abuse of rights in the frequent affirmation of the duty of States to act in good faith in the exercise of their rights.[49]

In the *Norwegian Loans* Case, Judge Lauterpacht observed that, 'Unquestionably, the obligation to act in accordance with good faith, being a general principle of law, is also part of international law.'[50] Fitzmaurice, a former Special Rapporteur on the Law of Treaties and Judge of the International Court of Justice, defined the principle as follows:

> The essence of the doctrine is that although a State may have a strict right to act in a particular way, it must not exercise this right in such a manner as to constitute an abuse of it; it must exercise its rights in good faith and with a sense of responsibility; it must have bona fide reasons for what it does, and not act arbitrarily and capriciously.[51]

Schwarzenberger included good faith among the 'seven fundamental principles' of international law.[52] Commenting on the 'prohibitory or mandatory character' of the rules underlying the principle of good faith, he observed:

> It is possible to hold that, within the limits in which the principle of good faith is incorporated in international law, any deviation from these rules constitutes a breach of rules prohibiting the interpretation of legal duties of abstention as *jus strictum* or in outright bad faith. It is, however, equally

[48] M Virally, 'Review Essay: Good Faith in Public International Law', 77 *American Journal of International Law* (1983), p 130, at p 133. Moreover, as Rosenne states: 'Its normative content is to be distinguished from the role of good faith against the broader background of international relations .... Without denying... that good faith, as a concept, is *also* one of public and of private morality, the view that it is *only* a moral or a metaphysical concept is one that cannot be entertained ... .' (S Rosenne, *Developments in the Law of Treaties. 1945–1986*, (Cambridge, 1989), pp 135–36.)

[49] H Lauterpacht, *The Development of International Law by the International Court of Justice*, (London, 1958), p 163. See also Rosenne, above n 48, pp 139–40.

[50] *Certain Norwegian Loans Case, ICJ Reports*, 1957, p 53.

[51] G Fitzmaurice, 'The Law and Procedure of the International Court of Justice, 1951–54: General Principles and Sources of Law', 27 *British Year Book of International Law* (1950), p 1, at pp 12–13.

[52] G Schwarzenberger and E Brown, *A Manual of International Law*, 6th edn (London, 1976), pp 35–36.

> permissible to put the emphasis on the positive regulative functions which the rules underlying the principle of good faith fulfil in delimiting the respective spheres of competing rights.[53]

2.2. Aspects of Good Faith Distinguished

It is necessary to distinguish the various aspects of what is a *general* principle of international law. So far as State responsibility is a matter of *objective* conditions (on which, see Section 2.4 below), good faith is also to be distinguished from bad faith ('dolus'). 'Good faith' operates as a legal principle in different contexts, including the obligations of States, (1) to settle disputes in good faith;[54] (2) to negotiate in good faith;[55] (3) having signed a treaty, not to frustrate the achievement of its object and purpose prior to ratification;[56] (4) having ratified a treaty, to apply and perform it in good faith and not to frustrate the achievement of its object and purpose;[57] (5) to interpret treaties in good faith, in accordance with their ordinary meaning considered in context and in the light of their object and purpose;[58] (6) to fulfil in good faith any obligations arising from other sources of international law;[59] and (7) to exercise rights in good faith.[60] Of these, the fourth, sixth and seventh are considered for the purposes of the present discussion.

2.3. Good Faith and the Law of Treaties

Three articles of the 1969 Vienna Convention on the Law of Treaties are relevant to the good faith implementation of treaty obligations: Article 18 (Obligation not to defeat the object and purpose of a treaty prior to its

[53] *Ibid*, p 99. See also B Simma et al, *The United Nations Charter: A Commentary*, 2nd edn (Oxford, 2002), p 91.
[54] Manila Declaration on the Peaceful Settlement of International Disputes, General Assembly resolution 37/10, 15 November 1982, Annex; and *Aerial Incident Case (Pakistan v India), Jurisdiction of the Court, ICJ Reports*, 2000, para 53.
[55] See, for example, *Gabcíkovo-Nagymaros Case (Hungary/Slovakia), ICJ Reports*, 1997, paras 141–142.
[56] Art 18, Vienna Convention on the Law of Treaties, 1155 *UNTS*, p 331.
[57] Art 26, *ibid*.
[58] Art 31, *ibid*.
[59] Art 2(2), UN Charter.
[60] This is a non-exhaustive list. In addition, the provisions of the 1969 Vienna Convention on the Law of Treaties relating to fraud (Art 49), corruption (Art 50), coercion (Art 51), and fundamental change of circumstances (*rebus sic stantibus*—Art 62), all derive from the principle of good faith.

entry into force); Article 26 (*Pacta sunt servanda*); and Article 31 (General rule of interpretation).[61]

2.3.1. *Obligation Not to Defeat the Object and Purpose of a Treaty*

Writing in 1989, the Soviet scholar, Lukashuk noted as follows:

> The principle of good faith fulfilment of obligations requires not only that states implement what has been provided for by a rule imposing an obligation, but also that they refrain from acts that could defeat the object and purpose of such a rule. This interpretation was confirmed by the Vienna Convention on the Law of Treaties of 1969, which obliges states to refrain from acts that would defeat the object and purpose of a treaty prior to its entry into force (Article 18). The prescription takes on even greater significance with respect to treaties that have already entered into force. It cannot but apply also to customary norms having equal status with treaty norms.... Thus, states are under an obligation to refrain both from acts defeating the object and purpose of a rule and from any other acts preventing its implementation.[62]

During the course of drafting the Vienna Convention on the Law of Treaties, the International Law Commission located the obligation of a State to refrain from acts which would defeat the object and purpose of a treaty in two contexts. The first instance, in what became Article 18 as mentioned by Lukashuk,[63] was the obligation of a *signatory* State to refrain from such acts before the treaty entered into force. The Special Rapporteur, Sir Humphrey Waldock, noted in this context that, 'good faith was the foundation of an obligation which did not, strictly speaking, arise out of the treaty itself.'[64] The ILC eventually decided to drop the specific reference to 'good faith'. In Ago's view,

[61] 1969 Vienna Convention on the Law of Treaties: 1155 *UNTS*, p 331.

[62] I I Lukashuk, 'The principle *pacta sunt servanda* and the nature of obligation under international law', 83 *American Journal of International Law* (1989), p 513, at p 515. Although written at a time of major change in Soviet/Russian institutions (the article was published in a section of the *American Journal of International Law* entitled 'Agora: New Thinking by Soviet Scholars'), it is submitted that this is an accurate description of the principle of good faith as relevant to the issues under discussion.

[63] As initially drafted, the then text (Art 17, para 2) provided that even before a treaty comes into force a State that has established its consent to be bound by the treaty is under an obligation of good faith to 'refrain from acts calculated to frustrate the objects of the treaty, if and when it comes into force'.

[64] *Yearbook of the International Law Commission*, 1964, vol I (Summary records of the 16th Session), 727th Meeting, 20 May 1964, p 70. See also *Yearbook of the International Law Commission*, 1965, vol II (Documents of the first part of the 17th Session), pp 43–44; *Yearbook of the International Law Commission*, 1965, vol I (Summary records of the first part of the 17th Session), 788th Meeting, 21 May 1965, pp 87–88.

> ... admittedly the rule stated was an application of the principle of good faith, but there was no need to mention good faith expressly. The essential point was that the State was bound to refrain from acts calculated to frustrate the object of a treaty ... .[65]

The second instance in which the ILC identified the obligation not to frustrate the object and purpose of a treaty lay in its formulation of the fundamental principle, *pacta sunt servanda.*[66] Referring to the ILC's recognition of 'pre-conventional' obligations, the Special Rapporteur commented,

> *A fortiori,* when the treaty is in force the parties are under an obligation of good faith to refrain from such acts. Indeed, when the treaty is in force such acts are not only contrary to good faith but also to the undertaking to perform the treaty according to its terms which is implied in the treaty itself ... .[67]

And again on the topic,

> ... the intended meaning was that a treaty must be applied and observed not merely according to its letter, but in good faith. It was the duty of the parties to the treaty not only to observe the letter of the law, but also to abstain from acts which would inevitably affect their ability to perform the treaty.[68]

The ILC redrafted the principle as follows:

> A treaty in force is binding upon the parties to it and must be performed by them in good faith. [Every party shall abstain from any act incompatible with the object and purpose of the treaty.]

It had unanimously agreed on the first sentence, while opinion was divided as to whether the sentence in brackets should be retained. Some

[65] *Yearbook of the International Law Commission*, 1965, vol I (Summary records of the first part of the 17th Session), 813th Meeting, 29 June 1965, para 102; other members agreed (see *ibid*, paras 104, 106, 109, 111, 113). In the words of a recent commentator, the legal basis of pre-treaty obligations is to be found in the principle of good faith ('Le fondement juridique des obligations préconventionnelles réside dans le principe de bonne foi'): R Kolb, *La bonne foi en droit international public,* (Presses Universitaire de France, 2000), p 206.

[66] In the 1964 draft, the then Art 55 provided: '*Pacta sunt servanda*. 1. A treaty in force is binding upon the parties and must be applied by them in good faith in accordance with its terms and in the light of the general rules of international law governing the interpretation of treaties. 2. Good faith, *inter alia,* requires that a party to a treaty shall refrain from any acts calculated to prevent the due execution of the treaty or otherwise to frustrate its objects ... .' (*Yearbook of the International Law Commission*, 1964, vol II (Documents of the 16th Session), p 7.)

[67] *Yearbook of the International Law Commission*, 1964, vol II (Documents of the 16th Session), p 8.

[68] *Yearbook of the International Law Commission*, 1964, vol I (Summary records of the 16th Session), 727th Meeting, 20 May 1964, p 70.

members considered that the principle was implicit in the first sentence, whereas others regarded the two sentences as complementary, believing it advisable to stipulate that States must refrain from acts not expressly prohibited by the terms of the treaty, but incompatible with its object and purpose.[69]

Replying to a question from Mr Lachs, the Polish representative, the Special Rapporteur said that the phrase 'the object and purpose of the treaty',

> ... was used with the same meaning as in paragraph 1(d) of article 18, on reservations. It had been taken from the advisory opinion of the International Court of Justice on *Reservations to the Convention on the Prevention and Punishment of the Crime of Genocide*. The purpose of the second sentence was to deal with the problem of certain acts which, although not prohibited by the letter of the treaty, would, if accomplished, render its performance much more difficult. It was meant to strengthen the first sentence by going beyond its literal provisions.[70]

It was finally agreed to drop the explicit reference to the obligation of the State to refrain from acts incompatible with the object and purpose of the treaty, because the obligation was implicit in the statement of the principle, and it would be inadvisable to stress one of the applications of the principle to the exclusion of the others.[71] Moreover, the link in Article 31 of the 1969 Vienna Convention on the Law of Treaties ('VCLT69') between good faith and the need to respect the meaning and purpose of a treaty emphasises the

[69] *Yearbook of the International Law Commission*, 1964, vol I (Summary records of the 16th Session), 748th Meeting, 18 June 1964, Articles submitted by the drafting committee, p 52 *et seq*.

[70] *Yearbook of the International Law Commission*, 1964, vol I (Summary records of the 16th Session), 748th Meeting, 18 June 1964, p 55.

[71] *Yearbook of the International Law Commission*, 1964, vol I (Summary records of the 16th Session), 748th Meeting, 18 June 1964, p 55. See, for example, the views of Messrs Rosenne (*ibid*, p 63), de Luna (*ibid*, p 71), Yasseen (*ibid*, p 75); and also *Yearbook of the International Law Commission*, 1966, vol I (Summary records of the 18th Session), Messrs. Castrén (*ibid*, para 24), and Ago (*ibid*, para 32). With regard to Article 26 (then Article 23 in the draft), the ILC's 1966 Commentary states: '(1) *Pacta sunt servanda*—the rule that treaties are binding on the parties and must be performed in good faith—is a fundamental principle of the law of treaties ... (2) There is much authority in the jurisprudence of international tribunals for the proposition that in the present context the principle of good faith is a legal principle which forms an integral part of the rule *pacta sunt servanda*. ... (3) Some members felt that there would be advantage in also stating that a party must abstain from acts calculated to frustrate the object and purpose of the treaty. The Commission, however, considered that this was clearly implicit in the obligation to perform the treaty in good faith and preferred to state the *pacta sunt servanda* rule in as simple a form as possible' (ILC Commentaries on Draft Articles, paras 1, 2 and 5 on (then) draft Article 23, *Report of the ILC on the work of its 18th Session*, *Yearbook of the International Law Commission*, 1966, vol II, pp 42–43).

objective function of the principle. As Reuter observed with regard to then Article 17, the Commission had a choice between adopting an objective criterion or a subjective criterion; in conformity with the Commission's wishes, the Special Rapporteur had adopted an objective criterion by referring to the treaty—a solution which linked the obligation created to the treaty itself.[72]

Thus, good faith requires conduct which is objectively compatible with meaning, object and purpose. This conclusion is consistent with the jurisprudence, which also has based itself on objective considerations in determining whether a State has deprived a treaty of its object and purpose before its entry into force. Judgments on good faith or otherwise have thus looked at the conduct of the State and its consequences in fact, rather than at its intentions.

In the *Conditions of Admission to the United Nations Case,* Judge Azevedo considered abuse of rights as being related to good faith. In his separate opinion, he remarked:

> [It] has now been freed from the classical notions of *dolus* and *culpa;* in the last stage of the problem an inquiry into intention may be discarded, and attention may be given solely to the objective aspect; i.e. it may be presumed that the right in question must be exercised in accordance with standards of what is normal, having in view the social purpose of the law.[73]

The International Court of Justice approached the 'object and purpose' aspect of certain types of standard-setting agreements, such as in the area of human rights and refugee matters, in the context of its Advisory Opinion on *Reservations to the Genocide Convention.* Its remarks are particularly significant, in view of the question as to who may invoke the responsibility of the State. The Court stated:

> The objects of such a convention must also be considered. The Convention was manifestly adopted for a purely humanitarian and civilizing purpose. It is indeed difficult to imagine a convention that might have this dual character to a greater degree, since its object on the one hand is to safeguard the very existence of certain human groups and on the other to confirm and endorse

[72] *Yearbook of the International Law Commission*, 1965, vol I (Summary records of the first part of the 17th Session), 788th Meeting, 21 May 1965, p 88 (paras 38–39). See also A Aust, *Modern Treaty Law and Practice,* (Cambridge, 2000), p 94: the test is objective, and it is not necessary to prove bad faith.

[73] *Conditions of Admission to the United Nations, Advisory Opinion, ICJ Reports*, 1947–8, p 80. Commenting on this decision, Rosenne concludes that, '... the court rightly turned itself away from any attempt to explore the depths of the "mind" of a collectivity such as a State and shifted the focus of its attention from such an elusive object to actual conduct.' (Rosenne, above n 48, p 171.)

> the most elementary principles of morality. In such a convention the contracting States do not have any interests of their own; they merely have, one and all, a common interest, namely, the accomplishment of those high purposes which are the *raison d'être* of the convention. Consequently, in a convention of this type one cannot speak of individual advantages or disadvantages to States, or of the maintenance of a perfect contractual balance between rights and duties. The high ideals which inspired the Convention provide, by virtue of the common will of the parties, the foundation and measure of all its provisions.[74]

The object and purpose of the Refugee Convention, in this sense, certainly calls for attention in the present context; arguably, it is to extend the protection of the international community to refugees, and to assure to refugees 'the widest possible exercise of ... fundamental rights and freedoms';[75] the minimum content of protection is illustrated by the category of impermissible reservations.[76]

2.3.2. *Lack of Good Faith and Violation of Treaty Distinguished*

Lack of good faith in the implementation of a treaty must be distinguished from a violation of the treaty itself. A State lacks good faith in the application of a treaty, not only when it openly refuses to implement its undertakings, but more precisely, when it seeks to avoid or to 'divert' the obligation which it has accepted, or to do indirectly what it is not permitted to do directly.

> As Lord McNair has observed, A State may take certain action or be responsible for certain inaction, which, though not in form a breach of a treaty, is such that its effect will be equivalent to a breach of treaty; in such cases a tribunal demands good faith and seeks for the reality rather than the appearance.[77]

Among various examples, he suggests that, 'the making of regulations by one party which in substance destroyed or frustrated the right of the other party would be a breach of good faith and of the treaty.'[78]

[74] *Reservations to the Genocide Convention, Advisory Opinion, ICJ Reports*, 1951, p 15, at p 23. Cf the jurisprudence of the European Court of Human Rights, which illustrates the importance of 'object and purpose' when assessing the validity of State policy and practice. See, for example, *Anguelova v Bulgaria,* 13 June 2002, para 109; *Prinz Hans-Adam II of Liechtenstein v Germany,* 12 July 2001, para 48; *Z v United Kingdom,* 10 May 2001, para 103; *Chassagnou v France,* 29 April 1999, para 100.

[75] Preamble to the 1951 Convention relating to the Status of Refugees, 189 *UNTS*, p 150.

[76] Thus, reservations are not permitted to, among others, Art 1 (refugee definition), Art 3 (non-discrimination), Art 4 (religious freedom), Art 16(1) (access to courts of law), and Art 33 (*non-refoulement*): see Art 42 CSR51, *ibid.*

[77] A McNair, *The Law of Treaties,* (Oxford, 1961), p 540.

[78] *Ibid*, p 550.

In the *Free Zones Case,* France was under treaty obligations to maintain certain frontier zones with Switzerland free from customs barriers. The Permanent Court of International Justice, while recognising that France had the sovereign and undoubted right to establish a police cordon at the political frontier for the control of traffic and even for the imposition of fiscal taxes other than customs duties, held that,

> A reservation must be made as regards the case of abuses of a right, since it is certain that France must not evade the obligation to maintain the zones by erecting a customs barrier under the guise of a control cordon.[79]

The *North Atlantic Coast Fisheries Case* (Great Britain–United States of America) recognised the right and duty of Great Britain as the local sovereign to legislate in regulation of fisheries. However,

> ... treaty obligations are to be executed in perfect good faith, therefore excluding the right to legislate *at will* concerning the subject-matter of the treaty, and limiting the exercise of sovereignty of the State bound by a treaty with respect to that subject-matter to such acts as are consistent with the treaty.[80]

In the *Rights of US Nationals in Morocco Case,* the International Court of Justice considered that while the power of making the valuation of import goods for customs purposes vested with the customs authorities, '... it is a power which must be exercised reasonably and in good faith.'[81]

2.4. Duty to Exercise Rights in Good Faith and the Objective Aspects of Responsibility

Writing in 1953 on the general principles of international law, Bin Cheng concluded:

> The principle of good faith which governs international relations controls also the exercise of rights by States. The theory of abuse of rights (*abus de droit*), recognized in principle both by the Permanent Court of International Justice and the International Court of Justice, is merely an application of this principle to the exercise of rights.
>
> ...
>
> Good faith in the exercise of rights ... means that a State's rights must be exercised in a manner compatible with its various obligations arising either

[79] *Free Zones of Upper Savoy and the District of Gex Case, (France v Switzerland)* (Merits), *PCIJ Reports*, Ser A/B, No 46, p 167.
[80] *RIAA*, vol XI, (1910), p 167, at p 188. Emphasis in original.
[81] *Rights of US Nationals in Morocco Case, ICJ Reports*, 1952, p 212.

> from treaties or from the general law. It follows from this interdependence of rights and obligations that rights must be reasonably exercised.[82]

Modern jurisprudence, particularly in the field of human rights, applies corresponding notions of reasonableness and proportionality.[83]

The principle of good faith is essentially *objective* in application. Consistent with the general principles of international law on the responsibility of States for internationally wrongful acts, good faith looks to the *effects* of State action, rather than to the (subjective) intent or motivation, if any, of the State itself.[84]

Fitzmaurice, reviewing the law and procedure of the International Court of Justice, considered whether the subjective element was essential. He noted:

> There is always a natural reluctance to ascribe bad faith to States, in the sense of a deliberate intention knowingly to circumvent an international obligation. Is this subjective element an essential ingredient of the concept of bad faith? Possibly, in the case of bad faith considered purely in and of itself, it is such an ingredient. But this would not seem necessarily to apply to an abuse of rights—and it is largely through abuses of rights that actions that may give the impression of being in (deliberate) bad faith are carried out .... A State which, though not with the actual object of breaking an international obligation as such, uses its right to apply certain laws, or to apply them in a certain way, in such a manner that the obligation is not in fact carried out, may be said to have committed an abuse of rights.[85]

3. THE PRACTICAL APPLICATION OF THE PRINCIPLE OF GOOD FAITH

It was suggested above that the United Kingdom's actions in Prague may have violated its duty to implement the 1951 Convention and 1967

[82] B Cheng, *General Principles of Law as applied by International Courts and Tribunals*, (London, 1953), pp 121, 131.

[83] Cf also Art 300 of the 1982 United Nations Convention on the Law of the Sea (Good faith and abuse of rights) which provides that: 'States Parties shall fulfil in good faith the obligations assumed under this Convention and shall exercise the rights, jurisdiction and freedoms recognized in this Convention in a manner which would not constitute an abuse of right.'

[84] Brownlie states that, 'provided that agency and causal connection are established, there is breach of duty by result alone'; and he also notes the irrelevance of intention to harm, or of *dolus* as a condition of liability. (I Brownlie, *Principles of Public International Law*, 6th edn (Oxford, 2003), pp 423, 426–427.) See also Crawford, commenting on attribution in particular as an element of responsibility, who states: 'In the absence of any specific requirement of a mental element in terms of the primary obligation, it is only the act of the State that matters, independently of any intention.' (Crawford, above n 1, p 84.)

[85] G Fitzmaurice, 'The Law and Procedure of the International Court of Justice, 1951–54: General Principles and Sources of International Law', 35 *British Year Book of International Law* (1959), pp 183, 209.

Protocol in good faith. It was further argued that the responsibility of the United Kingdom might be invoked by an international organisation, the UNHCR, having a legal interest in compliance. If such is indeed the case, then the principle of good faith implementation, being in the nature of a series of cumulative obligations of conduct, its breach could most easily be determined by reference to and against the standard which is the object and purpose of the 1951 Convention, considered in light of its text and context, including supporting institutions, rules, and practices.

In addition to conformity with the object and purpose of the relevant treaty, good faith requires that a State's actions in a field regulated by treaty must also be consistent or compatible with its international obligations at large; and, in appropriate circumstances, that such actions should be proportionate.

3.1. The Consistency or Compatibility of a State's Actions with its International Obligations at Large

The requirement of 'consistency' is a well established principle, applicable in times of emergency as much as in normal times. Article 15 of the European Convention on Human Rights provides a clear statement of the principle:

> In time of war or other public emergency threatening the life of the nation any High Contracting Party may take measures derogating from its obligations under this Convention to the extent strictly required by the exigencies of the situation, *provided that such measures are not inconsistent with its other obligations under international law*.[86]

The requirement of consistency can be usefully illustrated by reference to other provisions of the European Convention on Human Rights, to which both the United Kingdom and the Czech Republic are party. For example, the Czech Republic is also a party to the Fourth Protocol to the Convention, which the United Kingdom has signed but not yet ratified. The Czech Republic consequently has accepted the following obligations, pursuant to Article 2 of the Fourth Protocol:

> 2. Everyone shall be free to leave any country, including his own.
> 3. No restrictions shall be placed on the exercise of these rights other than such as are in accordance with law and are necessary in a democratic

[86] Emphasis added. See also Art 4, 1966 International Covenant on Civil and Political Rights, which adds the further qualification that such measures should not 'involve discrimination solely on the ground of race, colour, sex, language, religion or social origin'.

> society in the interests of national security or public safety, for the maintenance of *ordre public*, for the prevention of crime, for the protection of health or morals, or for the protection of the rights and freedoms of others.

Article 6 of the Fourth Protocol (Relationship to the Convention) provides:

> As between the High Contracting Parties the provisions of Articles 1 to 5 of this Protocol shall be regarded as additional articles to the Convention, and all the provisions of the Convention shall apply accordingly.

The Czech Republic is thus obliged under the Convention to recognise the freedom of its citizens to leave the country and may only restrict that freedom consistently with the exceptions mentioned in Article 2(3) of the Fourth Protocol, and subject to the overriding requirements of non-discrimination set out in Article 14 of the Convention. Moreover, as a signatory to the Fourth Protocol, the United Kingdom is, in the words of Article 18 VCLT69, 'obliged to refrain from acts which would defeat the object and purpose' of the treaty.

Other treaties ratified by the United Kingdom contain obligations relevant to its actions in the migration and refugee protection field. In addition to the 1966 International Convention on the Elimination of All Forms of Racial Discrimination, referred to briefly above,[87] the United Kingdom is party to the 1966 International Covenant on Civil and Political Rights,[88] which also protects freedom of movement and lays down the general principle of non-discrimination and equal protection of the law.[89]

On the other hand, it may be argued that no State is obliged to facilitate the travel to its territory of those who wish to seek asylum. Yet in 1948, and even as they were not prepared to recognise a right on the part of the refugee to be *granted* asylum, States adopting the Universal Declaration of Human Rights did acknowledge in principle 'the right of everyone *to seek* ... in other countries asylum from persecution'.[90] Beyond the Universal Declaration, the options available to a State wishing to frustrate the movement of those who seek asylum are limited by specific rules of

[87] See text corresponding to above nn 18–22.

[88] 999 *UNTS*, p 171. The UK ratified the Covenant with reservations on 16 Sep 1968.

[89] See Arts 12 and 26. The United Kingdom's reservation to Art 12 reads in part: 'The Government of the United Kingdom reserve the right to continue to apply such immigration legislation governing entry into, stay in and departure from the United Kingdom as they may deem necessary from time to time ... .'

[90] Art 14(1), 1948 Universal Declaration of Human Rights, General Assembly resolution 217A (III), 10 December 1948.

international law and by the State's obligation to fulfil its international commitments in good faith. These commitments, illustrated above, include obligations towards refugees and asylum seekers, obligations in relation to racial discrimination and freedom of movement, and obligations generally with regard to treaties. The 'legitimate purpose' of immigration control may only be pursued within the law.[91]

3.2. Proportionality and Choice of Means

Wherever the actions of a State, taken in pursuit of a lawful aim, such as migration management, run the risk of undermining the object and purpose of a particular treaty or of infringing the internationally protected rights of those affected, including other States party to multilateral treaties, it is submitted that the principle of good faith 'conditions' the legality of those actions on the taking of certain steps. In particular, it requires the State to consider, among others, the availability of reasonable alternatives which are proportionate to the purported objective (such as alleged abuse of the asylum process) and which are least likely to violate its international obligations.

According to the general principles of State responsibility, a plea of necessity,

> ... may not be invoked by a State as a ground for precluding the wrongfulness of an act not in conformity with an international obligation of that State unless the act:
> (a) Is the only way for the State to safeguard an essential interest against a grave and imminent peril; and
> (b) Does not seriously impair an essential interest of the State or States towards which the obligation exists, or of the international community as a whole.[92]

As a matter of general principle, and in view of the applicability of international obligations deriving from a variety of sources to the exercise of the

[91] Cf the European Court of Human Rights case of *K-H W v Germany*, a claim arising out of the prosecution and conviction of the applicant for intentional homicide in the death of a person trying to escape from the German Democratic Republic (East Germany). The European Court of Human Rights included as 'relevant international law' the 1966 International Covenant on Civil and Political Rights, including Art 12(2), (3) on freedom of movement, and found that GDR State practice was in breach of its international obligations. (*K-H W v Germany* (Application no 37201/97), Grand Chamber, 22 March 2001, paras 62–7, 92–101).

[92] Crawford, above n 1, Art 25 and Commentary, pp 178–86. See also Art 26 of the ILC Articles (on compliance with peremptory norms) which provides: 'Nothing in this chapter precludes the wrongfulness of any act of a State which is not in conformity with an obligation arising under a peremptory norm of general international law.' (*Ibid*, pp 187–88.)

powers in question, the State must therefore provide objective justification for the course of conduct chosen and show its consistency with international law.[93]

It might be argued that there is no difference between the implementation of a policy of pre-entry clearance and the administration of a visa system, under which prospective travellers are required to seek authorisation to enter from the diplomatic or consular authorities of the prospective receiving country; and that as the visa system is generally accepted in the practice of States, even with regard to those who may be seeking to leave their country of origin by reason of a well-founded fear of persecution, so a system of pre-entry clearance requiring the submission of prospective passengers to immigration control immediately before boarding an aircraft in their country of origin should also be accepted.

However, the long history of visas in the administration of international travel movements is not conclusive of their lawfulness in all instances. Thus, a visa regime can be unlawful, both in domestic and in international terms, for example, where visas are introduced or required for the purpose of maintaining a policy of racial discrimination; or where they are in fact used for the purpose of assisting the government of another State to commit an internationally wrongful act. The expulsion or deportation of non-citizens is likewise a matter of sovereign competence, but the discretion must be exercised in good faith and not for an ulterior motive. Expulsion may well constitute an internationally wrongful act, for example, when it infringes the principle of non-discrimination, or when carried out in life-threatening circumstances.[94] In each case, the purpose is relevant. It may be difficult to draw the line between clear instances of unlawful purposes, and instances where the harm to individuals is incidental to the practice; but the line is there.

Passive regimes, such as visas and carrier sanctions, are readily distinguishable in the first instance from the active interdiction or interception of persons seeking refuge from persecution or protection of their human rights. Depending on the circumstances, including the knowledge of the acting State, the scope and extent of that State's international obligations, and the availability of reasonable alternatives (including screening and referral), such practices are clearly capable of violating international law.

One of the best deterrents to 'abuse' of the asylum process, for example, is a fair, efficient and expeditious procedure for the determination of claims to refugee status, combined if necessary with bilateral or regional arrangements for the return to their countries of origin of those found not to be in

[93] Cf the European Court of Human Rights case of *Former King of Greece v Greece*, Judgment, 23 Nov 2000, para 98.
[94] Brownlie, above n 84, p 499.

need of protection. On the other hand, a system in which decisions are delayed or so flawed as to require regular correction on appeal or review,[95] is most likely to attract numbers of applications from persons not in need of protection.[96]

4. CONCLUSIONS

The principle of good faith requires that a State contemplating action within the area of its sovereign authority, for example, in controlling the movement of persons, must ensure that its actions are compatible with its international obligations. Good faith regulates the area between the permissible and the clearly impermissible. The mere fact that a certain matter falls within the sovereign competence of the State does not imply unfettered discretion. Certain things may not be done, even in pursuit of the 'legitimate aim' of migration management,[97] and the principle of good faith requires that the actions of the State are consistent with its other obligations under international law.

It is submitted that the principle thus requires the State to identify in good faith the actual circumstances and interests affected by its proposed action; to select the course of action to be adopted in good faith; to ensure that policies and practices are implemented in a manner compatible with

[95] In recent years, very high numbers of first instance asylum decisions by Home Office officials have been overturned on appeal: Home Office statistics note that 22% of appeals before immigration adjudicators were allowed in 2002: 'Asylum Statistics United Kingdom 2002', HOSB 08/03, para 26. A considerable proportion was also either conceded by the Home Office, overturned by the Immigration Appeals Tribunal, or following judicial review. The Refugee Legal Centre, a not-for-profit non-governmental organisation providing advice and representation to refugees and asylum seekers, reported a 34% success rate for its London office at appeals before adjudicators in 2001–2002, and even higher rates at regional offices; in the same period the Tribunal team were granted leave to appeal in 47% of applications, and of the cases that went to the Tribunal for hearing, 68% were allowed: *Annual Review 2001–2002*, pp 9–11.

[96] See *Conka v Belgium* (Application no 51564/99, 5 Feb 2002) in which the European Court of Human Rights recalled the principle of effectiveness of remedies (*ibid*, para 75) and went on to state: 'As to the overloading of the *Conseil d'Etat*'s list and the risks of abuse of process, the Court considers that, as with Article 6 of the Convention, Article 13 imposes on the Contracting States the duty to organise their judicial systems in such a way that their courts can meet its requirements.' (*Ibid*, para 84.) The case arose out of a Belgian Government proposal for the 'collective repatriation' of asylum seekers from Slovakia, following a sharp increase in numbers (*ibid*, paras 30–31). The Court cited reports on the situation of Roma in Slovakia which indicated that they were disadvantaged, often the victims of skinhead violence and regularly subjected to ill-treatment and discrimination by the authorities (*ibid*, paras 32–33). The Government claimed that its measures were justified, *inter alia*, by the numbers and 'major abuses of process which undermined [the] effectiveness' of the *Conseil d'Etat* (*ibid*, para 74). The Court found that the Applicants did not have a remedy available that satisfied the requirements of Art 13 to air their complaint under Art 4 of Protocol No 4 (*ibid*, para 85).

[97] For example, shooting people or deliberately sinking boats suspected of carrying illegal migrants.

the letter and spirit of international obligations that bind the State; to define in good faith the scope of its policies and practices so as not to apply them in such a way as to cause damage to the rights and lawful interests of other subjects of international law, including protected persons; and to refrain from or avoid abuse of rights.

If that indeed is what the principle of good faith requires, then in circumstances such as those litigated in the *ERRC* case, a State proposing, in respect of another State known to be the origin of people in search of refuge or protection of their human rights,[98] to introduce pre-entry clearance or similar methods of extra-territorial interception of persons, is obliged as a matter of law,

(1) to take into account the facts relating to conditions in the country of origin, including evidence relating to the protection of human rights, discrimination and persecution;
(2) to take into account the impact of its proposed measures on:
  (a) the rights and obligations of other States, in particular, where the area of action is the subject of a convention-based regime; and
  (b) the rights and interests of individuals, in particular, where these are protected by treaty or by general international law;
(3) to ensure that its actions are compatible with its international obligations, including
  (a) obligations expressly accepted by treaty;
  (b) the object and purpose of treaties to which it is party; and
  (c) obligations deriving from general international law.
(4) to act in accordance with the rules of general international law, especially with regard to methods and mechanisms of revision and modification of treaties, and the requirements for consultation and co-operation;[99] and
(5) to exercise its rights reasonably, that is, proportionately to a lawful purpose, and with due regard to alternatives.

The UK Court of Appeal did not accept this argument, or indeed that the Prague scheme violated the law prohibiting racial discrimination. Simon Brown LJ set out the submissions made on behalf of UNHCR as intervener.[100] He was of the view that the 'Convention challenge' raised

[98] As mentioned above, numbers of Czech Roma have been recognised as refugees; see above n 8.

[99] Cf Art 41 of the 1969 Vienna Convention on the Law of Treaties (see above n 56) on the modification of multilateral treaties between certain of the parties.

[100] *European Roma Rights Center v Immigration Officer, Prague Airport and Secretary of State for the Home Department* [2003] EWCA Civ 666 (Court of Appeal), §29.

two distinct issues, namely, the question as to the UK's obligations, having regard to the Convention; and secondly, 'the justiciability of this question given the limited extent to which the obligations have been incorporated into domestic law.'[101] His judgment focused on Article 33 CSR51, which he found had no direct application to the Prague operation because the Convention refugee definition applied necessarily to persons outside their country of origin, and because Article 33 prohibited *refoulement* to the 'frontiers' of other States.[102] In his view, the Convention did not 'concern itself ... with enabling people to escape from their own country by providing them with a right of admission to another country'.[103] Simon Brown LJ laid great stress on admission to the United Kingdom as the apparently necessary consequence of a successful challenge to pre-clearance; this prospect led him to hold, 'not merely [that] the Home Secretary [is] under no obligation to facilitate the arrival of asylum seekers but rather he is entitled to take steps to prevent their arrival.'[104] He concluded:

> It seems to me to be important to recognize that in entering international treaties states are undertaking limited obligations only and that the courts must recognize and respect such limitations. The good faith allegation should be approached with this in mind.[105]

Simon Brown LJ also invoked the ICJ's dictum in *Cameroon v Nigeria,* cited above:

> Although the principle of good faith is 'one of the basic principles governing the creation and performance of legal obligations ... it is not in itself a source of obligation where none would otherwise exist'.[106]

Mantell LJ agreed with the judgment of Simon Brown LJ on both the Convention and discrimination grounds. Laws LJ agreed on the Convention

[101] *Ibid*, §30.
[102] *Ibid*, §31.
[103] *Ibid*, §37.
[104] *Ibid*, §43. Simon Brown LJ's reasoning considerably overstates both the argument and the scope of the rule of *non-refoulement* in international law. It implies that admission to a State is the necessary and only consequence of the rule and, further, that admission is required even of those who are not Convention refugees, but merely claim to be so. What *non-refoulement* in fact requires, of course, depends very much on the circumstances. In one case, for example, a State may fully discharge its responsibilities under the Convention by sending a refugee to a third State willing to admit him or her; in another, by determining, prior to admission, that the person concerned is not entitled to protection as a refugee. By choosing the *non-refoulement*/admission reading of the law, Simon Brown LJ effectively foreclosed consideration of the lawfulness of measures which fall short of violating specific treaty obligations, but the consequence (and intent) of which is to prevent claims to protection ever being made.
[105] *Ibid*, §45.
[106] See above n 44.

ground, but dissented on the issue of direct discrimination. Laws LJ nevertheless added comment on the justiciability issue,[107] reemphasising the responsibility of the executive in making treaties, and the rule that 'no treaty comes within the body of the law of the land unless it is specifically incorporated by Act of Parliament'. In his view, the only elements of the Convention to have been incorporated were those to be found in the immigration rules,[108] the exact position being described in section 2 of the Asylum and Immigration Appeal Act 1993 ('Nothing in the immigration rules ... shall lay down any practice which would be contrary to the Convention'). Given that nothing in the immigration rules so provides, and that on the facts no one was facing removal from the United Kingdom in violation of the Convention,[109] Laws LJ concluded that the appellants necessarily were driven to argue, 'that the 1951 Convention has distinct and enforceable effects in the domestic law of England which transcend the reach of its incorporation by Parliament.'[110] That was a 'constitutional solecism', and 'we must not be seduced by humanitarian claims to a spurious acceptance of a false source of law.'[111]

Overall, the judgment of the Court of Appeal is not surprising. Among others, the Court was asked to deal with international law issues of some complexity, and on which there is little jurisprudence. The approach adopted by Simon Brown LJ and endorsed by Mantell LJ left little opportunity to examine the substantive aspects of the good faith argument, the idea of reviewing UK procedures overseas against the panoply of international obligations may have been somewhat daunting, and there is a natural reluctance to find that a State is acting in bad faith.[112] Questions nonetheless remain; the implied interpretation of the Convention in the narrowest of terms is worth further discussion, and the connection between *non-refoulement* and non-rejection at the frontier, in itself and in relation to the responsibility of the State for its extra-territorial activities, will call for greater in-depth analysis.[113]

[107] *ERRC*, above n 100, §§95–101.
[108] *Ibid*, §98.
[109] *Ibid*, §99.
[110] *Ibid*.
[111] *Ibid*, §100. Laws LJ was also not prepared to admit that ratification without or before incorporation could give rise to a legitimate expectation on which the public could rely. He observed: 'The proposition that the act of ratifying a treaty could *without more* give rise to enforceable legitimate expectations seems to me to amount, pragmatically, to a means of incorporating the substance of obligations undertaken on the international plane into our domestic law without the authority of Parliament.' (*Ibid*, §101. Emphasis in original.) The obligation in international law for a State, having signed a treaty, not to frustrate its object and purpose prior to ratification, suggests a more sophisticated approach than English law is presently prepared to countenance.
[112] But see Fitzmaurice, quoted in text corresponding to above n 85.
[113] The European Court of Human Rights has recognized that the implementation of Convention obligations may involve the responsibility of more than one State, and that,

As already indicated above, the majority judgment's focus on 'facilitation' and 'admission' leaves many questions begging. The argument put to the Court was intended precisely to show that no *additional* obligation, such as admission, was in fact involved; but rather to emphasize the narrowing of options that follows, as a matter of good faith, from the ratification of a treaty in an area of human rights protection.

Laws LJ followed (and endorsed perhaps even more firmly than necessary) the traditional United Kingdom approach to international law obligations which might be prayed in aid of domestic litigation. In theory, it might yet be thought that some room for review remains in regard to the exercise of executive discretionary power which displays egregious disregard of obligations solemnly undertaken, for example, in relation to the protection of human rights generally, or the prohibition of racial discrimination specifically, or which appears otherwise unreasonable and disproportionate. That may be wishful legal thinking, but the evident lack of control and review mechanisms and of opportunities to invoke the responsibility of the State confirms a worrying tension between national systems and international law. There are clear deficiencies where human rights or individual rights are concerned, and if certain claimants are not to remain beyond the pale of legal protection, both national approaches and the system of State responsibility itself must be further and substantially developed.

'Where States establish international organizations, or mutatis mutandis *international agreements*, to pursue co-operation in certain fields of activities, there may be implications for the protection of fundamental rights. It would be incompatible with the purpose and object of the Convention if Contracting States were thereby absolved from their responsibility under the Convention in relation to the field of activity covered ... ': *TI v the United Kingdom*, Application No 43844/98, Decision on Admissibility, 7 March 2000, emphasis supplied. See also *Prince Hans-Adam II of Liechtenstein v Germany,* 12 July 2001, para 48. In *Bankovic v Belgium and 16 Other Contracting States*, the European Court of Human Rights accepted that jurisdiction (and hence responsibility under the Convention) was primarily, though not exclusively, territorial. It recalled, however, that it had also recognised extra-territorial jurisdiction, for example, 'when the respondent State ... *through the consent, invitation or acquiescence of the Government of [the relevant] territory, exercises some or all of the public powers normally to be exercised by that Government.*' (*Bankovic v Belgium and 16 Other Contracting States*, (Application no 52207/99), 12 Dec 2001, para 71). The Court mentioned other recognised instances of the extra-territorial exercise of jurisdiction by a State, which 'include cases involving the activities of its diplomatic or consular agents abroad ... .' (*Ibid*, para 73). The decision in *Bankovic*, clearly distinguishable as to the facts, is nevertheless authoritative as to the principles of responsibility. That case involved acts of war against a State that was not party to the European Convention on Human Rights. The *ERRC* case (above n 100) involved a co-operative engagement by two parties to the European Convention to take or to tolerate action in the common legal space (*espace juridique*: *Bankovic*, *ibid*, para 80) which affects the international obligations of at least one of those parties.

7

For the 'Common Good': Rights and Interests in the Law of State Responsibility

MATTHEW CRAVEN*

WHEN THINKING ABOUT the relationship between general rules on State responsibility and the activities of various international courts and tribunals one is naturally drawn to articulate that relationship in terms of a set of oppositions: between the general and the particular, the local and the universal, the foreground and the background, the primary and the secondary, and so forth. Indeed the very project on State responsibility, with which the International Law Commission was engaged for so many years,[1] was evidently shaped by the difficulties of developing a singular set of systemic rules in face of an increasingly diverse array of practice, including that emanating from a multiplicity of international courts and tribunals. The opposition between the need for homogeneity in general rules of responsibility on the one hand, and the apparent heterogeneity of particular regimes of obligation (in terms of their textual specificity or their teleology) on the other, seemed hard to avoid.

The dialectics underlying such a project, however, are far from simple. At one level, the task facing the ILC, in this respect, was a reductive one, involving the distillation of essentials from the diversity of practice (the identification of the general in the particular, and the universal in the local). At another, it was eminently constructive, in the sense of relying not only upon certain assumptions being made as to the character, shape, or tenor of that diversity (assumptions, for example, as to the 'nature' of certain types of regime, or classes of obligation), but also upon certain critical

* Reader in International Law, SOAS.

[1] Articles on the Responsibility of States for Internationally Wrongful Acts, UN Doc A/CN 4/L 602/Rev 1 (2001). Approved by the General Assembly in Resolution 56/83, 12 Dec 2001.

suppositions as regards the social setting in which those rules and regimes may be thought to operate. The dialectics of system-building, in other words, would seem to involve both the essentialisation of particular projects and processes and the removal of ambivalence, dissonance, or ambiguity as regards their place or function within international society. It would also involve the constructive articulation of the society in which those projects would acquire their meaning—a society which would have to be simultaneously reflective of, and independent from, the particular projects and processes in question.

It is with a view to exploring the complexities of this process, and in particular the way in which regimes for the protection of human rights both appeared to configure, and be configured by, the articulation of systemic rules on State responsibility, that this chapter is written. It is argued that despite the attempt to avoid the ambivalence associated with inter-State human rights agreements—to reduce them to a singular characteristic 'form' for purposes of elucidating the general rules of responsibility—that ambivalence only reappears when one stands back to contemplate the nature of the society in which they are deemed to operate.

1. HUMAN RIGHTS REGIMES AND STATE RESPONSIBILITY

The relationship between general principles of State responsibility and the operational characteristics of regimes for the protection of human rights is not immediately obvious. We are, after all, not simply dealing with rules or principles that operate at a different conceptual level—the latter having the characteristic of primary rules of behaviour, the former secondary, residual, principles that govern the attribution for and effect of internationally wrongful acts[2]—but the elucidation of a framework that directs itself primarily to the entitlements and reactive capacity of injured States following a breach of a primary obligation seems to miss the point. Even if one should admit that compliance with human rights obligations remains premised upon the 'mobilisation of shame' in which States themselves may assume a not inconsiderable role,[3] the everyday life of human rights

[2] Higgins remarks that '[t]here seems to be no topic that is not embraced by "State responsibility". It covers, in the view of some, the law of every substantive obligation; the law of "instrumental consequences" to breach of obligations; and the detail of the law of reparation. It is my opinion that it is exactly this tendency to make State responsibility "the law of everything" that has led to such problems in achieving a concluded programme of work on the topic in the ILC.' (R Higgins, *Problems and Process: International Law and How We Use It* (Oxford, 1994), p 162.)

[3] Krasner argues that '[i]nternational regimes for human rights are designed to encourage some States to adopt policies that they would not otherwise pursue. The question of whether States adhere to such regimes is not a function of the extent to which a regime enhances information

(encompassing the enunciation of claims and their advancement through, or within, national and international fora) seems to be largely independent of any generalised argument as to the legal capacity of States to react to breaches. Not only may it be regarded as inappropriate, given the nature of the issues in question, to confine one's attention solely to the activities of States to that end, but the paucity of inter-State claims brought before human rights courts or tribunals itself, despite the availability of inter-State mechanisms to that end,[4] seems to suggest that for States at least the rhetorical potential of human rights is usually regarded as more important than the technicalities of enforcement.

It is not altogether implausible to suggest that such considerations may have played a part in the International Law Commission's approach to the question of State Responsibility. The articles on State responsibility, drafted with such great deliberation by the ILC over many years, eschew dealing either with the issue of individual responsibility[5] or indeed with the capacity of individuals or groups to invoke State responsibility. They are, furthermore, articulated as essentially residual principles that come into operation only where matters are not otherwise regulated by conventional agreement,[6] suggesting thereby that their relevance for human rights treaty regimes is strictly limited. By the same token, it is apparent that the practice of human rights institutions exercised a not inconsiderable influence upon both the structure and content of the ILC Articles not least in relation to the vexed issues of crimes of States and *erga omnes* obligations.[7] Even some of the more prosaic elements of the Articles have been affected by practice in relation to such treaties. One might mention here the avoidance of a distinction between obligations of conduct and result,[8] the

or discourages cheating; rather it is a function of the extent to which more powerful States in the system are willing to enforce the principles and norms of the regime.' (S Krasner, 'Sovereignty, Regimes and Human Rights', in V Rittberger, *Regime Theory and International Relations* (Oxford, 1993), pp 140–41.)

[4] See eg, International Covenant on Civil and Political Rights (1966), Art 41; International Convention on the Elimination of All Forms of Racial Discrimination (1965), Art 11; Convention Against Torture and Other Cruel, Inhuman or Degrading Treatment or Punishment (1984), Art 21; European Convention of Human Rights and Fundamental Freedoms (1950); American Convention on Human Rights, (1969, Art 55).

[5] Art 58 provides: 'These articles are without prejudice to any question of the individual responsibility under international law of any person acting on behalf of a State.'

The articles, furthermore, do not deal with the responsibility of individuals whether or not they are acting on behalf of a State.

[6] Art 55 provides that the articles 'do not apply where and to the extent that the conditions for the existence of an internationally wrongful act or the content or implementation of the international responsibility of a State are governed by special rules of international law.'

[7] On the way in which crimes of States were ultimately addressed see, E Wyler, 'From "State Crime" to Responsibility for "Serious Breaches of Obligations under Peremptory Norms of General International Law"', 13 *European Journal of International Law* (2002), p 1147.

[8] The Commentary to Art 12 uses the case of *Colozza and Rubinat v Italy* (ECHR, *Series A*, No 89, 1985) to demonstrate the relative lack of utility of the distinction: see J Crawford,

recognition given to 'continuing wrongful acts' in general international law,[9] and the determination that countermeasures should not be restricted to reciprocal action.[10] One also finds the text replete with references to the fact that the beneficiaries of the obligation breached may be other than the 'injured' State itself (as, for example, is found in the commentary to Articles 33 and 54).[11]

One of the areas in which the practice of human rights institutions may be regarded as having most significance, however, was in the development of special rights of invocation as found in Article 48 of the ILC draft, and the related provision concerning the adoption of 'lawful measures' by way of response (Article 54). Under the terms of Article 48, provision is made for a right of invocation of responsibility on the part of States parties to treaties established in the 'collective interest', even in absence of any claim that they may be regarded as injured by the breach. It draws, in that sense, upon the existence of mechanisms for the receipt of inter-State communications as found in sundry human rights treaties, and is at least partly reflective of the practice of the European Court of Human Rights.[12] The terms of Article 48, however, are to be contrasted with the more general right to invoke responsibility on the part of injured States as spelled out in Articles 42 to 47, and its existence may largely be accounted for by reason of the perception that many international obligations established in the collective interest could not easily be accommodated within a framework of responsibility that was essentially bilateral in nature.

The International Law Commission's Articles on State Responsibility: Introduction, Text and Commentaries (Cambridge, 2002).

[9] Reliance was placed upon *Papamichalopoulos and Others v Greece*, ECHR, *Series A*, No 260–B (1993); *Loizidou v Turkey, Merits, ECHR, Reports* 1996–VI, p 2216; and *Lovelace v Canada*, decision of 30th July 1981, 36 GAOR, Supp. No 40 (A/36/40), p 166.

[10] Commentary to Chapter II, para 5 in Crawford, above n 8.

[11] Art 33 clarifies the scope and effect of part II making clear that responsibility may extend, in virtue of particular obligations, to 'several States, or to the international community as a whole'. This is further qualified by the second paragraph that notes that such responsibility 'is without prejudice to any right, arising from the international responsibility of a State, which may accrue directly to any person or entity other than a State'. Thus, the Commentary observes that a 'State's responsibility for the breach of an obligation under a treaty concerning the protection of human rights may exist towards all the other parties of the treaty, but [it continues] the individuals concerned should be regarded as the ultimate beneficiaries and in that sense as the holders of the relevant rights.' (Art 33, Commentary, para 3 in Crawford, above n 8.)

[12] See eg Commentary to Art 48, para 12 in Crawford, above n 8. In the case of *Austria v Italy* (App No 788/60, 4 *European Yearbook of Human Rights* (1961), p 116, at p 140), for example, the European Commission concluded that 'the obligations undertaken by the High Contracting Parties in the European Convention are essentially of an objective character, being designed rather to protect the fundamental rights of individual human beings from infringements by any of the High Contracting Parties than to create subjective and reciprocal rights for the High Contracting Parties themselves.'

2. The Background

The development of the principle in Article 48, had its roots in extensive discussions within the ILC dating back to the inclusion of a broad definition of the 'injured State' by Special Rapporteur Riphagen in Article 5 part II of the 1985 draft articles (later to become Article 40 of the 1996 draft).[13] The definition was regarded as a crucial bridge between Parts I and II of the articles insofar as it provided the conceptual framework for the articulation of rights arising as a consequence of a breach of an international obligation. The definition in Article 40 endeavoured to be both broad and complete—at least in the sense that whilst the list of 'situations' enumerated in which a State may be said to be injured were not intended to be exhaustive there was no intention of leaving anything out.[14] Despite concerns of certain members of the ILC to the effect that the broad conception of injury did not discriminate effectively enough between the differing intensity of State interests as regards any particular breach, or between the consequences of the breach of different types of obligation, Article 40 provided inter alia that a State may be regarded as injured not only if the right infringed arose from a bilateral treaty or if it had been deliberately created or established in its favour, but also if:

> the right infringed ... arises from a multilateral treaty or from a rule of customary international law ... [and] if it is established that ... (iii) the right has been created or is established for the protection of human rights and fundamental freedoms (Article 40(2)(e)).

Article 40(3) provided, in addition, that in case of international crimes, 'all other States' could be regarded as 'injured' for such purposes.

A particularly curious aspect of Article 40(2)(e)—and one that was criticised by Sir Ian Sinclair at the time[15]—was the description of injury in terms of the infringement of a right. This was premised, as the commentary to Article 40 confirms, on the assumption that 'to each and every obligation corresponds *per definitionem* a right of at least one other State'. In the context of human rights, despite the fact that individuals are evidently the ultimate beneficiaries, this would either suggest that obligations incurred are matched by rights of performance on the part of each and every other State party (in the case of treaties) or every other member of the international

[13] It arguably goes back further than this. See generally, G Nolte, 'From Dionisio Anzilotti to Roberto Ago: The Classical International Law of State Responsibility and the Traditional Primacy of a Bilateral conception of Inter-State Relations', 13 *European Journal of International Law* (2002), p 1083.

[14] See eg Mr Calero Rodrigues (Chairman of the Drafting Committee), 1929th mtg, 1985 *ILC Yearbook*, Vol I, p 308.

[15] See, 1929th mtg, 1985 *ILC Yearbook,* Vol I, p 311.

community (in the case of custom), and irrespective of any link they may have with the injured party. Apart from assuming that it would do no harm to the idea of human rights to transform them into rights of States, the resulting provision gave rise to an extremely broad competence to invoke the legal consequences of a violation (irrespective of the nature or gravity of that violation[16]). The breadth of this provision was further reinforced by the decision to exclude any requirement of damage in the identification of responsibility itself—a factor which might have had the effect of narrowing the parameters of 'invocability' had it been present.

It was precisely the failure to distinguish between States which could properly be regarded as 'injured' by a wrongful act and other States possessing a mere 'legal interest' in performance of the obligation in question, that led to vociferous criticism not only of the terms of Article 40(2)(e), but also of paragraphs (2)(f) (concerning obligations under multilateral treaties for the protection of the 'collective interest') and (3) (concerning international crimes).[17] The ILC, in response, sought to reformulate the terms of Article 40[18] by seeking to differentiate, in a general manner, between injured States who are entitled to seek reparation for a wrongful act in their own right, and States possessing a mere 'legal interest in performance' who are entitled to claim the cessation of the wrongful conduct and for reparation to be made in favour of the injured party. In his Third Report, Professor Crawford emphasised, furthermore, that in the case of human rights a distinction should be drawn between 'the rights of the victims and the responses of States'. Even in case of systematic violations, where different rules on admissibility may apply, he warned that:

> [t]he States concerned may be representing the victims, but they are not to be identified with them, and they do not become the rights-holders because they are recognized as having a legal interest in the author State's compliance with its human rights obligations.[19]

[16] This despite the Commentary which urges that 'not every one of the rights enumerated in these instruments, not every single act or omission attributable to a State which could be considered as incompatible with the respect of such rights ... must necessarily be qualified as giving rise to the application of the present provision.' (Commentary to Article 40[5] in Crawford, above n 8, p 27 (para 22).)

[17] For discussion of this problem see eg, K Sachariew, 'State Responsibility for Multilateral Treaty Violations: Identifying the "Injured State" and its legal Status', 35 *Netherlands International Law Reports* (1988), p 273; D Hutchinson, 'Solidarity and Breaches of Multilateral Treaties', 59 *British Yearbook of International Law* (1988), p 273; B Simma, 'Bilateralism and Community Interest in the Law of State Responsibility', in Y Dinstein and M Tabory, (eds), *International Law at a Time of Perplexity: Essays in Honour of Shabtai Rosenne* (Bordrecht, 1989), p 821; J Frowein, 'Reactions by Not Directly Affected States to Breaches of Public International Law', 248 *Hague Recueil* (1994), p 349; and C Dominicé, 'The International Responsibility of States for Breach of Multilateral Obligations', 10 *European Journal of International Law* (1999), p 353.

[18] *ILC Rep* 1999, 45 UN GAOR, Supp No 10 (1999) p 10 (para 29).

[19] A/CN.4/507, p 39 (para 87).

'Just because' he continues,

> human rights obligations under multilateral treaties or general international law are not 'allocatable' or owed to any particular State does not make it necessary that all States concerned should be considered as obligees, and certainly not 'in the first instance'.[20]

In respect of this latter concern, the preferred approach was to regard human rights treaties as imposing obligations for the protection of 'a general common interest'[21] rather than the interest of any individual State[22] in respect of which States may have an indirect, and limited, right to invoke responsibility other than by way of claiming themselves to be 'injured' by the act in question.

In seeking to make the appropriate distinctions alluded to above, the ILC set about completely re-drawing the terms of Article 40. The way it did so is quite important. At the outset, a distinction was drawn between bilateral and multilateral obligations. In case of bilateral obligations the position was regarded as relatively simple: as a matter of definition there are only two parties, and, as a direct consequence, a breach of obligations on the part of one would give rise to responsibility in respect of the other which could, for purposes of taking action in response, regard itself as 'injured' by the act or omission concerned. In the case of multilateral obligations, several further distinctions were required. First, there are those obligations owed to the international community as a whole (hence *erga omnes* in the *Barcelona Traction* sense[23]); second there are those owed to all parties to a particular regime (*erga omnes partes*); and third, there are those owed to many States but in respect of which particular States are recognised as having a 'special interest'.[24]

The initial distinction between obligations *erga omnes* and obligations *erga omnes partes* corresponded in part to a distinction between different sources of law (between custom and treaty law; and between general and local custom), but its effect was to make clear, in any particular context, the circle of obligees to whom the obligation is owed, and to determine, therefore, who may have some justifiable interest in compliance (and whether or

[20] *Ibid*, para 88.
[21] Note the subtle shift in language that was to later occur—'common interests' were to become in the final version of Art 48 'collective interests'. One might suggest that the distinction between the two is of some importance: a common interest supposes that the interest is jointly owned by a plurality of States concerned, whilst a collective interest, by contrast, supposes that the group enjoys some degree of corporate identity. Action taken pursuant to a common interest may still remain essentially 'private' whereas that taken in the collective interest assumes a public aura.
[22] Above n 18, p 41 (para 92).
[23] *Barcelona Traction, Light and Power Co* case, *ICJ Reports*, 1970, p 3, at p 32 (para 33).
[24] Above n 18, pp 46–53 (paras 106–18).

not their rights in respect of a breach are identical). The second distinction between multilateral obligations of a common or collective nature (whether *erga omnes* or *erga omnes partes*), and multilateral obligations in which only certain States may be said to have a legal interest in default is less obvious, but essentially relates back to the initial distinction between bilateral and multilateral treaties and seeks to reflect the possibility of distinguishing between those who were injured by a breach of a multilateral obligation and those to whom an obligation was owed but who were not so injured.

In the event, such ideas were expressed in the respective language of Articles 42 and 48 which sought to differentiate between the position of injured States (Article 42) and other States possessing a legal interest in performance but which are unable to regard themselves as 'injured' (Article 48). Under the terms of Article 42 a State may regard itself as 'injured' in one of three circumstances: a) where the obligation breached is owed to that State 'individually'; b) where, in case of a multilateral obligation, the breach is such as to 'specially affect' that State; or c) where the multilateral obligation is essentially of an 'integral' nature such that breach of the obligation 'is of such a character as radically to change the position of all the other States to which the obligation is owed'. Considerable emphasis was placed, in the construction of this typology, upon the terms of Article 60 of the Vienna Convention on the Law of Treaties from which the distinctions in cases b) and c) above were directly drawn.[25] Article 48, by contrast, elucidates a more limited framework of entitlements in respect of States to which an obligation is owed in respect of a multilateral obligation established in the collective interest, but which are not in a position to regard themselves as injured by the act in question.

3. ARTICLES 42 AND 48 COMPARED

The significance of the distinction between Articles 42 and 48 is found primarily in the respective entitlements of injured States and States 'invoking' responsibility following the breach of an international obligation. States invoking responsibility under either Articles 42 or 48 may regard themselves as having a legal interest in performance simply in virtue of the fact that they are parties to the same treaty. To speak about a State having a legal interest in performance, therefore, fails to capture the distinction.[26] Similarly, in neither case are the States concerned the necessary beneficiaries of any subsequent remedy. Even in cases in which a State claims as an

[25] Commentary to Art 42 in Crawford, above n 8, paras 4–5. It was noted that although Articles 60 of the Vienna Convention is exclusively concerned with treaty obligations and is limited to 'material breaches', the parallelism was thought justified.
[26] Commentary to Art 48 in Crawford, above n 8, para 2.

injured State, as the ILC points out in its commentary to Article 33, the obligation of reparation will not necessarily accrue to that State's benefit.[27] Where the distinction has importance is in the idea that the injured State should essentially control the process by way of enjoying a right to determine the form of reparation provided (Article 43) or, in certain contexts, to waive the claim (Article 45). More importantly, injured States are entitled to take countermeasures in certain defined circumstances, whereas the right of States identified in Article 48 to take such measures is expressly reserved under the terms of Article 54.[28] The corollary to this, of course, is that other States parties' entitlements under Article 48 essentially derive either from a notion of 'solidarity', or from what might be invested in the idea of the 'collective interest'.

What is not entirely clear in this account is the relationship between the two sets of entitlements: for example, whether States may invoke responsibility under the terms of Article 48 even in absence of any claim being made on the part of the putatively injured party?[29] And whether a decision to waive a claim may affect the entitlement of other States to invoke responsibility?[30] If Article 48 were strictly conceived as giving rise to rights by way of 'solidarity' understood in a 'strict' sense as condoning action in support of the injured party, they would surely remain contingent upon the maintenance of the claim by that party. Recognition of the entitlement as being expressive of a 'collective interest' by contrast (such as the interest States may have in a particular interpretation of a treaty's provisions, or in the more general effects flowing from compliance/non-compliance[31]) may well argue in favour of the maintenance of a right to invoke responsibility even in the absence of such a claim being made by an injured party. Another way of

[27] Commentary to Art 33 in Crawford, above n 8, para 2.
[28] Art 54 provides: 'This Chapter does not prejudice the right of any State, entitled under Article 48, paragraph 1, to invoke the responsibility of another State, to take lawful measures against that State to ensure cessation of the breach and reparation in the interest of the injured State or of the beneficiaries of the obligation breached'.
[29] See proposal of UK, UN Doc A/CN.4/488, p 99. This scenario was expressly excluded by Professor Crawford in his Third Report, see, UN Doc A/CN.4/507, p 42 (para 94).
[30] The UK argued, for example, that a waiver of a claim would extinguish other States' entitlement to invoke responsibility. (State Responsibility: Comments and Observations Received from Governments, UN DocA/CN.4/515 (2001), p 72.) The Netherlands and Korea, by contrast, argued that where the obligation is owed to the international community as a whole, any waiver by the injured State extinguishes only its own claim, but leaves intact those of other interested States. (*Ibid*, pp 67–68.) See I Scobbie, 'The Invocation of Responsibility for the Breach of "Obligations under Peremptory Norms of General International Law"', 13 *European Journal of International Law* (2002), p 1201, at pp 1213–14.
[31] In the sense outlined by the ICJ in the *Diplomatic and Consular Personnel* case, *ICJ Reports*, 1980, p 3, at pp 42–43 (para 92): 'Such events cannot fail to undermine the edifice of law carefully constructed by mankind over a period of centuries, the maintenance of which is vital for the security and well-being of the complex international community of the present day, to which it is more essential than ever that the rules developed to ensure the ordered progress of relations between its members should be constantly and scrupulously respected'.

expressing this might be to say that Article 48 can be conceived as either a limited extension of the broad rights of invocation enjoyed by injured States, or as a restriction upon a more generalised entitlement to ensure compliance with multilateral obligations. Whilst the text of the draft articles does not necessarily resolve the issue one way or another, one senses that the former understanding is the operative one, not least insofar as Article 48(2)(b) speaks about interested States claiming performance of the obligation of reparation 'in the interest of the injured State or of the beneficiaries of the obligation breached'. The important feature, however, is that the entitlement is not thought to arise from any notion that the State concerned has been injured by non-compliance on the part of another State, nor simply by the fact that they are parties to the same multilateral agreement. The entitlement arises, rather, from the fact that the agreement is both multilateral and held to be constituted in the 'collective interest' or for the 'common good'.

What is meant by the 'common good', or the 'collective interest', in such a context, is not immediately clear. Almost any multilateral treaty could be regarded as being constituted in the 'collective interest' at some level, and one might argue that the very resort to 'multilateralism' itself supposes as much.[32] It is apparent, however, that the 'collective interest' was to be understood less as a positive affirmation of a sociological reality—that there is a well defined 'community' to which one may refer, or a coherent set of values adherence to which serves to describe that community—but rather as a negative counterpoint to an essentially bilateralist frame of reference. Accordingly, certain obligations (included here are substantive obligations under most human rights treaties) seem to do more than simply create a series of bilateral commitments for each State (party) in respect of each and every other State (party). They either are not, or cannot be reduced to, a series of synallagmatic relationships of rights and obligations as between States, but rather impose obligations that transcend such relationships in significant ways. This follows through into the subsequent relations of responsibility which are similarly forced to take account of the transcendent nature of obligations imposed, and allow opportunity for invocation on the part of members of the 'community' in the apparent interests of that community.

4. MODELLING THE TREATY

Whilst it is easy to begin with the proposition that reliance upon an essentially bilateral framework for the articulation of relations of responsibility

[32] Cf Allott, who defines the 'common interest' as 'society's self-interest, a self-interest which may conflict with the self-interest of society-members in their capacity as individual human beings, but which is in their interest in their capacity as society-members.' (P Allott, 'The Concept of International Law', in M Byers, (ed), *The Role of Law in International Politics* (Oxford, 2000), p 69 at p 73.

may not be particularly fruitful when one is dealing with human rights treaty obligations, it is far more difficult to elucidate an appropriate framework that does not either tend to overextend the capacity to invoke responsibility on the part of other States, or reduce it to the point of disappearance. The ILC clearly sought to adopt a posture somewhere between these two extremes, and for which it is not necessarily to be faulted. The main difficulty, however, concerns the manner in which it sought to articulate its position and the debatable assumptions made as to the innate character of different international obligations.

As a starting point, however, it would appear necessary to articulate more clearly the perceived deficiencies of bilateralism in respect of human rights treaties. Whilst there are a considerable number of ways in which the issue might be approached, two particular characterisations stand out: one focusing upon the apparent non-reciprocal nature of human rights treaties, the other upon the non-individuated nature of their obligations.

4.1. Reciprocity

The issue of non-reciprocity was not necessarily central to the ILC's approach to the problem of responsibility, but it is certainly a recurrent feature of claims concerning the peculiarities of human rights treaty obligations. As a general matter, the function of reciprocity in the construction of contractual relations may clearly be understood in various different ways—whether that is by reference to the formal element of *quid pro quo*, the substantive 'fairness' of the exchange, the conditional nature of the agreement to be bound, or the dyadic relationship between rights and obligations. Given the diversity of provisions within human rights treaties (including not merely substantive obligations, but 'procedural' commitments in relation to implementation or dispute resolution), it is extremely difficult to substantiate a claim to the effect that they are either entirely reciprocal or entirely non-reciprocal. Seeking to do so often involves shifting one's attention from one dimension of such regimes to another.[33] They are in that regard both complex, in the sense that they appear to invoke a variety of 'interests', and conceptually overdetermined, in the sense that they may respond to a number of different constructions in terms of their structure or operational theory. One could simply contrast, at this point, the description of human rights treaties advanced by the Inter-American Court of Human Rights in the *Effect of Reservations Case* in which States were regarded as having submitted themselves 'to a legal order within which they, for the

[33] See M Craven, 'Legal Differentiation and the Concept of the Human Rights Treaty in International Law', 11 *European Journal of International Law* (2000), p 489.

common good, assume various obligations, not in relation to other States, but towards all individuals within their jurisdiction',[34] with that of the European Court in *Ireland v UK* in which it was stated that the Convention created 'over and above a network of mutual bilateral undertakings, objective obligations ... which benefit from a "collective enforcement" '.[35] Alternatively, one could contrast the oft repeated assertion by the ICJ in the *Reservations Case* to the effect that 'the contracting States do not have any interests of their own ... [but only] a common interest' in the accomplishment of the objectives that form the *raison d'etre* of the Genocide Convention,[36] with its subsequent decision in relation to reservations to the effect that a State may ultimately be regarded as a State party in respect of some, but not all States parties.

If one starts from the proposition that human rights treaties, like any other treaty, are more than merely a formalised set of unilateral commitments, and therefore involve a series of legal engagements as between each and every State party (a proposition that seems to be endorsed by the ICJ's approach to the Genocide Convention) one might conclude that the notion of non-reciprocity merely adverts to the fact that the performance or non-performance of obligations on the part of one State will not necessarily benefit or disadvantage any another State party. As Simma explains, the peculiarity of human rights treaties is found in the idea that, whilst the relationship of legal rights and obligations (legal reciprocity) is properly construed as a series of bilateral engagements, it is not simultaneously supported by a corresponding sociological reciprocity. He suggests that:

> On the normative level, the treaties under consideration set forth reciprocal rights and obligations in precisely the same way as their more traditional counterparts. The difference lies in the fact that, in the case of pure social or humanitarian conventions, the mutual rights of the States parties are not accompanied by any material benefits accruing to them.[37]

This does not exclude one State from invoking responsibility in its own right as an injured State when, for example, the breach affects the rights of

[34] *The Effect of Reservations on the Entry into Force of the American Convention on Human Rights (Arts 74 and 75)*, Advisory Opinion OC–2/82 of 24 Sep 1982, *Inter-Am Ct H R (Ser A)* No 2 (1982), para 30.

[35] *Ireland v United Kingdom* ECHR, Series A, No 25, Judgment of 18th Jan 1978, 2 *EHRR*, p 25.

[36] *Reservations to the Convention on the Prevention and Punishment of the Crime of Genocide* case, *ICJ Reports*, 1951, p 23

[37] B Simma, 'From Bilateralism to Community Interest', 250 *Hague Recueil* (1994), p 401. In the same context he points out (*ibid*, p 369) that '[t]o recognize that in the case of a human rights treaty States parties do not exchange any tangible benefits is one thing. But then to assert that such absence of factual, or 'sociological' reciprocity, as it were, leads to the absence of reciprocal legal rights and duties proper is quite another matter. By no means is the second claim a necessary conclusion from the first'.

one of its nationals, but suggests that such situations are exceptional: more often than not, States will not experience disadvantage by the fact of non-compliance. This conception of non-reciprocity explains therefore both the resort to non-State centred mechanisms of implementation, and the conceptualisation of inter-State procedures as essentially concerned with performance of obligations rather than vindication of rights.[38] By the same token, speaking about a 'community' interest in such circumstances would appear to be simply shorthand for the idea that the practice of bilateralism (*qua* the vindication of subjective entitlements on the part of injured States) would be deficient as a means of securing the ends of the treaty in question. It says very little about the origin, nature or content of the community/collective interest, and in fact says a great deal more about the supposed limited nature of State 'interests' or 'motivations' as regards compliance.

4.2. Non-Individuation

Another way of approaching the same issue—and this approximates that adopted by the ILC in respect of the division between Articles 42 and 48—is to focus upon the nature of the legal obligations themselves. It appears to be argued, in that respect, that obligations in treaties such as those for the protection of human rights tend not to be 'differentiated' or 'individuated'. In other words, whilst one may admit the existence of a legal engagement between one party and each and every other party, the substance of those relationships are principally indistinguishable. Hence, in case of breach it would rarely be possible to say that one State was more or less affected than any another: they are all both equally affected, and equally unaffected, by the breach (barring, again, the possibility that the injured party may be a national of another State).

This idea of individuation clearly lies behind the ILC's sharp distinction between bilateral and multilateral treaties. It also explains its attempts to differentiate between classes of multilateral treaties—some of which apparently impose obligations of an individuated nature, others of which do not. An exception here is that the ILC recognised the possibility that even in case of non-individuated obligations, one State may still regard itself as 'injured' by way of being 'specially affected' by the breach. This admission somewhat undermines the ILC's general stance insofar as, in such a case, the fact of non-observance of the obligation is, in its own

[38] In *Ireland v United Kingdom* (above n 35), for example, the European Court noted that Art 24 'allows Contracting States to require the observance of those obligations without having to justify an interest deriving ... from the fact that a measure they complain of has prejudiced one of their nationals'.

right, not enough. In addition, the demonstration of some measure of damage will have significance—and this, despite the apparent 'revolution' associated with eliminating damage from the law of State responsibility.[39] It is also, and incidentally, difficult to square with the observation of the ICJ in the *South West Africa* case to the effect that 'a legal right or interest need not necessarily relate to anything material or tangible, and can be infringed even though no prejudice of a material kind has been suffered'.[40]

In contrast to the non-reciprocity argument, that of non-individuation generally suggests that the main location of the problem in case of human rights agreements is found in the nature of the obligations assumed by States rather than in the underlying sociology of response—the inability to distinguish between obligations owed in respect of each and every other party individually, rather than the lack of material interest in compliance. In case of non-individuation, furthermore, the notion of the collective seems to have more meaning. It is not simply shorthand for the ineffectiveness of a bilateral response system, but partly descriptive of the overlapping or common interest other States may be deemed to have in performance. The argument as to the need for collective mechanisms for enforcement (if that is how inter-State communication procedures are to be understood) derives from the common nature of the entitlement, rather than simply the inadequacies of a bilateralist response system.

5. UNDERLYING ASSUMPTIONS

Lying behind both of these accounts of the particularities of human rights agreements (or more broadly human rights obligations) are two main assumptions. The first assumption is that relations of responsibility under such agreements are essentially framed by non-legal (ethical, political, or prudential) accounts of State interests. Those interests are regarded either as insufficiently extensive (under the argument from non-reciprocity) or of a collective rather than an individual character (under the argument from non-individuation). The essential point being, in either case, that a bilateral framework of responsibility premised upon individuated interests would fall short of providing an effective system of enforcement. For one reason or another, States would have insufficient motive to respond to a breach of obligations by way of invoking responsibility. The second assumption is that the problem lies in the nature of those 'primary' obligations (as being either non-reciprocal or non-individuated) and that the difficulties

[39] Cf A Pellet, 'La codification du droit de la responsibilité', in L Boisson de Chazournes and V Gowlland-Debbas, (eds), *Liber Amicorum Georges Abi-Saab* (The Hague, 2001), p 290.
[40] *South West Africa* case, *Second Phase, ICJ Reports*, 1966, p 6.

envisaged may be overcome by dint of classification—differentiating at the outset between types of customary or conventional obligations and instituting, in relation to them, different schemes of responsibility.

Whilst both of these assumptions may be regarded as inextricably linked, in the sense that it is the motivational deficit that seems to lead one to question the salience of the bilateral-delictual relationship in case of human rights, it is important to recognise the different thrust of each of these assumptions. The first naturalises a particular international sociology and articulates the problem as one of seeking to institutionalise the move from a society based upon coexistence (premised perhaps upon a thin, 'liberal', version of the rule of law) to one based upon co-operation in which the recognition, enunciation and enforcement of common values is of critical importance.[41] The second naturalises a particular legal architecture, and understands the problem as being found in the extension of that framework to cover variegations in the legal landscape of primary obligations.

5.1. State Interests

As suggested above, both accounts rely upon particular assumptions as to the nature of State interests or motivations in respect of human rights agreements. In the argument from non-reciprocity, States are imputed with a limited field of vision—an ocular sclerosis—that effectively disables them from responding to breaches of human rights obligations except in cases where there is a pre-constituted relationship of nationality/allegiance. The argument from non-individuation, by contrast, views those interests as being either common or collective in nature with the effect that any invocation of responsibility must necessarily involve the assumption of a public, as opposed to a private, role. These two approaches are, of course, perfectly compatible on one view: the insufficiency of motive on the part of States to invoke responsibility individually may itself be related to the common/collective nature of the obligations in question. By the same token, they are not necessarily so connected—it does not follow simply because the rights of invocation are recognised as being collective in nature, that one or more States may not see it as being in their particular interests to avail themselves of those rights. Nor does it follow, merely because no individual State may be regarded as prejudiced by the wrongful act (and hence not have any motive for enforcement), that the obligations are necessarily collective in nature (and there is certainly some reason to doubt the conflation of the interests of the beneficiaries of a human rights regime with those of the international community writ large).

[41] See, Friedmann W, *The Changing Structure of International Law* (New York, 1964) pp 60–71.

The suggestion that States do not have an interest in the observance of human rights norms on the part of others may be plausibly descriptive, in the sense that one State may not obviously be materially advantaged or disadvantaged by how another State treats its own nationals (it has not, in that sense, been 'harmed' by the breach). But again it may not be. States seem to demonstrate on a daily basis their concern as to the treatment of non-nationals abroad, and seem to regard the limits on their capacity to respond as being in some respects predicated by features of the legal system itself—whether that be principles of sovereignty, non-intervention or domestic jurisdiction—rather than by reference to innate, or prudential, accounts of their presumptive interests. Witness, for example, recent debates as to the existence of a unilateral right of humanitarian intervention, which have largely turned upon the question whether those evident interests may be authorised, legitimised, or tolerated within the international system.[42] Indeed, one may say that it seems to overlook the very fact that, in standard accounts at least, the creation of human rights regimes in the aftermath of the World War II was premised upon the idea that they should operate as early warning systems—it being presumed that State interests go somewhat further than merely a concern for the treatment meted out to a local or domestic political constituency.[43]

The point would seem to be not that one account of the pathology of State behaviour is necessarily better than any other (one may recall EH Carr's warning that any description of State innate 'interests' is liable to be excessively deterministic[44]) but that to rely upon a particular account of those interests (in terms of either what States actually think, or what they should think if acting rationally) for the purpose of discriminating between legal institutions will, at best, be speculative. Where such arguments fail is in the tendency to assume that the interests in question are largely a priori, or 'given', rather than constructed in complex understandings as to the relationship between local politics and the international environment, and as to the interaction between law and power on the international plane.[45] The argument, in other words, that human rights treaties are non-reciprocal in a sociological sense works only to the extent that one has in mind the view that the constitutional relationship between State of nationality and citizen

[42] See eg, S Chesterman, *Just War or Just Peace?* (Oxford, 2001); N Wheeler, *Saving Strangers: Humanitarian Intervention in International Society* (Oxford, 2000); and T Franck, *Recourse to Force* (Cambridge, 2002), pp 135–73.
[43] This understanding is, of course, perfectly expressed in the Preamble to the UN Charter which couples an express concern to 'save succeeding generations from the scourge of war' with a commitment to 'reaffirm faith in fundamental human rights'.
[44] EH Carr, *The Twenty Years' Crisis 1919–1939*, 2nd edn (New York, 1946), pp 42–88.
[45] Allott points out that 'the human actual, including the social actual, is the product of human choice, that is to say, moral choice. To rationalize or naturalize the human actual is to empty it of its moral content, to neutralize it' (above n 32, p 87).

is fully determinative. Similarly, the argument that they represent an instantiation of a common or collective interest falls prey to the supposition that States do not 'naturally' have individual motivations that extend beyond a concern for the treatment of their own nationals (such as a concern for the treatment of particular ethnic groups in neighbouring States). Once one admits, as constructivists amongst others would certainly argue, the possibility that legal regimes may play a role in the construction of interests and identities on the part of significant actors (and whether or not in a determinative way),[46] it becomes increasingly implausible to rely upon a 'naturalised' account of those interests for purposes of delineating between types of normative regime.

Whilst there may well be difficulties associated with reliance upon such descriptive accounts of State interests, there is an underlying point here. However extensive a State may claim or perceive its interests to be in any particular context, the invocation of law supposes that there exist parameters within which it may legitimately act in pursuit of those interests. If that is the case, however, one is speaking less about whether States have sufficient motivation to pursue breaches of fundamental obligations, whether their 'interests' are sufficiently extensive, and more about the extent to which doing so may allow States rather too much, or too little, discretion by way of responding to such breaches. The argument from sociology, in other words, is difficult to separate from an essentially normative argument as to the permissible scope of State action by way of response to breaches of human rights obligations.

5.2. The Legal Architecture

As suggested above, the second main assumption underlying both theses is the idea that the issue hinges upon the perceptible variations in primary rules of behaviour, rather than in the secondary rules concerning invocability. It is clear that the importance placed upon the ideas of both individuation and reciprocity, seem to rely upon the demonstration of prejudice to personal, as opposed to general (or common), legal interests. This may suggest, as the ILC assumed, that the issue of differentiation arises primarily in case of multilateral treaties, and, furthermore, multilateral treaties of a particular kind—bilateral treaties are presumptively individuated as are certain obligations in multilateral treaties. Ultimately, this method of analysis is not entirely persuasive. To begin with, even if one might assume

[46] See eg, A Wendt and R Duvall, 'Institutions and International Order', in E-O Czempiel and J Rosenau, (eds), *Global Changes and Theoretical Challenges: Approaches to World Politics for the 1990s* (Lexington, MA, 1989), p 51; A Wendt, 'Anarchy is What States Make of it: The Social Construction of Power Politics', 46 *International Organization* (1992), p 391.

that bilateral treaties are necessarily individuated, this doesn't seem to follow from the language of obligations in question. One might, for example, consider the case of a (fictitious) bilateral human rights treaty that in phraseology is identical to its multilateral counterparts. In such a case any differentiation between the bilateral agreement and its multilateral counterparts can only be maintained by way of reading something more into the treaty than is evidently there. To the extent that bilateral agreements may confer rights on third party beneficiaries, just as much as multilateral treaties occasionally do, suggests that individuation cannot be presumed, or if it is, a distinction premised upon the number of parties to the agreement is insufficiently explanatory.

Furthermore, in case of multilateral obligations, unless one party is specifically designated as the rights holder, it seems the obligation is personalised only by a particular construction being placed upon the general rules of conduct (that the general rules are simply shorthand for a series of bilateral commitments). The example chosen by the ILC to illustrate the individuation of obligations within a multilateral setting is Article 22 of the Vienna Convention on Diplomatic Relations. That article obliges States parties 'to take all appropriate steps to protect the premises of the mission against intrusion or damage', and use of the definite article within this provision would seem to disclose the fact of individuation. Nevertheless, bearing in mind the possibility of multiple accreditation,[47] in which a breach of that obligation may result in a plurality of injured parties whose injuries may not be tangibly dissociated, the strongest argument is clearly the contextual one: breach of this or that particular obligation would undoubtedly be 'felt' more strongly by one party than another. The experience of damage following breach, however, says rather less about the nature of those obligations at the outset, and a good deal more about what may, or may not, be a legitimate basis for invoking responsibility. To work Simma's distinction (between legal and sociological reciprocity) round the other way, it could thereby be argued that the fact that harm or disadvantage might be experienced on an individual basis is not such as to render the legal obligations similarly individual.

Similar arguments operate in respect of other categories of treaty obligations to which the ILC refers. In case of treaties imposing 'integral' obligations in the sense of Article 42(b)(ii) (the examples provided being a disarmament treaty or a treaty establishing a nuclear free zone treaty) the assumption is that any breach 'must be considered as affecting per se every other State to which the obligation is owed'. It is palpably evident that such classification relies not upon any formal recognition of such an idea in the terms of the agreement, nor would the teleology of the

[47] Cf Art 6 Vienna Convention on Diplomatic Relations.

agreement necessarily point in that direction—it should not immediately be supposed, for example, that the objective of disarmament is an 'all or nothing' affair. The rationale, it would seem, lies primarily in a motivational analysis, to the effect that States would not willingly consider themselves bound by such an agreement in absence of similar steps being taken by other significant parties. Two considerations may seem to undermine the security of this assumption. First of all, whether or not such a motivational analysis is a valid basis for instituting different regimes of responsibility in light of the observations above, categorisation of such obligations clearly does not work purely by reference to the structure of obligations themselves. Rather it is a question of placing some conceptual framework over those obligations, or of construing them in a particular way. Secondly, it is no more evident that a disarmament treaty should be regarded in an 'all or nothing' manner than it is of a human rights treaty or a treaty protecting the environment. Seen from the perspective of each State entering the regime, it might plausibly be maintained that such limitations upon their freedom of action as are required by the terms of the agreement, may only be acceptable so long as a certain number of other States are equally so bound.[48]

6. THE RETURN OF DAMAGE

To the extent that the projected classification of obligations adopted by the ILC may be thought somewhat tenuous, or perhaps overly deterministic, it is worth returning to the basis upon which that particular approach to the question of responsibility was adopted. Ultimately it appears to have been the immediate result of an apparently neutral decision to exclude any requirement of damage or harm from the definition of responsibility. As explained in the ILC's commentary to the articles, the decision was taken on the basis that since the matter was one falling within the scope of primary obligations, and since primary obligations themselves were divergent on the point, 'no general rule in this respect' could be discerned.[49] The ILC continues by explaining that, for example,

> the obligation under a treaty to enact a uniform law is breached by the failure to enact the law, and it is not necessary for another State party to point to any specific damage it has suffered by reason of that failure.[50]

[48] Simma suggests, for example, that the explanation as to why States assume humanitarian obligations in treaty form despite the absence of any tangible advantages that might accrue to them, may be found in the 'interest each contracting party has in every other party keeping step by accepting identical obligations'. (Above n 37, p 401.)
[49] Commentary to Art 2 in Crawford, above n 8, para 9.
[50] *Ibid.*

Whilst this example might be perfectly appropriate by way of demonstrating the necessity of separating the issue of harm from that of 'objective' responsibility, it does nevertheless pose the question as to the circumstances (if any) in which any other State might justify a claim that it was 'injured' by the breach. It is, after all, by no means obvious that the elimination of the requirement of damage from Part I of the articles, would simultaneously necessitate its irrelevance to the principles elaborated in Part II concerning the consequences of responsibility for other parties.

In the event, it appears that the element of damage has reappeared interstitially in the terms of Part II of the ILC Articles as the basis for distinguishing between the respective capacities of other States to respond to a breach. Although, as has been pointed out, this distinction is articulated in terms of the differing characteristics of international obligations (the extent of individuation), behind the differentiation lies the clear belief that, in case of multilateral obligations at least, a State would have to demonstrate some prejudice to its interests resulting from the breach in order for it to maintain that it has been injured. What is key, here, however, is not simply the requirement that the harm be something more than the general collateral effect of non-compliance on the interests of other State parties, but that there is a demonstrable link between the harm caused and the State claiming to be injured. In that context, the terms of Article 44 which stipulate that responsibility may not be invoked if the claim is 'not bought in accordance with any applicable rule relating to the nationality of claims' is of considerable significance. Far from merely being an affirmation of the existence of the rule as regards the jurisdiction or admissibility of claims before judicial bodies, it is articulated as a principle that is generally applicable and which defines the conditions for invocation of responsibility in any circumstance.[51] If this is so, however, one may suspect that the concept of individuated obligations is largely illusory: even if a State may be able to claim that an obligation was owed to it personally, it would be precluded from pursuing that claim absent any demonstrable 'bond' of nationality on the part of the injured party.[52] Far from being a matter determined by the nature or content of primary obligations, in other words, the concept of the 'injured State' is determined at the very outset by generalised rules which circumscribe the

[51] Reference is made, in that respect, to the Permanent Court's decision in the *Mavrommatis Palestine Concessions* case, (1924, PCIJ, *Series A*, No 2, p 12) in which it stated that: 'It is an elementary principle of international law that a State is entitled to protect its subjects, when injured by acts contrary to international law committed by another State, from whom they have been unable to obtain satisfaction through the ordinary channels.'

[52] On the relationship between Art 48 and the ILC's work on Diplomatic Protection see generally, I Scobbie, 'The Invocation of Responsibility for the Breach of "Obligations Under Peremptory Norms of General International Law"', 13 *European Journal of International Law* (2002), p 1201, at pp 1215–18.

capacity to act by way of drawing presumptive lines around each States' natural patrimony.

An interesting facet of this shift in emphasis is the move from an essentially inductive approach—one drawing upon demonstrable consistencies in the various regimes of primary obligations—to one that is essentially deductive, in which those regimes are conceptualised and ordered by reference to pre-existent secondary principles, albeit principles supposedly awaiting articulation. It privileges, thereby, certain structures and processes and wraps all else around them. It also, and importantly, creates obvious difficulties as regards the management of legal obligations the breach of which would not give rise to any tangible injury to other States or their nationals. This, of course, extends not merely to obligations under human rights agreements, but also to other types of agreement such as those protecting the environment or promoting disarmament.

A general question here is whether human rights agreements might be regarded as something of a special case insofar as they deliberately attempt to sever the connection between entitlements on the one hand and nationality on the other. Taken to a logical conclusion this would suppose either that all States parties to the regime may regard themselves as 'injured' by non-compliance (on the basis that the notion of nationality is either generalised under the regime or deemed inapplicable) or that none may do so. The latter possibility clearly involves a limitation of the scope for response far beyond that currently recognised either in the terms of general international law or under specific treaty regimes, and clearly falls short of what many might regard as desirable by way of enforcement. The former, by contrast, is generous to the opposite extreme. Two considerations, however, underpin the evident unwillingness of the ILC to develop this idea (that is if, one supposes, they actually gave it much thought). The first is that, as the ILC took great pains to point out, the primary beneficiaries, and perhaps even 'rights holders', under such regimes are always the individual subjects. It may seem somewhat strained, in those circumstances, to speak about other States parties being 'injured' by any breach of obligations, and certainly where they have little or no connection with the injured individual. More significantly, however, is the fact that the rights enjoyed by injured States under the regime of Part II are extensive—to the point at which they enjoy a right to take counter-measures in case of injury. This clearly opens up the possibility for abuse by dominant powers in a way that may undermine the integrity of the obligations sought to be protected.[53] The evident choice underlying such capacity could well result in the development of a highly selective policy not only as regards the rights sought to be protected, but also in respect of the regimes that become the targets of such action.

[53] See eg M Koskenniemi, 'Solidarity Measures: State Responsibility as a New International Order?', 72 *British Yearbook of International Law* (2001), p 337.

7. BY WAY OF CONCLUSION: COSMOPOLITANISM AND THE REALITIES OF POWER

Lying behind the apparent policy choices made in the articles on State Responsibility, one senses the presence of (at least) two conflicting narratives as to the significance of human rights within the realm of State responsibility. One narrative is that of enlightened cosmopolitanism, that regards the instantiation of human rights within the international legal order as a thoroughly revolutionary initiative designed to foster a reconfiguration of traditional principles of sovereignty and domestic jurisdiction and to provide the basis for the development of an international 'community' (and not simply a 'community of States') under a new regime of collaboration and co-existence. Reliance upon the practice of human rights institutions throughout the articles on State responsibility (despite the obvious objection that they could be regarded as purely epiphenomenal in the articulation of secondary rules), and the attempts to elucidate the consequences of the idea of *erga omnes* obligations, is illustrative of the extent to which they are thought to have become (or at least should be) ingrained more deeply in the structures of international law. From this vantage point, the initiative is one concerned with casting off the shackles of a bilateral, delictual, framework of responsibility that assumes that every breach of an obligation must be articulated in terms of the violation of some subjective right on the part of another State, and of providing, by contrast, for a regime which allows for a generalised right of response on the part of the international community or members thereof, albeit in attenuated form.

Another narrative, of course, is the traditional narrative of power grounded in the 'realities' of a world comprised of governments possessing highly differentiated capacities that are only barely obscured by the formalities of sovereign equality. Even if the instantiation of human rights might be regarded as responsive to a cosmopolitan agenda concerned with re-articulating the boundaries of power and control between and within States in the international community (it clearly doesn't have to be seen in this light, however[54]), such initiatives necessarily take place within the framework of the *ancien régime*. As such, developing the capacity of States to assume a public function by way of responding to breaches of human rights obligations on the part of other States might be thought to be constrained by the palpable dangers of providing greater access or opportunity for the exercise of that power internationally, especially in the absence of sufficient procedural or substantive constraints. The building of the new order, in such circumstances, would seem to be contingent upon the complete

[54] Cf M Wa Mutua, 'Politics and Human Rights: An Essential Symbiosis', in Byers, above n 32, p 149.

dismantling of the old. Such an understanding, no doubt, informed not only the determination to distinguish between the respective capacities of States under Articles 42 and 48, but also the implicit unwillingness to extend the right to adopt counter-measures to States possessing a mere legal interest (as opposed to those demonstrably injured).

To the extent that both such narratives are woven into the same regime with contrasting effect, the articles of State responsibility might be considered to reflect the transitional State of international law in general. They might, in that regard, be thought reflective of the manner in which common utopian ambitions associated with the development of an international community (of ideas, institutions and expectations) outstrip the concrete possibilities inherent within current realist understanding of international relations. There is, however, a certain ambivalence underlying such an approach to the issue, which stems from the 'thinness' of the sociology that underpins it. Can one be sure, for example, that the cosmopolitan initiative is not merely a function of a Foucauldian shift in the technology of power? To what extent, in other words, may it be thought simply reflective of a subtle shift in the way power is exercised, rather than a change in the fundamental order of power (ie as an extension of realism, rather than its antithesis)? Perhaps, by contrast, what is understood by realism in this context is less as a State-centric hangover from an outdated epoch, and more as a persistent claim in defence of the integrity of local politics as against the supercession of the global? In any case it is apparent that evaluation of the initiative, whether as an achievement or as a loss, as a necessary expedient or a transitional step, will be hampered by the absence of a clear, or univocal, understanding of the society (of its nature or needs) in which it is deemed to operate, or of the interplay of relations of power in which it is implicated. To the extent, however, that international society will always be capable of being described alternatively as a domain for antagonistic power-play or as a locale for the development of co-operative endeavours, means that any project concerned with the articulation of systemic rules such as those on State responsibility, will assume a highly ambivalent nature. The point to be made, nevertheless, is surely not that one should seek to obscure that ambivalence, or suppress it, or indeed seek an alternative 'totalising' account of international society in which it is dissipated, but rather to place it centre stage, and make clear from the outset the contingent and hesitant nature of the legislative endeavour.

8

Exploring the Strasbourg Case-Law: Reflections on State Responsibility for the Breach of Positive Obligations

BENEDETTO CONFORTI*

THE EUROPEAN COURT of Human Rights (the 'Court') has very often used the notion of positive obligation, ie the obligation of the State to protect a person against violations of human rights committed by individuals or other entities. Positive obligations may also be called obligations of prevention, if the terminology of the International Law Commission is adopted. In the words of the Commission, obligations of prevention '... require States to take all reasonable or necessary measures to prevent a given event ... .'[1]

In some cases the Court has inferred a positive obligation from articles of the European Convention on Human Rights (the 'Convention') that were exclusively couched in terms of a negative duty. This is the case, for instance, in relation to Article 3, the prohibition of torture and inhuman or degrading treatment, or Article 8—non-interference with private and family life. In some other cases, the State is expressly bound by the Convention either to abstain from itself infringing directly the human right or to prevent someone else's infringement of the right. The best example of an

* Professor of International Law, University of Napoli; and Former Judge, European Court of Human Rights.

[1] International Law Commission (the 'ILC'), 53rd session, 2001, Doc A/56/10, Draft Articles on State Responsibility, Commentary to Art 14, para 3. See also The Report of the International Law Commission on the work of its fifty-third session which contains draft articles on responsibility of States for internationally wrongful act, Official Records of the General Assembly, Fifty-sixth Session, Supplement No10 and corrigendum (A/56/10 and Corr 1) and the Resolution adopted by the General Assembly, A/RES/56/83 taking note of the articles.

express obligation of prevention is offered by Article 2, first sentence of § 1, according to which 'everyone's right to life shall be protected by law. . . .'

This essay is focused specifically on the case-law of the Court regarding Article 2, since it offers the most interesting examples of decisions in the matter of positive obligations.[2] There is reference made to other articles of the Convention where relevant. Moreover, the conclusions reached in relation to Article 2 could be applied, *mutatis mutandis,* to positive obligations pertaining to other parts of the 'Convention'. The case-law of the previously existing European Commission of Human Rights (the 'Commission') will also be taken into account.

The ultimate goal of this paper is to contribute to the theory of State responsibility for internationally wrongful acts, in particular as far as the role of the principle of causation is concerned.

1. THE CASE-LAW OF THE COURT

The Court has defined the positive obligation under Article 2 in the following terms:

- The first sentence of Article 2 § 1 enjoins the State not only to refrain from the intentional and unlawful taking of life, but also to take appropriate steps to safeguard the lives of those within its jurisdiction.[3]
- This involves a primary duty on the State to secure the right to life by putting in place effective criminal-law provisions to deter the commission of offences against the person backed up by law enforcement machinery for the prevention, suppression and punishment of breaches of such provisions.[4]
- For a positive obligation to arise, it must be established . . . that the authorities knew or ought to have known at the time of the existence of a real and immediate risk to the life of an identified individual from the criminal acts of a third party and that they failed to take measures within the scope of their powers which, judged reasonably, might been expected to avoid that risk.[5]

[2] Judgments and decisions on admissibility of the Court will be quoted by mentioning the date and the name of the parties only, since they can easily be found on the web-site of the Court at: www.echr.coe.int/Eng/Judgments.htm.
[3] See, among others, the following judgments: *LCB v UK*, 9 June 1998, para 36; *Osman v UK*, 26 Oct 1998, para 115; *Kiliç v Turkey*, 28 March 2000, para 62; *Keenan v UK*, 3 April 2001, para 88; *Mastromatteo v Italy*, 24 Oct 2002, para 67. See also the decision as to the admissibility n° 33747/96 of *Bromiley v* UK, 23 Nov 1999.
[4] *Keenan* case, *ibid.*
[5] *Ibid*, para 89, quoting *Osman v UK*, above n 3, para 116.

The second among the above cited dicta is self-evident. If relevant criminal legislation does not exist or is even inadequate, an individual cannot be deterred from committing an act which amounts to a violation of Article 2. The same can be said of Article 3 and, as far as the protection of private and family life so requires, Article 8.

As far as Article 2 is concerned, no evident cases exist wherein the lack or the inadequacy of the legislation has been taken into account. Perhaps the only case which can be quoted is *Kiliç v Turkey*.[6] Here the Court decided that the life of the applicant's brother—a journalist working in the South-Eastern part of Turkey for a newspaper voicing Kurdish opinions and who was found shot dead on his way home from work—had not been properly protected. The Court observed in its decision that many defects, and in particular the lack of serious investigations when murders of alleged supporters of the PKK occurred in the South-Eastern part of Turkey (and they occurred very often), undermined the effectiveness of criminal law protection in this region.[7] This part of the decision can, it is argued, be interpreted in the sense that the provisions of Turkish criminal law were unable *to deter* people from committing these kinds of murders in the South-Eastern region of the country.[8]

By contrast, a clear case of inadequacy of criminal legislation, leading to a finding of violation of Article 3, is *A v UK*.[9] Here the Court was asked to find a violation of Article 3 because of the failure on the part of the State to protect a child from ill-treatment by his step-father. After having decided that the ill-treatment reached the level prohibited by Article 3 (the child had been severely beaten), the Court noted that under English law it is a defence to a charge of assault on a child on the part of his parents if the treatment in question amounted to 'reasonable chastisement'. It also noted that, in the trial before the national court, the jury had acquitted the step-father and that even the Government 'accepted that the English law currently fails to provide adequate protection to children and should be amended.' In conclusion, the Court decided that the positive obligation under Article 3 had been breached.[10]

Similarly, *X and Y v The Netherlands*[11] is a case involving breach of a positive obligation owed by the State, pursuant to Article 8, due to the lack of relevant criminal legislation. Miss Y, a handicapped 16 year old girl, had

[6] See above n 3.
[7] *Ibid*, paras 71–75.
[8] As a second argument, the Court held that Turkey had failed to provide for individual and preventive measures of protection, notwithstanding the frequent request of protection by the victim. (*Ibid*, §§ 65–68). This part of the decision fits rather in the third dicta of the Court quoted in the text.
[9] *A v UK*, Judgment of 23 Sep 1998.
[10] *Ibid*, paras 9–24.
[11] *X and Y v The Netherlands*, Judgment of 26 March 1965.

been allegedly raped, but was unable, due to her mental condition, to bring the complaint herself. Acting on her behalf, her father had filed a complaint with the local police station in order to institute criminal proceedings. However, the proceedings had been discontinued since according to the Netherlands Criminal Code in force at the time of the incident, the legal representative of the victim was not allowed to lodge a complaint if the victim was over the age of sixteen or placed under a guardianship. The Court held that respect for private life, in a case like the one above, can only be assured by criminal-law provisions, since it is only these kind of provisions that provide the 'effective deterrence [which] is indispensable in this area'. As such, the Court concluded that the positive obligation of the State to protect the private life of the second applicant had been violated.[12]

According to the third of the above quoted dicta, a test of 'foreseeability of the event' and a test of 'reasonableness' of preventive measures are applied by the Court in order to find a breach of Article 2. The State is responsible if the authorities 'knew or ought to have known' the risk to the life of a person and they failed to take measures which, 'judged reasonably', might have prevented the occurrence of the lethal event.

The Court has applied these two tests on a number of occasions. However, to the knowledge of the present author, only once has it reached the conclusion that Article 2 was violated because of the lack of measures necessary to avoid a foreseeable risk. This was already exemplified by the above-mentioned judgment in *Kiliç v Turkey*, concerning the murder of a journalist in the South-Eastern part of Turkey. Additionally, the Court held that Turkey had not taken preventive and appropriate measures of protection, notwithstanding the frequent requests for protection by the victim. In the opinion of the Court, the event was predictable due to the situation in the South-Eastern region where security forces were accused of committing all kinds of illegal activities, including the elimination of alleged supporters of the PKK.[13]

No cases concerning other obligations of prevention, in particular obligations to prevent torture or inhuman or degrading treatment (Article 3) or interference in private or family life (Article 8) can be mentioned.

Sometimes the Court—in addition to or—as a specification of the test of 'foreseeability' has used the test of causality. By applying Article 2, it has tried to ascertain whether a causal link between the event and the

[12] *Ibid*, paras 23–30. The Court was also asked to find a violation of Art 3. In the opinion of the present author it was exactly a case of breach of the obligation to protect a person against inhuman or degrading treatment inflicted by another person. On the contrary, the Court examined the case under Art 8, and consequently held that it had not to examine the application under Art 3 (*Ibid*, para 34).
[13] *Kiliç v Turkey*, above n 3, paras 65–68.

omission—ie, between the death of a person or a severe life-threatening injury, and the omission of preventive measures on the part of the State—could be established. The case of *LCB v UK*[14] is an example of this approach.

In *LCB v UK* the applicant claimed that she had developed leukaemia, during her childhood, due both to her father's exposure to radiation (he was a serviceman stationed on Christmas Islands at the time of nuclear testing) and the failure of authorities in the UK to warn her parents of the possible risks for the health of their subsequently conceived children. The Court stated that:

> having examined the expert evidence submitted to it, the Court is not satisfied that it has been established that there is a causal link between the exposure of a father to radiation and leukaemia in a child subsequently conceived .... The Court could not reasonably hold, therefore, that ... the UK authorities could or should, on the basis of this unsubstantiated link, have taken action in respect of the applicant.[15]

Another clear reference to causality appears in the case-law of the abolished Commission. In the case of *Tugar v Italy*, the Commission declared inadmissible the application of an Iraqi national who stepped on a mine while clearing a minefield in the Chowman Valley in Iraq after the first Gulf war. The applicant—having suffered severe injuries and the amputation of a leg—contended that since Italy was the State that had permitted the sale of mines to Iraq without adopting any controls or effective arms transfer licensing system (the seller had also been found guilty of illegal arms trafficking to Iraq), that it had failed to take preventive measures against the risk of an 'indiscriminate' use of such arms. The Commission held:

> In the present case ... the applicant's injury can not be seen as a direct consequence of the failure of the Italian authorities to legislate on arms transfers. There is no immediate relationship between the mere supply, even if not properly regulated, of weapons and the possible 'indiscriminate' use thereof in a third country, the latter's action constituting the direct and decisive cause of the accident which the applicant suffered.[16]

With some hesitation the case of *Mastromatteo v Italy*[17] can also be cited for present purposes. In this case the Italian authorities were accused by a father of having violated Article 2 in relation to the murder of his son by

[14] See above n 3.
[15] *Ibid*, para 39.
[16] Decision N° 22869 of 18 Oct 1995, DR, vol 83A, p 29.
[17] See above n 3.

three criminals during a bank robbery. The criminals, when leaving the bank, encountered a car driven by the applicant's son. They attempted to take control of the car, but it appeared that the applicant's son tried to escape whereupon he was shot dead. At the time of these offences, two of the three criminals had been granted prison leave—as part of a 'semi-custodial' regime—when serving sentences for armed robbery and other offences; and the third was not in prison at the material time although he had a number of convictions for armed robbery. According to the applicant, the authorities (ie the judge granting the prison leave and the semi-custodial regime) should have foreseen that the lethal event would happen and that they had failed to take reasonably available measures to prevent it from occurring. The Court expressly applied the test of 'foreseeability' and did not find a violation in the case.[18] Incidentally, however, it also pointed out that the tragic death of the applicant's son had been 'a result of the chance sequence of events which occurred in the present case', a sequence which the authorities were unable to predict.[19]

In conclusion, it may be said that in their case-law the Court and the previously existing Commission have set out the elements of the concept of a positive obligation, or what can alternatively be called the obligation of prevention. However this elaboration has not been of much importance in practice, since a violation of the Convention has been declared in very few cases. The breach of an obligation of prevention is easy to ascertain if it is the result of the lack or inadequacy of legislation - that is, of legislative provisions deterring individuals from behaving in a way that is condemned by the Convention. By contrast, a finding of violation is difficult to reach when the breach is, or should be, solely the result of the negligence of the authorities in protecting a person against the wrongful action of other persons. In such cases the Court is satisfied only if the 'foreseeability' of the wrongful event and the 'reasonableness' of the preventive measures can be proved. Moreover, it is necessary for a link of causality to exist between the behaviour of the authorities and the event.

The role of causality has to be stressed in ascertaining the breach of a positive obligation, since, in the view of the present author, it is the most problematic element under consideration in this essay. A conclusion that can be drawn from the Strasbourg case-law is that no violation is found in cases where there is lack of a casual link between the behaviour of the State and the event. The same reasoning applies to cases where the event is not 'the immediate consequence' of State behaviour, ie where the State omission is too remote in the chain of the various circumstances which led to the final wrongful event. Of course, the remoteness (understood in this essay in

[18] *Ibid*, paras 74–79.
[19] *Ibid*, para 76.

the literal sense as something referring to what is far in time or space) can be ascertained only empirically, taking into account the concrete circumstances of each and every case. It is quite impossible, and even unnecessary in a review of the case-law of the Court, to enter into all the theoretical and philosophical discussions and the technicalities of the doctrine of causation in criminal and civil law, including the numerous views that have been expounded on the question whether an omission can be a cause.[20] Couched in simple terms, in the opinion of the present author, the causation, as it appears in the case-law of the Court concerning the obligations of prevention, is strictly linked to the 'foreseeability' of the wrongful event. It is an *ex post* test of 'foreseeability' of the event: even if the event was predictable, there is still room, even after the wrongful event occurred, for verifying its place in the chain of events. It seems that, in these three cases reported in the preceding paragraphs, the event was per se predictable and the reason why the Court reached a finding of no violation was exactly the absolute lack of a causal link between the omission and the event.

2. THE CASE-LAW OF THE COURT AND THE THEORY OF STATE RESPONSIBILITY

In this Section some conclusions will be drawn regarding the theory of State responsibility for internationally wrongful acts from the above review of the case-law of the Court.

Looking at the work of the International Law Commission on the subject, it is worth noting that a reference, although very loose, to the causal link between the omission and the internationally wrongful event was contained in the commentary to Article 23 of the previous Draft Articles on State Responsibility, the Draft inspired by the late Italian scholar Roberto Ago.[21] The entire Article 23 was expressly devoted to the breach of an obligation to prevent a given event and perhaps one of the reasons why it was there was exactly the necessity to stress that 'a certain causal link—indirect, of course, not direct—must exist between the occurrence of the event and the conduct adopted in the matter by the organs of the State'.[22] The rule of Article 23 has disappeared in Articles that were inspired by the Special Rapporteur James Crawford,[23] and with it vanished as well the reference to the causal link. A reference to causation can now be found in Article 31 and its Commentary concerning the reparation, wherein the obligation is

[20] On the subject, see A Honoré, 'Causation and Remoteness of Damage', in A Tunc (ed), *International Encyclopedia of Comparative Law*, XI, 1, Ch VII (Tübingen, 1971), paras 13, 44.
[21] *Yearbook of the ILC*, 1978, II, 2, p 81.
[22] *Ibid*, p 83.
[23] See above n 1.

laid down to repair the damage 'caused' by a wrongful act of the State. Clearly this is a different aspect of causation from the one being considered at present. The former aspect—an aspect which has been treated by international tribunals, including the Court,[24] and deeply explored in legal doctrine[25]—corresponds to the parallel aspect in the law of tort in national legal orders. On the contrary, the aspect dealt with in this essay pertains to the structure of the internationally wrongful act itself, like the parallel aspect in national criminal law.

In the view of this author the reason for the disappearance of the old Article 23 and of any reference to the causal link, as well as the disappearance of many rules already contained in the previous Draft, is that the present members of the Commission are of the opinion that such rules do not pertain to State responsibility (they were not secondary rules) but rather belong to the realm of primary rules.[26] The present author confesses many difficulties in accepting the distinction between primary and secondary rules. Unfortunately, the elaboration of such a large subject exceeds the scope of this study.[27] It is enough to stress that what has been said thus far in this essay, shows that the problem of the causal link—like the parallel problem in criminal law—is an element of the internationally wrongful act. In this regard it seems appropriate to quote another Italian scholar, the late professor Rolando Quadri, who opposed consistently the so-called (by Ago) 'subjective element of the internationally wrongful act', ie the attribution of the wrongful conduct to the State under international law.[28] His contrasting view was that only the element of causation was pertinent to establish State responsibility for actions or omissions contrary to international law.[29] No doubt, this is an extreme and exaggerated opinion. Perhaps the best conclusion is one in the middle, ie that the causal link can

[24] For a review of the case law of the Court on the subject, see P Kempees, *A Systematic Guide to the Case-Law of the ECHR (4 vols),* (The Hague, 1996-2000), *sub* Art 50: Of course, the decisions relevant to causation are those allowing, or refusing to allow, pecuniary damages for material loss suffered as a consequence of a violation of the Convention. Normally the Court awards also a sum as compensation for damage of a non pecuniary nature, wherein a problem of causal link does not arise.

[25] Especially in the slightly outdated, but still very stimulating, book by B Bollecker-Stern, *Le préjudice dans la théorie de la responsabilité internationale*, (Paris, 1973), p 179. As far as the reparation for violations of the Convention is concerned, see M Enrich Mas, 'Right to compensation under Article 50', in R St J MacDonald, F Matscher and H Petzold, (eds) *The European System for the Protection of Human Rights*, (Dordrecht, 1993), p 784.

[26] Cf J Crawford, 'Revising the Draft Articles on State responsibility', 10 *Journal of European Law* (1999), p 441.

[27] Reference is made to observations submitted by the present author in the book on *International Law and the Role of Domestic legal Systems* (English version of the General Course on public international law delivered at the Hague Academy in 1988) (Dordrecht, 1993), p 171.

[28] This subjective element is maintained *tel quel* in the new Draft of the ILC (cf Art 2 (a)).

[29] R Quadri, *Cours général de droit international public*, in *Recueil des Cours*, vol 111 (The Hague, 1964), p 457.

be taken into consideration as one of the conditions of the subjective element, the other one being, according to Ago, the fact that the action or the omission is committed by an organ of the State. In other words, it is not sufficient—as it is said in the general remarks to Chapter II, Article 4, of the Articles on State Responsibility—that the act shall be considered an act of that State under international law when:

> the organ exercises legislative, executive, judicial or any other functions, whatever position it holds in the organisation of that State, and whatever its character as an organ of the central government or a territorial unit of that State.[30]

It is also necessary that a certain link exists, as it was explained, between the conduct and the wrongful event.

[30] Articles on State Responsibility: see above n 1.

9

State Responsibility and the European Convention on Human Rights: Role and Realm

MALCOLM D EVANS*

THERE IS SOMETHING decidedly peculiar about the manner in which State responsibility edges its way into the operation of treaty systems of human rights protection. The entire enterprise of protecting human rights through international treaty regimes is a recognition of 'State responsibility', understood in the layman's sense of reflecting the belief that States are to be held accountable for the manner in which they treat those over whom they exercise power.[1] This, however, has little—if anything—to do with State responsibility as an aspect of international law and as now reflected in the ILC's Articles on State Responsibility.

And why should it? The concepts which are bundled up into the rubric of State responsibility in international law are said to be a means to an end, that end being the establishment of responsibility at the international level for international wrongs. State responsibility is not concerned with defining what comprise international wrongs that are capable of being addressed on the international level. This is now[2] the orthodoxy, ILC style, and Crawford has written that 'the law of State responsibility, as articulated in the Draft Articles provides the framework—those rules,

* Professor of Public International Law, University of Bristol.

[1] The word 'power' is used here in order to avoid the use of the words 'jurisdiction' or 'control' (effective or otherwise) and the reasons for avoiding these terms in this context are considered below.

[2] It was not always the case. As is well known, the Reports produced by Garcia Amador, the ILC's first Rapporteur on State Responsibility (1955–61), addressed a considerable range of substantive issues. Indeed, his final Report was entitled 'Responsibility of States for Injuries caused in its Territory to the Person or Properties of Aliens'. (See *ILC Yearbook* 1961, Vol II, p 46.)

denominated 'secondary', which indicate the consequences of a breach of a primary obligation'.[3] As far as the Articles themselves are concerned, doubtless this is the case. From a human rights perspective, however, the claim seems unconvincing since in the human rights arena in general—including the jurisprudence of the European Court of Human Rights—the language of State responsibility has been used in a quite different fashion: it has been employed quite deliberately to broaden the scope of substantive legal obligations.[4] This is not orthodox at all, unless one is a human rights lawyer, when it is your principal occupation. Yet this discrepancy should neither disturb nor surprise.

It should not disturb because if the consequences of international law generating secondary principles concerning the responsibility of States were limited to those achieved by the application of the Articles, then it is to be doubted whether the more egregious violators of primary human rights obligations would have reason for concern. Indeed, it is surely to be hoped that the effect of more clearly articulating the circumstances that engage responsibility under international law would indeed have an unsettling effect on those who are responsible for violations of primary obligations, be they human rights obligations or otherwise. Whether the bright line between primary and secondary rules that is reflected in the Articles is the product of principle, pragmatism or practicality is largely irrelevant: what matters is whether the Articles facilitate the holding to account of those who are responsible for breaching international obligations.

It should not surprise because human rights have had a thoroughly unsettling effect on almost all aspects of international law. This in itself is hardly a surprise since the classic Westphalian model of international society was constructed precisely in order to minimise the opportunities for States to be legitimately interested in questions concerning the treatment by a State of its own nationals. Though rarely remarked on, this is quite obvious from the conceptualisation of an entire body of 'substantive' law concerning the treatment of aliens abroad. International law has traditionally been all about boundaries—territorial and otherwise—which are not to be crossed, or crossed only on terms. The very idea of human rights being a matter of 'international concern' is an anomaly from the perspective of an international system built upon the foundations of the sovereign equality of States, the obligations and interactions of which are regulated by the rules generated by those States themselves.[5] The challenge of human rights—as

[3] J Crawford, *The International Law Commission's Articles on State Responsibility* (Cambridge, 2002), p 16.
[4] This will be considered further in section 3 of this chapter.
[5] Hence the endless fascination with the interplay between the role of the United Nations ('UN') in the protection of human rights and the preservation of the realm of the domestic jurisdiction of State under Art 2(7) of the UN Charter. See AWB Simpson, *Human Rights and*

with other fundamental assaults upon the systems and structures of the international legal system—are addressed at those boundaries themselves.[6] Thus the entire experience of international human rights protection has been one of taking hold of concepts well understood by international lawyers and, by deploying them in a context unknown to the traditional *locus* of international law, generating unforeseen outcomes and controversies that have then been carried back into the mainstream of international law itself.[7]

Of course, our understanding of the nature and function of the international system has moved a long way from the rather caricature-like portrayal given above, and other variously configured alternatives are now widely canvassed.[8] However, the dogmas and doctrines of the contemporary approach to State responsibility appear to remain something of a bastion of the more traditional underlying assumptions: nicely encapsulated in the title of Brownlie's work on the subject on State Responsibility, *System of the Law of States*.[9] Equally, it is perfectly true that the content of the

the End of Empire (Oxford, 2001), ch 5 for the reflection of this in the drafting process. Of course, this is not the only area in which the 'internationalising' of concerns traditionally within the exclusive purview of States has generated tensions with Art 2(7), the most obvious and well documented being the interplay with the outlawry of the unilateral use of force in accordance with Art 2(4). For an excellent analysis of those tensions in early UN practice see G Jones, *The United Nations and the Domestic Jurisdiction of States* (Cardiff, 1979). For a recent exploration of the issue in relation to the use of force see *eg* T Franck, *Recourse to Force* (Cambridge, 2002), pp 11–14. All three of these concerns—human rights, the use of force and domestic jurisdiction—combine to ensure that the issue of humanitarian intervention remains an irresolvable legal (though not necessarily moral) conundrum, the literature on which is now too voluminous to cite purposively.

[6] Cf the pertinently entitled feminist critique by H Charlesworth and C Chinkin, *The Boundaries of International Law* (Manchester, 2000).

[7] In addition to the matters mentioned in n 5 above, other high profile examples would include the debate over the approach to be taken to reservations made to human rights treaties, prompted in part by General Comment ('GC') No 24 adopted in 1994 by the UN Human Rights Committee ('HRC'). On this Comment, and the ensuing debate, see generally C Chinkin and others in P Gardner, (ed), *Human Rights as General Norms and a State's Right to Opt Out* (London, 1997). For practical application see the views of the HRC in *Rawle Kennedy v Trinidad and Tobago*, Case No 845/1999, Decision of 2 Nov 1999. See Report of the Human Rights Committee, 55th Session (A/55/40), Vol II, Annex XI, A (pp 258–71), discussed by D McGoldrick, 'Approaches to the Assertion of International Jurisdiction: the Human Rights Committee', in P Capps, M Evans and S Konstadinidis, (eds), *Asserting Jurisdiction. International and European Legal Perspectives* (Oxford, 2003), ch 11.

[8] These can range from calls for re-orienting our understanding of the dynamic of the system (as was the case with the New Haven School, and also Rosalyn Higgins in her calls for a more process-oriented vision of international law (See R Higgins, 'Policy Considerations and the International Judicial Process', 17 *International and Comparative Law Quarterly* (1968), pp 58–84)) to its whole-sale abandonment, in the hope and expectation that a Phoenix will arise from the ashes (eg P Allot, *Eunomia: New Order for a New World* 2nd edn, (Oxford, 2001). For a survey of contemporary thinking see I Scobbie, 'Some Common Heresies About International Law: Sundry Theoretical Perspectives', in M D Evans, (ed), *International Law* (Oxford, 2003), ch 2.

[9] I Brownlie, *System of the Law of States: State Responsibility Part 1* (Oxford, 1983).

rules concerning the responsibility of States now reflect the presence of human rights in numerous ways, both directly and indirectly. The direct reflections include in Article 50(1)(a) the idea that counter-measures must not affect 'obligations for the protection of human rights'. The indirect reflections include the various concepts that the international community has spawned or over-developed in its quest to accommodate the logic of human rights within its framework, that is, peremptory norms (*jus cogens*)[10] and community obligations (or obligations *erga omnes*).[11] Both of these concepts will be touched upon later but for now it is worth mentioning that these are, perhaps, the least objectionable manifestations—from a traditionalist's perspective—of the idea that Articles on the Responsibility of States for Internationally Unlawful Acts should reflect *stigma*, for that is what the inclusion of both these ideas seems to be about.[12] Some comfort, however, might be taken from the fact that the more objectionable element of international criminal responsibility of States—most clearly aimed at stigmatising forms of State conduct—has at least been exorcised from the current schema.[13] One may nevertheless remain profoundly sceptical about the value of norms of *jus cogens* and of obligations owed *erga omnes* as practical tools. If they fail in the context of human rights protection (and, to date, fail they have),[14] it is difficult to

[10] See Arts 26 and 40–41. Whilst acknowledging the existence of norms of *jus cogens*, the Arts themselves are scrupulously silent as to which norms enjoy such status. The origin is, of course, Art 53 of the 1969 Vienna Convention on the Law of Treaties. The ILC's Commentary to the original drafts of what became this Art 53 provided certain examples that are now taken up by the Commentary to Art 26, which notes that the prohibiting of aggression, genocide, slavery, racial discrimination, crimes against humanity and torture, and the right to self determination are clearly accepted examples, and there is further elaboration in the Commentary to Art 40, paras (3)–(6). (Crawford, above n 3, pp 245–47.)

[11] See Arts 42(b) and 48(1)(b).

[12] Thus norms of *jus cogens* are described as being 'those substantive rules of conduct that prohibit what has become to be seen as intolerable because of the threat it poses to the survival of States and their peoples and the most basic human values' (Commentary to Art 40, para (3)). (Crawford, above n 3, p 246.)

[13] This first found its way into the Draft Articles, ultimately as Draft Articles 19(2) and 40, in 1976 and has occasioned difficulties ever since. The concept was originally seen as a way of manifesting the idea of there being obligations owed to the international community. However, the lack of agreement over an appropriate penal sanction rendered their inclusion increasingly questionable and so in the final phases of the ILC's work, the stigma of criminalisation was removed in such cases. The practical consequences of this change for the malefactor, however, appear slight. For a succinct overview of the evolution and resolution of the issue, see Crawford, above n 3, pp 16–20. For a fulsome exploration of the issues see N Jorgensen, *The Responsibility of States for International Crimes* (Oxford, 2000). For robust criticisms of the deletion of the concept from the Articles, see, inter alia, G Abi-Saab, 'The Uses of Article 19', 10 *European Journal of International Law* (1999), p 339 (who in fact is arguing for the recognition of a form of aggravated State responsibility which does seem to have survived the deletion of the Article) and A Pellet, 'Can a State Commit a Crime? Definitely, Yes!', 10 *European Journal of International Law* (1999), p 425.

[14] This rather startling claim is doubtless in need of considerable support before it will be accepted. This is beyond the scope of a single footnote, but mention might be made of the well

see why they should have more potency in areas where the underlying ethical claim to override the orthodoxies of international legal formalism are weaker. Perhaps in time, but not just yet. In parentheses, it might be mentioned that there has been only limited success in utilising the relatively more orthodox concept of universal jurisdiction as a means of enforcing human rights standards against individuals, but even that has taken something of a battering at the hands of the ICJ of late.[15] It is, then, unsurprising that moves to make not individuals but States themselves susceptible to the jurisdiction of national courts in cases where their responsibility for violations of human rights has been raised have also been largely thwarted.[16]

known example of the *East Timor (Portugal v Australia)* case, *ICJ Reports*, 1995, p 90 in which the claim by Portugal against Australia based on its alleged breach of the *erga omnes* obligation regarding the self-determination of peoples fell foul of the *Monetary Gold* principle, taking the view that 'whatever the nature of the obligations invoked, the Court could not rule on the lawfulness of the conduct of a State when its judgment would imply an evaluation of the lawfulness of the conduct of another State which is not a party to the case. Where this is so, the Court cannot act, even if the right in question is a right *erga omnes*' (*Ibid*, para 102). Whilst not for a moment casting doubt on the existence of the obligation, or of standing to bring a claim, this rather closes down the ICJ as an available judicial forum—and, significantly, in respect of a norm of *jus cogens*. As regards *jus cogens* itself, one might point to the Judgment of the European Court of Human Rights in *Al-Adsani v UK*, Judgment, 21 Nov 2001, 34 *EHRR* 11 where the Court, whilst recognising the *jus cogens* nature of torture, refused to see in this a reason to accord primacy to the right of access to a Court for the determination a civil claim against a State under Art 6(1) of the European Convention on Human Rights with regard to acts of torture and upheld the immunity enjoyed by States in such circumstances. Both these judgments are perfectly capable of reconciliation with the concepts concerned, but the point of substance is that international judicial bodies do not seem overly keen to accord them the primacy and effect that, on the face of it, they would seem to call for.

[15] The Judgment of the ICJ in the *Arrest Warrant of 11 April 2000 (Democratic Republic of Congo v Belgium)* case, *Preliminary Objections and Merits, Judgment, ICJ Reports*, 2002, p 3, has had the practical effect of throwing into doubt many of the certainties that were crystallising around the applicability of universal jurisdiction, irrespective of the actual terms of the judgment itself. Although the Court was scrupulously silent on a question that it felt it unnecessary to address, it is difficult to avoid the conclusion that the Court was deeply divided on this issue (cf the remarkably restrictive approach of the President of the Court, Judge Guillaume).

[16] See, *eg*, the landmark case of *Siderman de Blake v Argentina*, 103 *ILR* 454 in the USA and *Al-Adsani v Government of Kuwait and others*, 107 *ILR* 536 in the UK. For the failure of the challenge before the ECHR in the latter case see *Al-Adsani v UK*, Judgment, 21 Nov 2001, 34 *EHRR* 11. Chinks in this armour are comparatively rare (*eg Prefecture of Voiotia v Federal Republic of Germany*, case No 137/1997, affirmed on this point on appeal, in case No 11/2000—though attempts to enforce the judgment were unsuccessful before the Greek Courts and resulting applications to the ECHR were declared inadmissible: see *Kalogeropoulou v Greece and Germany*, App No 59021/00, Decision of 12 Dec 2002, nyr) Alternatively, other breaches in this approach are very deliberately targeted for broader reasons of State policy, as is the case in the USA: see 94 *AJIL* (2000), pp 117–24; 95 *AJIL* (2001), pp 135–39; 96 *AJIL* (2002) p 463 for a presentation and discussion of various cases brought against both Cuba and Iran including *Flatow v Iran* (999 F Supp 1 (DDC 1998), *Cicippio v Iran* (18 F Supp 2d 62 (DDC 1998), *Anderson v Iran* (90 F Supp 2d 62 (DDC1998) *Eisenfeld v Iran* (No 98–1945, 2000 US Dist) and *Higgins v Iran*. See now also the 2000 'Victims of

Does this mean that international law should not have anything to do with human rights protection? The answer to this must be a resolute no. It is all a question of where and how. And is the concept of State responsibility significant for the implementation and development of international human rights protection? The answer to this must be affirmative. As Professor McGoldrick argues and demonstrates[17] human rights regimes reflect principles of State responsibility; they are found in, illustrated and amplified by them. However, that is not all that they do, and the gist of the argument presented here is that if we approach the question of State responsibility as found in the ILC Articles, and then seek to apply its approaches to the operation of human rights regimes, then we are going to get the answers to the questions 'where, and how?' very wrong indeed since State responsibility, ILC-style, does not provide an appropriate lens through which to analyse the practice of human rights bodies.

1. WHAT ARE INTERNATIONAL HUMAN RIGHTS?

It is necessary to take a few steps back in order to make sense of this. What are international human rights? I do not know what is their nature or their exact content and I doubt that anyone does—indeed, I doubt that anybody can. But rather than dwell on this conundrum, it is more useful to focus on the functions that human rights can play. Again, these are multitudinous, but for current purposes it is helpful to identify two points (some might say poles, or extremes) on the spectrum of possibilities. One function is that akin to 'Bills of Rights' within domestic constitutions. These provide the bases upon which the relationship between power and populace is policed, setting out principles which guide the examination of activities that take place in the borderlands between the acceptable and unacceptable conduct of both State and citizen, leaving their hinterlands—the heartlands of the public and the private spheres—untouched and untroubled. In this guise, they form a key component of a given form of 'constitutional compact'—that of democratic, constitutional governance. They are designed for and work within a given type of 'legal space'.[18]

Trafficking and Violence Protection Act' (P L No 106–386 ss, 2002 concerning recovery of damages) and the 2002 'Terrorism Risk Insurance Compensation Act' (PL No 107–297), for which see 97 *AJIL* (2003), pp 187–89.

[17] See ch 10 in this volume.

[18] Such is the model that is derived from Locke onwards, but couched in these terms it is without prejudice to the question of whether the liberal conception of rights is itself based on individualism or upon more communitarian impulses. For a succinct (but all the more useful for that very reason) presentation of these questions see J Donnelly, *Universal Human Rights in Theory and Practice* (Ithaca, 1989).

International human rights can also fulfil an entirely different function that flows from the perception that humans are being 'wronged'.[19] Whether this is 'true' is immaterial: indeed, it is (in human terms) unknowable. What is important is that such a claim is made and the case for a 'right' articulated. When such claims are made within a State and where they find acceptance—as, for example, in documents such as the French Declaration of the Rights of Man (sic) and the American Declaration of Independence—they may eventually become reflected and 'constitutionalized' within the relevant national legal order and they then appear in the guise of 'Bills of Rights', as described above.

It is perfectly possible that a similar process could happen on the international level and the image projected at the UN level by the use of terminology such as the 'Universal Declaration' and the 'International Bill of Rights' is that this is indeed the case. However, this is a complete misnomer since in reality the legal instruments that comprise that 'Bill' of rights do not effectively occupy the legal space between the UN and Member States. Neither the International Covenant on Civil and Political Rights ('ICCPR') nor the other UN-sponsored human rights treaties operate in a 'constitutional' fashion within the UN legal system at all, no matter what the original intention or aspirations were.[20] The international sphere has become an alternative forum in which to articulate claims which it is believed should be espoused at the national level and 'constitutionalised' in the manner described above.[21] Claims become 'internationalised' by being

[19] This is ultimately to take a 'victim' oriented approach that eschews the 'legal' characterisation of a norm in favour of its epistemological value: perhaps more easily characterised as a 'bottom' up approach. Although long-championed by many, this line of thinking found a natural and powerful outlet within the response to the 'Asian Values' debate and the question of universalism and cultural relativism. See, eg K Booth, 'Three Tyrannies', in T Dunne and N Wheeler, (eds), *Human Rights in Global Politics* (Cambridge, 1999), ch 1.

[20] See, *eg*, L Sohn, 'How American International Lawyers Prepared for the San Francisco Bill of Rights', 89 *American Journal of International Law* (1995), p 540; and AWB Simpson, *Human Rights and the End of Empire* (Oxford, 2001), chs 4 and 5.

[21] This is not to say that this process cannot happen within other forms of international order. The obvious example being the engrafting of the EU's Charter of Fundamental Rights into the structures of the European Union. To the extent that the EU represents a constitutionalised structure of governance, that Charter polices the relationships between its constituent elements, rather than 'simply' providing internationally binding legal obligations of conduct upon the constituent elements, which are to be respected in their relationships. A key question concerns the nature of the remedy offered by the international mechanism. Where the watchdog body can strike down domestic law, the 'constitutionalising' impact is most evident and this can certainly come about through a process of evolution within a human rights regime. It may already have done so in the Inter-American system. See, eg, the judgment of the Inter-American Court of Human Rights in *Castillo-Petruzzi* case, Merits, Judgment of 30 May 1999 Ser C, No 52, para 221, where the Court nullified the judgment of a Peruvian Court for want of due process (see J Bucherer, 95 *AJIL* (2001), p 171) and, more recently, the *Barrios Altos* case, Judgment of 14 March 2001, Merits, Ser C, No 75, para 44, where the Court declared Peruvian self-amnesty laws to be of no legal effect. In general, the Inter-American Court has been very directive in its demands on States in the face of findings of violations of the American

advocated and articulated within the international sphere and, should they be accepted and adopted at that level, this becomes a point of pressure upon that State to conform—pressure from without rather than from within. It is, of course, a form of pressure that is at odds with many of the presuppositions of the international legal system,[22] and will often have little to do with the articulation of a set of values deemed appropriate by a given society for policing the boundary between governors and governed. It is true that, to the extent that the State accepts the obligations contained in such legally binding international instruments, it may do so as a voluntary act,[23] but the addressees of that voluntary act are the other States parties to the instrument concerned, even if the beneficiaries of that act are those 'subject to the jurisdiction of the state'.[24] It is, then, hardly surprising that many States simply ignore their 'international human rights' commitments within their domestic legal orders. Although couched in the language of legal obligation and constructed within the forms of the international legal system, they can be seen as containing aspirational agendas,[25] commitments to realise a certain form of compact between the State and people.

As far as international human rights protection is concerned, the task, then, becomes one of ensuring that States honour their legal commitments and the international treaties have of course established various mechanisms

Convention. (See generally D Shelton, *Remedies in International Human Rights Law* (Oxford, 1999), pp 167–75 and for a recent example from the case law, see the *Barrios Altos* case, Reparations, Judgment of 30 Nov 2001, Ser C, para 50). The position under the European Convention on Human Rights is considered in section 3 below. For current purposes, the point is that even if this process is possible, and even if it has happened elsewhere, it has not yet happened in the UN system. It must also be remembered that this process of 'constitutionalisation' can (and usually is) generated by other pressures operating within a regional system. See, eg S Schnably, 'Constitutionalism and democratic government in the inter-American System', in G Fox and B Roth (eds), *Democratic Governance and International Law* (Cambridge, 2000).

[22] Such as non-intervention under Art 2(7) of the UN Charter, for which see above n 5.

[23] At least, as a matter of form. The reality is that many States are under an immense amount of diplomatic pressure—and often coercion—to ratify international human rights instruments and do so for a whole raft of reasons, the intention to implement their newly acquired obligations often not being one of them. See generally R Mullerson, *Human Rights Diplomacy* (London, 1997). To the extent that human rights obligations are generated by customary international law, the claim is even weaker.

[24] This being the position under the principal human rights treaties. See, eg, ECHR, Art 1, ICCPR, Art 2(1) and the American Convention on Human Rights, Art 1. Interestingly, the position under the African Charter on Human and People's Rights, Art 1, carries a slightly different nuance, seemingly giving greater significance to the State as opposed to the Charter as the source of the rights of the individuals. This is supported by some of the doctrinal writing concerning the Charter. See, eg R Murray, *The African Commission on Human and People's Rights* (Oxford, 2000), pp 51–53 and the literature sited therein at p 51, n 12.

[25] In saying this I do not intend to invoke the tired debate between the various 'generations' of international human rights and the question of whether some are of immediate obligation whilst others are of a programmatic nature. My point is that international human rights are in essence aspirational, irrespective of their legal nature.

of greater or lesser utility in achieving this objective.[26] For the purposes of the current argument, the essential point is that the principles of State responsibility—which are intended to provide a framework within which to address breaches of international obligations—currently seem to provide little assistance in this regard. It is of course perfectly true that where the victim of a 'violation' of a 'human rights abuse' is the national of another State, then the principles of State responsibility kick in to determine the circumstances in which that State may take up the claim. One may see this as 'protecting human rights' if one wishes, but it seems to be a category confusion to do so.[27]

What is critical is the ability of a State to respond to cases where those at risk are not its nationals. This is the true territory of human rights protection under international law and here the application of the principles of State responsibility do not seem to have played a significant role in the operation of the international system of human rights protection hitherto[28]: there is a distinct shortage of international claims arising from breaches of international human rights commitments per se.[29]

[26] It is also worth observing that an assumption of a high risk of non-compliance is entrenched in the very nature of the implementation machinery associated with the principal UN human rights instruments, the compulsory elements of which involve reporting procedures that, by and large, are concerned with ensuring that domestic law actually conforms to the international obligations undertaken. Even if it is argued that this is not the position in theory, it is certainly the case in practice. A full-scale review of the utility of the current UN system is clearly beyond the scope of this paper, let alone this footnote, but for a valuable overview see P Alston and J Crawford, (eds), *The Future of UN Human Rights Treaty Monitoring* (Cambridge, 2000). See also UN GA Res 57/300 calling for a review of procedures, and the Report of the Secretary General to the General Assembly, A/57/387, paras 52–54.

[27] Diplomatic protection of nationals abroad may be a way of protecting the 'human rights' of nationals (or not), but it is not really what international human rights law is all about. In any case, at this point one is speaking of the substantive rules concerning treatment of aliens, rather than with principles of State responsibility per se—and revisiting the problems posed by the earlier Reports to the ILC. See above n 2.

[28] The position may be changing. In this regard it is worth noting the current draft text of a new General Comment on Art 2 entitled 'the Nature of the General Legal Obligation Imposed on States Parties to the Covenant' which is under consideration by the UN Human Rights Committee. This provides that 'While Article 2 is couched in terms of the obligations of State parties towards individuals as the rights—holders under the Convention, every State party has a legal interest in the performance by every other State party of its obligations. This follows from the fact that the 'rules concerning the basic rights of the human person' are *erga omnes* obligations'. (See CCPR/C/74/CRP.4/Rev 3, para 1 *bis*.) This would seem to suggest a more prominent role for inter-State responsibility in the future. However, it is interesting to note that the remainder of the Draft moves on to deal with the broadening of the range of actions for which the State can be held responsible, and the extent of positive and procedural obligations that the Covenant imposes on States.

[29] This is reflected in the complete failure of States to take advantage of the machinery provided for in the UN human rights instruments to bring inter-State claims. Inter-State claims have, of course, been brought within the European Convention system but even here they tend to relate to situations of political tension between protagonists. There have been a relatively small number of cases—mainly against Turkey—in which the motives of the applicant States

At the end of the day, however, what matters is not merely 'compliance' with the international obligation (though that is certainly a good thing), but that the State 'buys into' the value of the 'human right' in question; that it accepts the ethical force of the argument and adopts it as a value within its internal legal order. So why are the principles of State responsibility so rarely called into play in the task of assisting in the realisation of the responsibility that States have assumed, or are under, at the inter-State level? Doubtless there are many reasons of a practical or pragmatic nature that can be legitimately canvassed. There is, however, a more fundamental reason: the type of 'space' which human rights are designed to occupy in the domestic sphere does not yet exist on the international plane. There simply is not an appropriate legal space in which the 'constitutional' model can operate. Despite claims to the contrary,[30] there is as yet no genuine international 'constitution' so there is, as yet, no 'constitutional role' for international human rights in the universal sphere although this is not necessarily true of the regional sphere.[31] It is difficult to avoid the conclusion that international human rights tend to operate in the international sphere at the 'ethical' end of the spectrum. Against this background, the paucity of international claims becomes more explicable, since State responsibility is about responding to, and holding States to account for, breaches of international law. It is not about enhancing the rhetorical quality of ethical claims. It therefore comes as no surprise that to the extent that the ILC's Articles directly bear upon human rights, they reflect—albeit weakly—this ethical component.[32] But even this appears to be little more than a sleight of hand since the true province of international human rights law does not lie within the realms of State responsibility at all.

might fairly be characterised as being primarily directed at the upholding of ECHR values, but even here the record of follow-through is not heartening: see, eg, the terms of the Friendly Settlement in *Denmark v Turkey*, 5 April 2000, *RJD* 2000-IV, 29 *EHRR* CD 35, the terms of which include the applicant funding training projects in the respondent State.

[30] Eg T Franck, *Recourse to Force* (Cambridge, 2002), p 5 ('quasi-constitutional'). *Cf* P Sands and P Klein, *Bowett's Law of International Institutions*, 5th edn (London, 2001), p 24, where a more orthodox approach is taken. Much of the argument revolves around UN Charter Art 103 concerning the effects of conflicts between obligations of members under the Charter and other obligations of international law. (B Simma, (ed) *The Charter of the United Nations: A Commentary*, 2nd edn, (Oxford, 2002) accepts that 'Article 103 is essential if the Charter is to be recognized as the 'constitution'; of the international community' but its analysis of practice under the Charter leads it to conclude that the Charter '*may become* a real and effective constitution for the international community.' (*Ibid*, p 1302, emphasis added.) Clearly, it has not yet done so.

[31] Even when there is evidence of an emergent legal space for a constitutionalised vision of international human rights—chiefly within regional systems—these tend to function within the confines of the specific treaty regimes that underpin them, rather than spreading out into the general international arena where the principles of State responsibility would provide the primary conceptual apparatus for addressing non-compliance.

[32] See text corresponding to n 9 above and following.

2. WHAT IS A VIOLATION OF AN INTERNATIONAL HUMAN RIGHT?

This rather controversial assertion is supported by reflecting upon what is meant by a 'finding' of a breach of an international human rights obligation. This reflection is also useful as a means of illustrating the difference between approaching international human rights from a 'constitutional' as opposed to an 'ethical' perspective. It seems to me that the mechanisms created by the various international human rights instruments reflect 'constitutionalist' assumptions: it is assumed that the obligations they contain are indeed reflected in States parties' constitutional arrangements and that the international mechanisms are to provide a means of oversight and external scrutiny of the manner in which States are fulfilling them.[33] The mechanisms are not designed to ensure compliance or to hold States to account for 'wrongs' that have taken place. Rather, they are designed to assist the State in the fine tuning of its internal apparatus, scrutinising compliance and indicating deviance. Within such a system, a 'finding' of a violation of a human rights obligation does not depend upon the act itself but turns on the nature of the agent and the response of that agent to the action in question. This is apt to confuse.

For example, probably no international human right is so well established as the absolute prohibition on torture, inhuman or degrading treatment or punishment,[34] and the leading definition in the human rights sphere, Article 1 of the UN Convention against Torture, stresses the need for a degree of official involvement in the act.[35] Article 3 of the European Convention on Human Rights ('ECHR') does not expressly require official involvement in the commission of an act for it to amount to torture but in its recent jurisprudence this element is becoming increasingly apparent.[36] This is perfectly consonant with the underlying idea of human rights being

[33] It might be tempting to try to distinguish between the 'reporting' and 'communications' procedures at this point and at first sight it is indeed plausible to argue that oversight through reporting is more reflective of the 'ethical' dimension by seeking to ensure that States do indeed live up to their commitments, whereas the communication procedures are more reflective of the 'constitutional' dimension. This, however, might be premature. In both instances, the outcome is still more akin to a declaratory remedy and, as has been argued above (above n 21), it is in the nature and the effect of the remedy that the true difference lies. To that extent, the future direction of international human rights protection lies in the hands of the human rights bodies, not all of which have yet attempted to seize the opportunities that are open to them.

[34] This is now well attested in domestic and international decisions as well as in the copious literature surrounding the subject. See generally N Rodley, *The Treatment of Prisoners under International Law*, 2nd ed. (Oxford, 1998), ch 2.

[35] For exploration of the definition of torture from a human rights perspective see Rodley, *ibid*, ch 3; N Rodley, 'The Definition(s) of Torture in International Law', 22 *Current Legal Problems* (2002); and MD Evans, 'Getting to Grips with Torture', 51 *International and Comparative Law Quarterly* (2002), p 365.

[36] There is an increasing tendency to draw on the UNCAT definition when differentiating between torture on the one hand and inhuman and degrading treatment on the other. See,

a reflection of the principles that guard the boundary between the State and the individual and a violation of a human right being a finding that that boundary has not been respected. However, the phenomena that 'is' torture is not dependent upon its being a 'human right' at all and, *a fortiori*, one can be 'tortured' without any human rights violation having occurred at all.[37]

For example, if I am 'tortured' it makes little difference who is torturing me and the official or unofficial nature of the act is not at the root of my sense of violation. Of course, one might think that the fact that one is being subject to acts of a torturous nature by a State official makes the matter ethically worse, because it is a breach of public trust as well. But this is not necessarily the case. What has hitherto anchored the legal definition of torture to State conduct has been the idea that human rights obligations are in fact restraints on the actions of States.[38] Although there is now an increasing willingness to recognise the responsibility of non-State actors for human rights abuses, this is still done as a matter of human rights law through the prism of State responsibility. In other words, it is

eg, *Selmouni v France* [GC] Judgment, 28 July 1999, *RJD* 1999–V, 29 *EHRR* 403, paras 97, 100; *Ilhan v Turkey* [GC] Judgment, 27 June 2000, *RJD* 2000–VIII, 34 *EHRR* 36, paras 85–88; *Salman v Turkey*, Judgment, 27 June 2000, *RJD* 2000–VIII, 34 *EHRR* 17, paras 114–16; *Akkoc v Turkey* Judgment, 10 Oct 2000, *RJD* 2000–X, 34 *EHRR* 51 para 115; *Aktas v Turkey*, 24 April 2003, *nyr*, para 313. There are also an increasing number of cases in which the failure to prove beyond reasonable doubt that the treatment received was imputable to the State has prevented a finding that that treatment amounted to a breach of Art 3 of the ECHR, even though there might be a breach of the procedural obligations to investigate under Art 3 itself, or of other Arts, such as Art 13 concerning the right to a remedy. See, *eg*, the recent case of *Tepe v Turkey*, Judgment, 9 May 2003, *nyr*, paras 175, 186, where the lack of proof beyond reasonable doubt of the involvement of the State or its agents in the actions was fatal to the claim that there had been a breach of the substantive provisions of both Art 2 and Art 3 of the Convention.

[37] Although not put in these terms, a similar conclusion can be drawn from developments in the field of international criminal law. Early Judgments of the *ad hoc* war crimes tribunals, eg, stressed the unity between the approaches to torture in the human rights and international criminal law sphere (*eg Prosecutor v Akayesu*, Judgment, Case ICTR 96–4 T, 2 Sept, 1998, para 593; *Prosecutor v Delalic*, case No IT 96–21–T, 16 Nov 1998, para 459). Later cases, however, have moved away from this, stressing the distinctive nature of international criminal law. From this perspective, the need for the involvement of the State is not at all necessary, and was repudiated in *Prosecutor v Kunarac*, Case IT 96–23–T, 22 Feb 2001, para 496 and in *Prosecutor v Kovcka*, Case No IT 98/30/1–T, 2 Nov 2001, paras 138–39, where the ICTY expressly said that 'the State actor requirement imposed by international human rights law is inconsistent with the application of individual criminal responsibility for international crimes ... '. The requirement of 'official capacity' has also been dropped from the Elements of Crimes, Art 8(2)(a)(ii) concerning the definition of torture as a war crime adopted by the Prepcom established under the auspices of the ICC Statute. (See K Dörmann, *Elements of War Crimes under the Rome Statute of the ICC* (Cambridge, 2002), pp 44–46, 55–59.)

[38] In the context of the UN Convention against torture, there is the added factor of the relationship with 'universal jurisdiction' *inter partes* under Art 5(2), a rationale for which is that the very fact that the acts of torture are committed by or with the acquiescence of State officials or under the colour of law makes the assertion of territorial jurisdiction improbable.

because the State has not prevented,[39] investigated[40] or provided a remedy[41] that there has been a human rights violation. This may provide a convenient route by which to find a State 'liable' before an international organ but as far as the victim is concerned it is perplexing, to say the least. For example, if I am whipped by a police officer in the course of an interrogation, then I will have been 'tortured'. If I am kidnapped by a gang of sadists and whipped in their presence and for their pleasure then I have not been 'tortured'. In both cases I have not yet been the victim of a human rights violation viewed as a legal concept (though doubtless the victim of an assault). It is only if the assault remains un-investigated or my assailant remains unpunished that I may find myself to have been the victim of a 'human rights' violation as far as an international body is concerned, and even then I might have been the victim of 'torture' in the first scenario, but not in the second. The stripes on my back would of course have been the same in all instances, as they would be if I had asked to be whipped for my own masochistic delight.[42] Put that way, what comprises a violation of a 'human right' becomes considerably less clear.

This, then, reinforces the need to distinguish between human rights as ethical claims and as 'constitutional' principles and to understand the manner in which a given instrument is being used. Failure to do so will only cause confusion, particularly as States may well be found not to be in breach of 'international human rights' obligations in situations where the actual forms of behaviour involved seem to cry out for moral condemnation *as* a breach of 'human rights'. Such outcomes are more readily explicable on a 'constitutional' than an 'ethical' approach.

[39] See *A v UK*, Judgement, 23 Sep 1998, *RJD* 1998–VI, 27 *EHRR* 611, para 22; *Z v UK*, 10 May 2001, para 73; *RJD* 2001–V, 34 *EHRR* 3; *DP and JC v UK*, Judgment, 10 Jan 2003, para 106, 36 *EHRR* 11, all of which stress that States are required 'to take measures designed to ensure that individuals within their jurisdiction are not subjected to torture or inhuman or degrading treatment, including such ill-treatment administered by private individuals'. This now provides a more general head within which to locate the many cases in which it is found that there would be a violation if a person were returned to a country due to there being substantial grounds for believing they would face a real risk of torture or ill-treatment, the '*Soering*' line of cases, which has always been couched in terms of 'State responsibility'. For an important recent decision determining that awards of interim measures issued by the Court in such cases are binding on the parties and that the failure to respect them entails a breach of Art 34 concerning the right of individual petition, see *Mamatkulov and Abdurasulovic v Turkey*, Judgment, 6 Feb, 2003, paras 110–11, nyr.

[40] Thus in cases such as *Aktas v Turkey*, Judgment, 24 April 2003, nyr, the State is not held responsible for the manner in which the person has been treated but it is held to be responsible for its failure to respond to the evidence of ill-treatment in an appropriate fashion. For the general growth of this area of responsibility see A Mowbray, 'Duties of Investigation under the ECHR', 51 *International and Comparative Law Quarterly* (2002), p 437.

[41] See, eg, *A v UK*, Judgement, 23 Sep 1998, *RJD* 1998–VI, 27 *EHRR* 611.

[42] In which case some might argue that there would be a violation of my human rights if the State *did* punish the person who fulfilled my wishes. See, eg, the arguments raised by the applicants in *Laskey, Jaggard and Brown v UK*, Judgment, 19 Feb 1997, *RJD* 1997–I, 24 *EHRR* 39.

3. THE EUROPEAN CONVENTION ON HUMAN RIGHTS?

Against this background, the role of the ECHR seems perfectly clear: it is projected as a form of constitutional settlement between a group of like-minded States adhering to common sets of values within a common legal space. Never has this been made clearer than in the Court's decision in the *Bankovic* case where it decided that an application brought in respect of those injured by the bombing of a radio station in Belgrade (a city not located within the territory of a contracting party to the ECHR) by the air forces of a number of contracting parties to the ECHR was inadmissible.[43] Previous decisions of the Court—notably *Loizidou v Turkey*[44] and *Cyprus v Turkey*[45]—had generated the impression that States parties were responsible under the Convention system for the acts of those subject to their jurisdiction, wherever committed, with the consequence that any victim of a violation would be able to bring a claim before the ECHR irrespective of their nationality or the place where that violation occurred.[46] It is difficult to think of a claim which more roundly supports the idea that the ECHR is reflective of the ethical view of human rights, made manifest and given institutional form: or, to put it another way, that State parties are responsible (in the layman's sense) for their actions. Such a claim transcends the 'constitutional' approach since it seeks to apply the Convention in spheres where there is no compact between the State and the populace, merely a straightforward understanding that a State will not act contrary to the principles set out in the Convention and may be held to account before Convention machinery if it does.

However, the Court did not see it that way at all. It declared that:

> The Convention is a multi-lateral treaty operating ... in an essentially regional context and notably in the legal space of the Contracting States. The Convention was not designed to be applied throughout the world, even in respect of the conduct of Contracting States.[47]

Of course, this does not mean that the Convention's writ does not run in places which are outside the jurisdiction of States parties, it simply means

[43] *Bankovic v Belgium* and others [GC], Decision, 12 Dec 2001. For critical comment see A Ruth and M Trilsch, 97 *American Journal of International Law* (2003), pp 168–72.
[44] *Loizidou v Turkey* (Preliminary Objections), Judgment, 23 March 1995, Ser A, No, 310, 23 *EHRR* 79.
[45] *Cyprus v Turkey*, Judgment, 10 May 2001, *RJD* 2001–IV, 35 *EHRR* 30.
[46] It has long been established that contracting States were responsible for the acts of their officials taken abroad. *Loizidou* decided that areas under the effective (military) control of a contracting State were under its jurisdiction for the purposes of Art 1. This was widely seen as a significant extension of the jurisdictional reach of the Convention (eg D Harris, M O'Boyle, C Warbrick, *Law of the European Convention on Human Rights* (London, 1995), pp 643–44), but it is better seen as a dramatic *application* of the pre-existing position.
[47] *Bankovic v Belgium* and others, above n 43, para 80.

that these instances are exceptions to the general rule of territorial application. The obvious exception is the application of the ECHR to the actions of Turkey in Northern Cyprus which the Court has been happy to hold Turkey responsible for in numerous cases, based—it was thought—on the principle of effective control.[48] But no longer. Although the argument in *Bankovic* that the NATO countries exercised such effective control over the skies above Belgrade was always veering towards the fanciful, the idea that the Convention could be used as a means of exercising what might be called an 'ethical oversight' of the actions of States parties was not.

The Court, however, took a different route, distinguishing the situation in Northern Cyprus on the grounds that 'the inhabitants of northern Cyprus would have found themselves excluded from the benefits of the Convention's safeguards and system which they had previously enjoyed'.[49] This is less than convincing as an argument and only works to the extent that part of a contracting State is effectively controlled by another State party to the Convention. If, for example, Iraq had supported the establishment of an independent Kurdish State in South East Turkey, the resulting 'regrettable vacuum in human rights protection' would not be filled, a position that the Court itself accepted.[50] Whatever the case, the Court was categorical:

> The Court's obligationn … is to have regard to the special character of the Convention as a constitutional instrument of *European* public order for the protection of individual human beings and its role … is to ensure the observance of the *engagements undertaken* by the Contracting Parties' …. It is difficult to contend that a failure to accept the extra territorial jurisdiction of the respondent states would fall foul of the Convention's *ordre public* objective, which in itself underlines the essentially regional vocation of the Convention system … .[51]

One can hardly put it any clearer than that. The EHCR is to be seen as an element of European public order, not a code of ethics for evaluating the conduct of contracting parties. It is 'in house' (but takes the occasional holiday). This has the merit of reflecting the reality that the judicial nature of

[48] *Cyprus v Turkey*, above n 45.
[49] *Bankovic v Belgium* and others, above n 43, para 80.
[50] There is an alternative approach, outlined in the Human Rights Committee's General Comment No 26, adopted in 1997 concerning the continuity of obligations, para 4 of which argues that 'The rights enshrined in the Covenant belong to the people living in the territory of the State party …. once the people are accorded the protection of the rights under the Covenant, such protection devolves with territory and continues to belong to them, notwithstanding change in Government or the State party, including dismemberment in more than one State or State succession or any subsequent action of the State party designed to divest them of the rights guaranteed by the Covenant'. The practicality of this approach is, obviously, open to debate in cases where territory of a contracting State is occupied by a non-contracting State.
[51] *Bankovic v Belgium* and others, above n 43, para 80. Emphasis in original.

the Convention mechanisms are not very appropriate for dealing with situations in which there are massive ruptures in the rule of law, and the fall out from such situations has been the cause of many of the logistical problems which the court now faces (and continues to face). It works best as a means of fine-tuning the operation of the domestic systems which by and large reflect and respect Convention values.[52]

What has any of this to do with State responsibility? It does not seem to me that the ECHR is directed towards holding States responsible for their actions *under international law* at all. True, the existence of inter-State cases at first sight seem to suggest otherwise, but a closer inspection suggests that even this is not the case. The result in *Cyprus v Turkey* was a finding that Turkey was in breach of a whole host of Convention obligations. However, the form of the outcome was a declaratory judgment and whatever relief is to be forthcoming is more likely to flow from the political process into which this judgment fits rather than from the judgment per se.[53] Hence the

[52] It should, however, be noted that the enlargement of the Council of Europe, which currently has 45 Member States, has had an impact on the role of the Convention in at least a part of the legal space to which the Convention's *ordre public* is supposed to extend. Admitting to the 'European home' countries which, in truth, do not respect and reflect these values in practice (irrespective of whether they genuinely aspire to do so) has placed the entire system under stress and called into question the true role of the ECHR in the European theatre. It is increasingly the case that the Convention is portrayed in an aspirational fashion, as the code to which those who wish to become 'members of the club' must promise to adhere, albeit that the reality is very different. Of course, these States subscribe to the ECHR as a matter of international legal obligation, but that is a very different thing. Many of the newly admitted States subscribe because they have to: these are sets of values which in truth have been imposed from the outside, rather than accepted from within. Against this background, the clear message given by the *Bankovic* case seems to be the wrong message, or at least only a part of the right message. The EHCR is indeed a constitutional instrument of European public order, but in at least part of the legal space covered by the Convention system it must be understood as fulfilling a chiefly rhetorical role, articulating values that are yet to be fully internalised by the States concerned. This presents an awesome challenge for the functioning of the Convention machinery which simply was not constructed to deal with such situations and which are currently under scrutiny once again. An element of that scrutiny—unsurprisingly—reflects this very debate: for an overview see L Wildhaber, 'A Constitutional Future for the European Court of Human Rights?', 23 *Human Rights Law Journal* (2002), pp 161–65. These issues have wider implications for the approach of the Court to its judicial functions, an issue explored in S Greer, 'Constitutionalizing Adjudication under the European Convention on Human Rights', 23 *Oxford Journal of Legal Studies* (2003), pp 405–33.

[53] The Court decided to adjourn issues under Art 41 of the Convention. This approach has historical precedent. Looking back to the first case brought by Cyprus against Turkey, the Commission found there to be numerous breaches of the Convention yet the Committee of Ministers ultimately resolved that 'The enduring protection of human rights in Cyprus can only be brought about through the re-establishment of peace and confidence between the two communities; and that inter-communal talks constitute the appropriate framework for reaching a solution of the dispute' (Res DH (79) 1 *QED*). Although it is within the framework of the Convention, the inter-State procedure has more to do with the politics of a situation of breakdown than with providing a means for addressing the illegality of the situation. This may account for the otherwise astonishing lack of interest in using inter-State complaints procedures for addressing human rights concerns: frankly, in most cases there are more potent political tools available. See further, above n 29.

Convention should not really be seen as being about holding States to account *as a matter of international law*. Of course, it will be seen as a means of doing so from the perspective of a domestic applicant and that is perfectly appropriate. But this does not really have anything to do with State responsibility, as international lawyers understand the concept. It is State responsibility in the layman's sense.

The real question, then, is whether it is possible for one State party to take measures against another State party outside of the ECHR framework for the failure of that State to secure to those within its jurisdiction the protections afforded by the Convention system. The reluctance to act within the Convention's own inter-State claims procedure seems to suggest that whatever the theoretical possibilities, it is simply not a realistic prospect.[54] Nevertheless, the ILC's Articles do seem to point towards this.

Article 48 (1) provides that States other than 'injured States' may invoke the responsibility of another State in either of two instances: (a) if 'the obligation breached is owed to a group of States including that State, and is established for the protection of a collective interest of the group' and (b) if 'the obligation breached is owed to the international community as a whole'. In both of these instances, the procedural right to pursue a claim is underpinned by the existence of a shared community interest. In Article 48(1)(a)—'obligations *erga omnes partes*'—that common, community interest is shared between a segment of the international community and the resulting procedural rights are only available to those States concerned. Article 48(1)(b)—obligations *erga omnes*, as described in the *Barcelona Traction* case,[55] that common, community interest is vested in the international community as a whole. The Commentary makes it clear that Article 48(1)(a) might embrace obligations flowing from 'a regional system for the protection of human rights'.[56] This does indeed hold out interesting possibilities. Could, for example, a State party to the ECHR choose to seek declaratory relief from, say, the ICJ (assuming of course it

[54] And the experience—or absence of experience—under the UN system tends to confirm this. States have shown greater willingness to raise issues through the more political channels of the OSCE mechanisms, as well as through more conventional diplomatic channels.

[55] *Barcelona Traction, Light and Power Company, Limited, Second Phase, Judgment, ICJ Reports*, 1970, p 3 (para 33).

[56] Commentary to Art 48, para 7 in J Crawford, *The International Law Commission's Articles on State Responsibility* (Cambridge, 2002), p 277. It is interesting to note that non-regional systems are not included in the example, which might indicate a belief that they are not 'collective' in nature in quite the same way and at first sight it is difficult to see why the possibility of holding States to account by the application of the principles of State responsibility should turn on the regional as opposed to universal character of the legal instrument in question. One answer might be that the UN systems are not seen as being of a 'constitutional' nature, there being no relevant 'legal space' at the global level for them to operate within, and therefore reinforcing the observations made earlier about the essentially 'ethical' thrust of these instruments.

had jurisdiction to hear the case), rather than using the ECHR's own inter-State mechanisms. And, if so, to what extent would the ICJ be bound by the interpretation placed upon the Convention by the European Court? It is not obviously the case that the European Court of Human Rights and the ICJ would speak with one voice on all matters, both procedural and substantive.[57] What is certain is that proceedings of this nature would breathe new life into the idea that States were accountable at the international level for fulfilling their human rights commitments. It would show there was a real role for the application of the principles of State responsibility in this field.

But do human rights obligations also give rise to procedural rights under Article 48(1)(b) as well? The *Barcelona Traction* case itself suggests that they do, but, doubtless prudently, the ILC Commentary refrains from lending much amplification, beyond reminding us that ICJ case law recognises the *erga omnes* nature of obligations relating to the outlawry of aggression and genocide, self determination, and 'the principles and rules concerning the basic rights of the human person, including protection from slavery and racial discrimination'.[58] Although any list will clearly be contentious, it is indisputable that, in theory, violations of some human rights obligations lay States open to international claims. What is equally clear is that, in practice, other States are generally not minded to make such claims.

Perhaps the real answer is that the international plane is not the appropriate *locus* for the enforcement of violations of international human rights obligations—properly understood—at all. It might be an appropriate place in which to articulate claims concerning human rights, and to encapsulate them in legally binding instruments. It might provide a means through which to construct avenues of accountability and means of oversight. But these applications of international legal paraphernalia do not require the application of principles of State responsibility, which remain a background noise: either a threat, or a promise—but given the nature of the international order, of little current practical utility.

[57] Cf The differences of approach to the issue of reservations between the ECHR, and human rights bodies in general, and the ICJ. For a broad-ranging appraisal see G McGrory, 'Reservations of Virtue? Lessons from Trinidad and Tobago's Reservation to the First Optional Protocol', 23 *Human Rights Quarterly* (2001), p 769. At the same time, it must be acknowledged that in other areas there have been moves towards a common approach, most notably in the recent case of *Mamatkulov and Abdurasulovic v Turkey*, Judgment, 6 Feb 2003, nyr, regarding the binding nature of awards of interim measures, which drew heavily on the reasoning of the ICJ in *LaGrand (Germany v United States of America), Merits, Judgment, ICJ Reports*, 2001, p 466.

[58] Commentary to Art 48, para 9 in Crawford, above n 3, p 278; quoting *Barcelona Traction, Light and Power Company, Limited, Second Phase, Judgment, ICJ Reports*, 1970, p 3 (para 33) and *East Timor,(Portugal v Australia), Judgment, ICJ Reports*, 1995, p 90 (para 29).

This brings us—finally—to the role that the idea of 'State responsibility' *does* play within the ECHR system. At first sight, it seems to play an entirely orthodox role, being chiefly concerned with the question of the attribution of conduct to the State.[59] However, this has been applied in a fashion that is quite at odds with the thrust of the ILC's Articles, under which the establishment of who is exercising governmental authority, or who is authorised to act by, or is acting under the direction or control of, the State is a key issue. The Commentary to Article 8 highlights the question of 'direction or control' as being the most problematic question, and then goes on to answer it in a restrictive fashion, saying that 'such conduct will be attributable to the State only if it [the State] directed or controlled the specific operation and the conduct complained of was an integral part of the operation'.[60] This would hardly be an apt way of describing the manner in which the European Court of Human Rights has extended the scope of the Convention's obligations with the effect that States are held responsible for those who are certainly not its agents or acting within the direction and control of the State, as understood by the ILC.[61]

First of all, there are numerous cases in which the Court accepts that there are positive obligations upon the State to act in order to prevent the violation of a Convention right.[62] In addition, there are cases in which 'we

[59] It must also be pointed out, however, that the Courts' approach to determining responsibility often involves the application of reverse burdens of proof or through the operation of fairly onerous sets of presumptions, and so attribution is often economically achieved. The latter can blur into 'positive obligations' when seen as a failure to provide a plausible explanation for treatment received when under the control of the State, a point noted in C Ovey and R White, *Jacobs and White: European Convention on Human Rights*, 3rd edn. (Oxford, 2002), p 67, in the context of *Sevtap Veznedarodlu v Turkey*, Judgment, 11 April 2000, 33 *EHRR* 1412. See also *Timutas v Turkey*, *RJD* 2000–VI, paras 82–83; *Orhan v Turkey*, Judgment, 18 June 2002.

[60] Commentary to Art 8, para 3 in Crawford, above n 3, p 110.

[61] Interestingly, however, this is also the path that the UN Human Rights Committee appears to be attempting to take. See above n 28.

[62] Charting the rise of positive obligations is a task beyond the scope of this chapter, let alone this footnote. (On positive obligations in the jurisprudence of the European Court of Human Rights, see ch 8 in this volume by Judge Conforti). Suffice to say that out of relatively modest origins in the jurisprudence under Art 8 (the right to family life) where there is a discrete obligation of 'respect', it has rippled out into the jurisprudence of other Articles of the Convention and is now a commonplace in cases under many Convention articles. The early 'foundational' cases on positive obligations under Art 8 were *Marckx v Belgium*, Judgment, 13 June 1979, Ser A, No 31, 2 *EHRR* 330 and *X and Y v Netherlands*, Judgment, 26 March, Ser A, No 91, 8 *EHRR* 235, for which see generally A Clapham, *Human Rights in the Private Sphere* (Oxford, 1993). For an example of a case concerning positive obligations under Art 2 see *Paul and Audrey Edwards v UK*, Judgment, 14 Mar 2002, 35 *EHRR* 19, paras 54–56, where, at para 54, the Court says that Art 2(1) 'enjoins the State not only to refrain from the intentional and unlawful taking of life, but also to take appropriate steps to safeguard the lives of those within its jurisdiction'. For a broad-ranging statement of the scope of positive obligations under Arts 1 and 3 see *Z v UK*, Judgment, 10 May 2001, *RJD* 2001–V, 34 *EHRR* 3, para 73, where it is said that they require States 'to take measure to ensure that individuals within their jurisdiction are not subjected to torture or inhuman or degrading treatment, including such ill-treatment administered by private individuals'.

all know' that the hand of the State is present, but that it is not possible to demonstrate it.[63] There are others in which it is not possible to show that the alleged harm actually occurred or is attributable to the State.[64] In both types of cases it is possible to point towards other failings for which the State can be held responsible that might account for this inability—such as the failure to conduct a proper investigation—with the result that the State is held responsible for its breach of a procedural obligation.[65] Quite where the combination of positive obligations and procedural obligations takes us—apart from into uncharted territory—is unclear. What is clear is that the Court is using the idea of the responsibility of the State to broaden the range of occasions upon which it can find the State in breach of its Convention obligations.

A different technique is suggested by cases such as those concerning the application of corporal punishment in schools that are not under the 'direction or control' of the State as such. In these cases the approach adopted has been to emphasise that education is an area in which the State has chosen to exercise a regulatory function and can therefore be held responsible under the Convention system for its permitting actions that breach Convention standards.[66] Once again, it seems easy enough to trace the hand of the State but it is not a novel insight to point out that there are very few areas of life over which the Convention does not exercise such a regulatory function.[67]

Both of these routes call into question in their separate ways the very idea that there are separate spheres of public/private life, one being the

[63] Some of the many cases concerning disappearances might arguably fall into such a category, but common prudence precludes citation.

[64] For a recent example of such a finding in a case concerning the alleged abduction and killing of the applicants' son by agents of the State, see *Tepe v Turkey*, Judgment, 9 May 2003, nyr.

[65] Thus in *Tepe v Turkey*, the Court went on to conclude that the investigation held had been inadequate and that this in itself amounted to a violation of the procedural provisions of Art 2. For an exploration of the relationship between substantive and procedural obligations in the jurisprudence of the Court see A Mowbray 'Duties of Investigation under the ECHR', 51 *International and Comparative Law Quasterly* (2002), p 437 and also MD Evans, 'Getting to Grips with Torture', 51 *International and Comparative Law Quarterly* (2002), p 365 at pp 378–81.

[66] See, *eg*, the approach of the Commission in its Report in *Costello–Roberts v UK*, 8 Oct 1991, an approach that was the subject of some dissent. The Court in its Judgment of 25 Mar 1993, Ser A, No 247–C, 19 *EHRR* 112 endorsed the finding of State responsibility for the disciplinary sanctions in the private education sector but did so in a somewhat more restrictive fashion—though by basing itself on fact-specific positive obligations to secure the right to education—it in fact assisted in the general opening up of this entire area.

[67] Similar examples can be found under other Convention articles, such as Art 9, where the State is increasingly seen as exercising a general regulatory function and States are examined for their stewardship in the light of Convention values. See, eg, *Serif v Greece*, Judgment, 14 Dec 1999, *RJD* 1999–IX, 31 *EHRR* 561 and *Metropolitan Church of Bessarabia v Moldova*, Judgment, 12 Dec 2001, 35 *EHRR* 3. For an analysis of these trends see MD Evans, 'Believing in Communities, European Style', in N Ghanea (ed), *Religious Discrimination at the Dawn of the New Millenium* (Leiden, (2004), p 133 2004).

stamping ground of the State, the other of the individual, and the human rights canon patrolling the borders. For the private sphere is only the private sphere *because* the State has not yet intruded into it. If the State is to be held responsible under the Convention for its failure to have done so, then the entire Convention edifice begins to crumble, or at least mutate. And where does this leave the *Bankovic* conception of the Convention as a tool of European *ordre publique*?

4. CONCLUSION

It seems that what is actually happening with the ECHR system is much more significant than the incremental development of the scope of Convention obligations premised upon the (mis)use of the language of State responsibility. What is happening is the adoption of an 'ethical' model of human rights, in which the Court is seeking to set out its vision of how the well-ordered State should be governed and individuals behave towards each other. The Convention becomes a '*cri de coeur*', an appeal to States parties to ensure that societies reflect the principles it espouses. It is a recognition that the 'constitutional' model has proved inadequate to address the sheer scale of the issues that are understood as falling within the scope of human rights concerns. We are increasingly being asked to examine all aspects of our public and private lives from the human rights perspective, and it is the State that is being held to account for the failures of us all. This makes something of a nonsense of the *Bankovic* decision, which moves in quite the opposite direction. Or perhaps it simply means that the ethical imperative is to be stressed within Europe, but not beyond.

Interestingly, it was in *Bankovic* itself that the Court stressed that, when interpreting the Convention,

> The Court must take into account any relevant rules of international law when examining questions concerning its jurisdiction and, consequently, determine State responsibility in conformity with the governing principles of international law, although it must remain mindful of the Convention's special character as a human rights treaty.[68]

Two points need to be made about this. The first is that it is the Convention's special character as a human rights treaty that makes the international principles of State responsibility *irrelevant* to its operation, so it is not clear why they should be referred to at all. Even if this is not accepted, it remains the case that the ECHR has recently called upon the 'governing principles of international law' in a series of controversial cases in which it has sought

[68] *Bankovic v Belgium* and others, above n 43, para 57.

to draw a line under the more purposive arguments that have sought to extend the parameters of the Convention system—*Bankovic* itself and *Al-Adsani v UK*.[69]

So there are two trends operating at the same time, though they are easily reconciled. Within the common 'legal space' the ECHR seems to be losing something of its technical, regulating function and adopting a more purposive voice that, whilst striving to respect traditional forms and structures, is in fact challenging them. Beyond that legal space, it is stressing the role of the Convention as a 'constitutional' instrument *for* that legal space, and resisting moves to extend its orbit beyond the well established list of exceptional circumstances. Whether this is driven by policy or pragmatism, it is difficult to say.

What does seem clear is that 'State responsibility' in the hands of the ECHR is a malleable instrument. It is being used to extend the scope of the Convention 'internally', reflective of the 'ethical' approach to human rights that breaks down the traditional boundaries. This is paradoxical since the ECHR has historically been premised upon the 'constitutional' model. At the same time, the orthodoxies of the international legal system, which presumably include the principles of State responsibility, are being used to justify the adoption of a more conservative approach at—what might fast become—the true 'international' level, that of relations between the European family of States and others. This too is deeply paradoxical, since the strength of the ILC's Articles from a human rights perspective seems to lie in their endorsement of community obligations and peremptory norms, matters that lie towards the 'ethical' end of the spectrum. Perhaps it is a pity that the ECHR did not choose to focus on these strands of thinking, or that the ILC did not tackle the human rights conundrum head on, rather than effect an accommodation with it. Either way, it is difficult to resist the conclusion that it would be for the best if the ECHR were to sort out quite what it means by 'State responsibility', and the role that it sees it playing within the Convention system. As for the principles of State responsibility as conceived by the ILC, for the time being it would seem best if they were to be seen as operating in an altogether different realm.

[69] *Al-Adsani v UK*, Judgment, 21 Nov 2001, 34 *EHRR* 11. The gist of the latter case was that traditional approaches to State immunity should be re-evaluated in the light of the principles of *jus cogens*. This was—narrowly—rejected, the Court appealing to the exigencies of the international legal order as a whole. This approach has been more recently endorsed in *Kalogeropoulou v Greece and Germany*, App No 59021/00, Decision on 12 Dec 2002, nyr.

10

State Responsibility and the International Covenant on Civil and Political Rights

DOMINIC MCGOLDRICK*

WHILE HUMAN RIGHTS law has been spreading at a revolutionary rate, the principles of State responsibility are in a process of continuous evolution. The challenge is to see how the primary and secondary rules impact and inter-react or appear to fail to connect.[1] The International Covenant on Civil and Political Rights ('Covenant') was adopted in 1966 but the approach to State responsibility under it has evolved. The famous decision of the International Court of Justice (ICJ) on *erga omnes* obligations came four years later in 1970, 'Every State, by virtue of its membership in the international community, has a legal interest in the protection of certain basic rights and the fulfilment of certain essential obligations'.[2] Among the examples given by the ICJ were 'the principles and rules concerning the basic rights of the human person, including protection from slavery and racial discrimination'.[3] The ICJ explained that, '[S]ome of the corresponding rights of protection have entered into the general body of international law ... others are conferred by international instruments of a universal or quasi-universal character'. The Covenant would be one of those international instruments.

* Professor of Public International Law, International and European Law Unit, Liverpool Law School. I am grateful to Fiona Beveridge for her comments on a draft of this essay and to Eric Donnelly for his assistance in editing it.

[1] See J Crawford, 'Revising the Draft Articles on State Responsibility', 10 *European Journal of International Law* (1999), p 435; D Shelton, 'Private Violence, Public Wrongs, and the Responsibility of States', 13 *Fordham Journal of International Law* (1990), p 1.

[2] *Barcelona Traction, Light and Power Company, Limited*, Second Phase, *ICJ Reports*, 1970, para 32. The ICJ has reaffirmed the idea in a number of subsequent cases.

[3] *Ibid*, para 34. See the discussion in T Meron, *Human Rights and Humanitarian Norms As Customary International Law* (Oxford, 1989), pp 192–201.

The thesis of this essay is that if international human rights law is based on general principles of State responsibility, it should be possible, empirically, to evidence that by a systematic examination of the principles against the terms of the Covenant and the jurisprudence of the Human Rights Committee (HRC). Similarly, if human rights law affects the evolution of the general principles of State responsibility, it should be possible to evidence that as well. In that context, it is notable that the ILC's Final Articles and the Commentary to them contain a number of references to human rights in general and to the Covenant and HRC in particular. This essay seeks to evidence the operation of the Final Articles by reference to the Covenant and the HRC's jurisprudence, in much the same way that the ILC's Commentary refers to the whole of international law. It is organised to follow the structure and language of the ILC's Articles, and evidence not just that the classic principles of State responsibility are alive and well, but that international human rights law has in fact played an important role in their continuing development.

Writing in 1989, Professor Meron stated that 'Unfortunately, the principles of State responsibility have often remained *terra incognita* for human rights lawyers'.[4] That was a strange but true state of affairs. It was a strange position for human rights lawyers to have reached given that some of the foundations of human rights law are traced from the system of diplomatic protection that was dominated by norms of State responsibility.[5] The early approaches of the International law Commission (ILC) to State responsibility were based on the system of diplomatic protection that was the forerunner of the modern human rights regimes.[6] Between 1957 and 1961 the ILC's Special Rapporteur Garcia Amador presented six reports on 'State Responsibility for Injuries to Aliens'.[7] However, the approach proved unacceptable and all of the subsequent Rapporteurs considered State responsibility in general. The '*terra incognita*' idea was true though. The details of quite how human rights fitted into the principles of State responsibility had proved problematic for successive Rapporteurs.[8] Even the redoubtable Professor Crawford, who sees problems merely as challenges,

[4] T Meron, 'State Responsibility for Violations of Human Rights', (1989) *Proceedings of the American Society of International Law*, p 373.
[5] See L Sohn and T Buergenthal (eds), *International Protection of Human Rights* (Indianapolis, 1974), pp 1–136.
[6] See R Lillich, *The Human Rights of Aliens in Contemporary International Law* (Manchester, 1984); and C Tiburcio, *The Human Rights of Aliens Under International and Comparative Law* (The Hague, 2001), Chapters II–III.
[7] See Vol II of the ILC Yearbooks from 1956–61.
[8] See J Crawford, *The ILC's Articles on State Responsibility: Introduction, Text and Commentaries* (Cambridge, 2002), pp 16–20 and pp 242–53 (on draft Art 19 and on serious breaches of obligations under peremptory norms of general international law). The ICJ has also found the issue problematic, see its much criticised decisions in the *South West Africa* cases, *ICJ Reports*, 1962, pp 425–33 and *ICJ Reports*, 1966, pp 325–42.

acknowledged the over-complexity, over-refinement, convoluted articles and levels of mystification in some of the ILC's texts.[9] Allott[10] and Higgins[11] had been severely critical of the ILC's approach to the project. Notwithstanding orthodoxy that State responsibility was fundamental to the discipline, the modern generation of public international lawyers in general, and international human rights lawyers in particular, were sceptical as to the meaning and relevance of State responsibility.

1. GENERAL CONCEPTS OF STATE RESPONSIBILITY AND THE COVENANT

The Covenant of 1966, which entered into force in 1976, is built on a classic structure of State responsibility.[12] Although Professor Nowak's *Commentary* on the Covenant[13] contains no index entry for State responsibility, there is clear reference to its principles.[14] Professor Ghandhi's text on The First Optional Protocol (OP1) has an index entry for State responsibility and twelve sub-categories.[15] The legal infrastructure of the Covenant is built on State responsibility. Only States can be parties.[16] Although the Preamble refers to the 'individual, having duties to other individuals and to the community to which he belongs', and being 'under a responsibility to

[9] Crawford, *ibid*, pp 16, 20, and 23.
[10] P Allott, 'State Responsibility and the Unmaking of International Law', 29 *Harvard International Law Journal* (1988), p 1.
[11] R Higgins, *Problems and Process* (Oxford, 1994), pp 146–68. For assessments of the Final ILC Articles, see 'Symposium: The ILC's State Responsibility Articles', 96 *American Journal of International Law* (2002), pp 773–890; and 'Symposium: Assessing the Work of the International Law Commission on State Responsibility', 13 *European Journal of International Law* (2002), pp 1037–56.
[12] Indeed, that is one of the reasons why international human rights law has been critiqued by feminist scholars, see C Chinkin and H Charlesworth, *The Boundaries of International Law: A Feminist Analysis* (Manchester, 2000); C Chinkin, 'A Critique of the Public/Private Dimension', 10 *European Journal of International Law* (1999), p 387; and R Cook (ed), *Human Rights for Women* (Philadelphia, 1994) (especially the essays by Charlesworth, Romany, Copelon, An-Na'im, Cook, Roth and Fitzpatrick).
[13] M Nowak, *UN Covenant on Civil and Political Rights: CCPR Commentary* (Kehl, 1993).
[14] Eg it is specifically discussed in relation to OP1, Nowak, *ibid*, pp 653–56. I have submitted elsewhere that 'The approach of the HRC is to apply the general international law rules of State responsibility', D McGoldrick, *The Human Rights Committee* (Oxford, 1991), p 169 in the context of *ratione personae* under OP1. In *Avsar v Turkey*, Application no 25657/94, the European Court of Human Rights stated that, '[r]esponsibility under the Convention is based on its own provisions which are to be interpreted and applied on the basis of the objectives of the Convention and in light of the relevant principles of international law' (10 July 2001, para 284).
[15] PR Ghandhi, *The HRC and the Right of Individual Communication* (Dartmouth, 1998). If asked, Members of the HRC and academic commentators would doubtless accept that they use the concepts of State responsibility almost unconsciously. At the October 2002 conference on which this book is based, Professor Crawford stated that, 'the whole of human rights is founded on the law of state responsibility' (authors' notes).
[16] See Art 48 Covenant.

strive for the promotion and observance of the rights recognized in the Present Covenant', the Covenant only expressly establishes obligations for States parties.[17] Only States parties can be responsible for violations of the Covenant.[18] The Covenant established three implementation mechanisms. Each of them are operated by the HRC:

1. A mandatory system of State reporting under Article 40. States report on the measures they have adopted to give effect to the rights in the Covenant. The HRC considers the report and engages in a constructive dialogue with a State party. A State may consult with NGO's about its report and NGO's may submit parallel critical reports that members will receive. Nonetheless, it is the State's report that is the key focus and it is on the basis of the report and the dialogue that the HRC will adopt its Concluding Observations.
2. An optional inter-State complaint mechanism (Articles 41–2). This can only be invoked by a State party which itself has made the necessary declaration accepting the HRC's competence to receive such a complaint. The mechanism has never been used.[19]
3. An optional individual petition system in the First Optional Protocol (OP1). This can only be invoked against a State party to the Covenant, which has also become a party to OP1. A complaint (called a communication) can only be submitted by an individual subject to the jurisdiction of a State party who claims to be a victim of a violation by that State party of a Covenant right.

As noted, only the first and third systems have functioned to date. Nonetheless, under each system it is necessary to apply the principles of State responsibility to establish whether a State party can be held responsible for an alleged violation of the Covenant. As noted above, the ILC Commentary uses a number of examples from the Covenant, OP1 and the jurisprudence of the HRC to illustrate the operation of the general rules of State responsibility set out in its Articles.[20]

The implementation mechanisms in the Covenant:

> apply without prejudice to the procedures prescribed in the field of human rights by or under the constituent instruments and the conventions of the

[17] Art 2 of the Covenant. Art 19(3) also refers to the 'special duties and responsibilities' that the exercise of the right of freedom of expression in Art 19(2) carries with it. See *Ross v Canada*, A/56/40, Vol II, p 69, para 11(6).

[18] See T Buergenthal, 'To Respect and to Ensure: State Obligation and Permissible Derogations', in L Henkin, *The International Bill of Rights—The Covenant on Civil and Political Rights* (New York, 1981), p 72, at p 77.

[19] See S Leckie, 'The Inter-State Complaints Procedure in International Human Rights Law: Hopeful Prospects or Wishful Thinking?', 10 *Human Rights Quarterly* (1988), p 249.

[20] See eg the ILC's commentaries to Arts 8, 14, 15, 20, 30, 33, 50 in Crawford, above n 8.

> United Nations and of the specialised agencies and shall not prevent the States parties to the present Covenant from having recourse to other procedures for settling a dispute in accordance with general or special international agreements in force.[21]

This suggests that the Covenant was not intended to be a self-contained regime.[22] This has been supported by State practice and UN practice.[23]

1.1. Primary and Secondary Rules

Fundamental to the ILC's Articles is the distinction between primary and secondary rules, as propounded by Special Rapporteur Ago.[24] One of the reasons why State responsibility appeared to remain as *terra incognita* for human rights lawyers is that their focus has been on the primary rules.[25] The Covenant provides the primary rules.[26] It established the obligations of States. Article 2 expresses the general obligation as an 'undertaking' by '[e]ach State party' to:

> respect and to ensure to all individuals within its territory and subject to its jurisdiction the rights recognised in the present Covenant, without distinction of any kind, such as race, colour, sex, language, religion, political or other opinion, national or social origin, property, birth or other status.

In addition there are a number of specific obligations. Article 2(2) contains an undertaking to introduce measures of domestic implementation where necessary to give effect to the Covenant. Article 2(3) contains three separate undertakings relating to remedies. Article 3 contains an undertaking to ensure the equal rights of men and women to the enjoyment of the rights set out in the Covenant. Articles 1 and 6–27 and OP2 set out the substantive rights for the purposes of the Covenant. The scope of the obligations of States parties is determined by the interplay of the language of the treaty, any valid and effective reservations, and the interpretation of the Covenant by the Human Rights Committee and by States parties.[27] The interpretation

[21] Art 44 of the Covenant.
[22] See B Simma, 'Self-Contained Regimes', 16 *Netherlands Yearbook of International Law* (1985), p 111.
[23] See M Kamminga, *Inter-State Accountability for Violations of Human Rights* (Philadelphia, 1992), pp 79–83, 186–90.
[24] See Ago's Second Report on State Responsibility, *Yearbook of the International Law Commission* (1970), Vol II, p 306; J Combeau and D Alland, ' "Primary" and "Secondary" Rules of State Responsibility: Categorising International Obligations' 16 *Netherlands Yearbook of International Law* (1985), p 81.
[25] See the essays by B Conforti (ch 8), M Craven (ch 7), and M Evans (ch 9) in this volume.
[26] So too does the Second Optional Protocol (OP2) to the Covenant on the death penalty.
[27] I leave aside the question of whether it is the HRC or only the States parties or both that have the power to interpret a treaty. In practice, the HRC has a critical role.

is developed under the dialogue with States parties, the HRC's Concluding Observations on State reports, the General Comments adopted by the HRC, and the HRC's decisions and views under OP1. The Covenant has been interpreted expansively by the HRC in relation to substantive rights. The rights are widely interpreted as to include positive obligations, for example to reduce infant mortality and to regulate private relations.[28] One area where human rights law and State responsibility might naturally seem to collide has been in respect of the right to an effective remedy. As the ILC sees it, remedies are a part of the secondary law of responsibility. However, in human rights law it is part of the primary law. Thus the 'right' to a remedy is found in Article 2 of the Covenant and in other regional human rights instruments.[29] The HRC,[30] the European Court of Human Rights[31] and the Inter-American Court of Human Rights[32] have all used this right to a remedy, alone or in conjunction with other rights, to hold the State responsible where it could not be established that the State itself was responsible for the violation of the substantive right, for example, to life or to security. The result has been a development of obligations to investigate, properly and effectively, alleged violations of human rights and to hold those responsible accountable.[33] The focus of human rights jurisprudence on the right to a remedy has not been accompanied by any attention on the responsibility of a State for failing to provide an effective remedy. For example, what is the appropriate remedy, in State responsibility terms, for a failure to provide a remedy?

An expansive approach has also been taken to the interpretation of procedural obligations such as the submission of State reports under Article 40 in the context of emergency situations and in the event of the dissolution of States,[34] and compliance with interim measures orders under OP1. The HRC has also asserted its competence to determine the validity and effect of reservations to the Covenant.[35] By contrast, the attention of the HRC and of human rights lawyers is rarely explicitly focused on

[28] See HRC's General Comment (GC) on Art 6.

[29] See D Shelton, *Remedies in International Human Rights Law* (Oxford, 1999); and D Shelton, 'Righting Wrongs: Reparations in the Articles on States Responsibility', 96 *American Journal of International Law* (2002), p 833.

[30] See McGoldrick, above n 14, pp 279–80, 285–87; GC 31 on Art 2 (adopted in March 2004); *Herrera Rubio v Columbia*, A/43/40, p 190.

[31] See A Mowbray, 'Duties of Investigation under the European Convention on Human Rights', 51 *International and Comparative Law Quarterly* (2002), p 437.

[32] *Velasquez Rodriquez v Honduras* case, Judgment, *Inter-Am Ct HR (Ser C)* No 4 (1988).

[33] See A/53/40, para 354 (concerning terrorist attacks in Algeria).

[34] See GC 26, text corresponding to n 112 below and *Weiss v Austria* (Apr 2003) (a failure to honour a request for interim measures amounted to a breach of a State party's obligations under OP1).

[35] See D McGoldrick, 'Approaches to the assertion of international jurisdiction: the Human Rights Committee', in P Capp, M Evans and S Konstadinidis, (eds,) *Asserting Jurisdiction* (Oxford, 2003).

State responsibility. The ILC Articles are virtually never explicitly mentioned in HRC discussions[36] or for that matter in those of other human rights treaty organs.[37] There is relatively little academic literature on State responsibility in the human rights context, outside of discussion of the ILC draft Articles.[38]

A second reason for the *terra incognita* of State responsibility for human rights lawyers arguably lay in the ILC's work of the idea of the 'criminal' responsibility of States. This may seem counter-intuitive given that, under its famous draft Article 19 (2), two of the examples where criminal responsibility could arise were in the human rights context, namely,

> (b) a serious breach of an international obligation of essential importance for safeguarding the right of self-determination of peoples ...
> (c) a serious breach of an international obligation of essential importance for safeguarding the human being, such as those prohibiting slavery, genocide and apartheid.

Given the attention and controversy that the proposed inclusion, and the subsequent deletion, of draft Article 19 attracted,[39] it is something of a paradox to then say that State responsibility for human rights is *terra incognita*. Nonetheless, it may be true. The article diverted attention away from the normality of State responsibility for breaches of international human rights obligations. In its Final Articles the ILC dropped its references to State criminal responsibility and so does not recognise the existence of any distinction between State 'crimes' and State 'delicts'. In its practice the HRC has not sought to assert any such distinction. Neither the inter-State mechanism under Articles 41–2 nor the OP1 are in any way limited to serious breaches of peremptory norms. The former extends to any obligation under the Covenant.[40] OP1 extends to any 'right' in the Covenant.[41]

[36] Cf below nn 86 and 88.

[37] There was a brief discussion in CERD in relation to the term 'reparation', see CERD/C/SR (1998), p 1269, paras 31–48.

[38] See Meron, above n 3; B Ramcharan, 'State Responsibility for Violations of Human Rights Treaties', in B Cheng and E Brown (eds), *Contemporary Problems of International Law: Essays in Honour of George Schwarzenberger* (London, 1988), p 242; Kamminga, above n 23; A Randelzhofer and C Tomuschat (eds), *State Responsibility and the Individual; Reparation in Instances of Grave Violations of Human Rights* (The Hague, 1999).

[39] See J Weiler *et al* (eds), *International Crimes of State: A Critical Analysis of the ILC's Draft Article 19 on State Responsibility* (Berlin, 1988); N Jorgensen, *The Responsibility of States for International Crimes* (Oxford, 2000); Crawford, above n 8, pp 16–20. The US and the UK had been heavily critical of the idea of criminal responsibility.

[40] Art 41(1) of the Covenant. Thus the inter-State mechanism may even cover procedural or institutional obligations, see Nowak, above n 13, pp 591–92.

[41] Art 1, OP1. The HRC has taken the view that Art 1 of the Covenant is not an individual right but that it can be taken account of in interpreting other rights in the Covenant, eg Art 25.

2. INTERNATIONALLY WRONGFUL ACTS

In the language of the ILC's Articles, a violation of the Covenant is an 'internationally wrongful act' for which a State party is responsible. The 'wrongful act' can be an act which violates a Covenant right: for example, an arbitrary deprivation of liberty contrary to Article 5 of the Covenant. The 'wrongful act' can also be an omission that violates a Covenant right. The omission could, for example, be in not providing an effective remedy for violation of a Covenant right (Article 2(3)).[42] In *Dermit Barbato v Uruguay*[43] the HRC held that the:

> inescapable conclusion is that in all the circumstances the Uruguayan authorities either by act or omission were responsible for not taking measures to protect his life, as required by Article 6(1) of the Covenant.[44]

In *Sanjuán Arévalo v Colombia*[45] the HRC found a violation of Article 9 of the Covenant in the State's failure to take appropriate measures to ensure an individuals right to security under Article 9 of the Covenant.[46] In addition, the HRC has repeatedly stated that the Covenant imposes positive obligations on State parties.[47] A State that does not take positive measures will, in certain circumstances, commit a wrongful act. The positive obligations can extend to the legal regulation and control of the activities of private individuals and non-State bodies.[48]

2.1. Subjective and Objective Responsibility

The ILC's Articles do not adopt the language of subjective and objective elements of responsibility.[49] In one decision, *Pinkey v Canada*,[50] the HRC used the language of 'objective responsibility'. P's appeal against conviction could not be heard for 34 months because the transcript of the original trial was not made available. P complained about the delay in holding the hearing. The HRC held that 'the authorities of British Colombia must be considered

[42] See above n 29.
[43] A/38/40, p 124.
[44] *Ibid,* para 9.2.
[45] CCPR/C/37/D/181/1984; A/45/40, Vol II, p 31.
[46] See also *Delgado Paez v Colombia*, A/45/40, Vol II, p 43 (failure to take measures against non-State actors); and *Chongwe v Zambia*, A/56/40, Vol II, p 137.
[47] See S Joseph, J Schultz and M Castan, *The International Covenant on Civil and Political Rights—Cases, Materials, and Commentary* (Oxford, 2000), pp 21–22.
[48] See *Nahlik v Austria*, below n 93. See generally A Clapham, *Human Rights in the Private Sphere* (Oxford, 1993).
[49] See Commentary to Art 2 in Crawford, above n 8, pp 81–85.
[50] A/37/40, p 101.

objectively responsible'.[51] The ILC's Articles lay down no general rule or presumptions as to fault, negligence etc. The appropriate standards are drawn from the text of the Covenant as interpreted by the HRC and by the States parties.

Under ILC Article 3:

> The characterization of an act of a State as internationally wrongful is governed by international law. Such characterization is not affected by the characterization of the same act as lawful by internal law.

The HRC has rejected a State's defence that the measures it had taken were in compliance with its constitution or national legislation. For example, in *Waldman v Canada*[52] the HRC began by noting that the fact that a distinction at issue was enshrined in the Canadian Constitution did not render it reasonable and objective. The distinction had been made in 1867 to protect the Roman Catholics in Ontario. The material before the HRC did not show that members of the Roman Catholic community or any identifiable section of that community were now in a disadvantaged position compared to those members of the Jewish community that wished to secure the education of their children in religious schools. Accordingly, Canada's argument that the preferential treatment of Roman Catholic schools was non-discriminatory because of its Constitutional obligation was rejected. In a number of cases, Uruguay and Colombia unsuccessfully sought to rely on their State security and impunity laws as a defence to violations of the Covenant.[53] In some cases, the violation lies not in the internal law per se, but in its discriminatory non-application to, for example, aliens. An example was *Gueye v France* where the pensions paid to retired soldiers from the French Army who were of Senegalese nationality were lower than those paid to retired soldiers of French nationality.[54] Compliance with national law can be part of an international human rights standard: for example, that contained in Article 9 of the Covenant on arbitrary deprivation of liberty.[55]

The same point, that State responsibility must be determined by reference to international law, also applies if national law is invoked as a justification by a State for its failure to comply with obligations of cessation and reparation.[56] In *Waldman v Canada*,[57] the Government of Canada informed the HRC that matters of education fell under the

[51] *Ibid*, para 22.
[52] A/55/40, Vol II, p 86.
[53] *De Guerrero v Colombia*, A/37/40, p 137, paras 14.5–14.6.
[54] A/44/40, p 189.
[55] See *A v Australia*, A/52/40, Vol II, p 125.
[56] ILC Art 32.
[57] A/55/40, Vol II, p 86.

exclusive jurisdiction of the provinces. The Government of Ontario had communicated that it has no plans to extend funding to private religious schools or to the parents of children that attended such schools, and that it intended to adhere fully to its constitutional obligation to fund Roman Catholic schools.[58] The HRC found Canada to be in violation of the ICCPR.

2.2. Responsibility of States

Under its implementation mechanisms the HRC is concerned with State responsibility. For example, under OP1 the HRC is only competent to consider alleged violations by a State party to the Covenant that has also become a party to OP1 (Article 1 OP). If a State validly denounces, terminates, suspends, or withdraws from the Covenant or OP1 the HRC loses its competence in respect of that State under OP1.[59] Communications have been submitted concerning States that have not been party to the Covenant or the OP. Under the HRC's Rules of Procedure, the HRC do not receive such communications. For a person to claim to be a 'victim' of a violation of a right protected by the Covenant, he or she must show either that an act or an omission of a State party has already adversely affected his or her enjoyment of such right, or that such an effect is imminent, for example on the basis of existing law and/or judicial or administrative decision or practice.[60]

The provisions of the Covenant extend to all parts of federal States 'without any limitations or exceptions'.[61] The responsibility of the State for the acts of a federal unit is well established—*Toonen v Australia*,[62] *Waldman v Canada*.[63] The State remains responsible for remedying the violation whatever the internal division of powers. This was an issue in *Waldman v Canada* where the Federal government claimed that all it could do was pass the decision to the provincial authorities and the provincial authorities refused to comply.[64] However, the existence of different laws and procedures in the different jurisdictions of a federal State will not necessarily raise an issue for discrimination under the Covenant.[65]

[58] A/56/40, para 187.
[59] There is no denunciation clause in the Covenant although one was considered. There is a denunciation clause in OP1 (Art 12). Where a state has denounced OP1 the denunciation becomes effective three months after the receipt of notification by the Secretary-General (Art 12(2) OP1). Until that date, the State continues to be subject to the application of OP1, see eg, *Glenroy Francis et al v Trinidad and Tobago*, A/57/40, Vol II, p 206, para 8.
[60] *EW et al v Netherlands*, CCPR/C/47/D/429/1990, para 6.4.
[61] Art 50 Covenant.
[62] A/49/40, Vol II, p 226.
[63] A/55/40, Vol II, p 86.
[64] *Ibid.*
[65] See *Hesse v Australia*, A/57/40, Vol II, p 364 (para 4.2.) (H had not substantiated for the purposes of admissibility that differences in the statute of limitations in different parts of a federal State would as such raise an issue under Art 26.)

The provisions of OP1 similarly extend to all parts of federal States without limitations or exceptions. The non-applicability of OP1 to any area within the jurisdiction of a State party to OP1 'cannot be assumed without any express indication (reservation/declaration) to that effect'.[66] In *Wan Kuok Koi v Portugal*[67] a majority of the HRC took the view that there was no such express indication on Portugal's accession to OP1 in 1983.[68] OP1 therefore extended to Macau which until 1999 was a territory under Chinese sovereignty and Portuguese administration. The territory then reverted to Chinese administration.[69]

States parties are liable for their own violations. They are not generally liable for violations of the Covenant by other States.[70] The implementation mechanisms cannot be used to hold international institutions responsible for their international acts. In *HvdP v Netherlands*[71] the author was an international civil servant with the European Patent Office (EPO) based in Munich, West Germany. He claimed that he was a victim of discrimination in the promotion practices of the EPO and, moreover, that the appeals procedures within the EPO did not constitute an effective remedy. The author, a national of the Netherlands, brought the communication against the Netherlands. He claimed that the HRC was competent to consider the case on the basis that five States parties to the EPO (France, Italy, Luxembourg, the Netherlands and Sweden) were also parties to OP1 and that the 'EPO, though a public body common to the Contracting States, constitutes a body exercising Dutch public authority'. The HRC took the view that the author had no claim under OP1 on the basis that:

> The author's grievances ... concern the recruitment policies of an international organization, which cannot, in any way, be construed as coming within the jurisdiction of the Netherlands or of any other State party to the International Covenant on Civil and Political Rights and the Optional Protocol thereto.[72]

[66] *Wan Kuok Koi v Portugal*, A/57/40, Vol II, p 333, para 6.3.
[67] *Ibid.*
[68] Three members of the HRC specifically dissented from this aspect of the decision. The communication was determined to be inadmissible by a majority of the HRC because domestic remedies had not been exhausted at the time of submission of the communication. When domestic remedies had been exhausted the author was no longer subject to the jurisdiction of Portugal because the territory was then under Chinese administration.
[69] UK practice is that extension of international treaties to UK British Overseas Territories only takes place by an express extension. See D McGoldrick and N Parker, 'The United Kingdom Perspective on the International Covenant on Civil and Political Rights', in D Harris and S Joseph (eds), *The ICCPR and UK Law* (Oxford, 1995), p 69.
[70] See *Kindler v Canada*, A/48/40, p 138.
[71] A/42/40, p 185.
[72] *Ibid*, para 3.2. *Cf Matthews v UK*, European Court of Human Rights (1999) (breach of Art 3 of Protocol 1 of ECHR by UK relating to an Act of the European Communities on elections to the European Parliament).

The ILC's Articles are 'without prejudice to any question of the responsibility under international law of an international organization, or of any State for the conduct of an international organization'.[73]

2.3. Responsibility of State Organs

Under ILC Article 4 (1):

> The conduct of any State organ shall be considered an act of that State under international law, whether the organ exercises legislative, executive, judicial or any other functions, whatever position it holds in the organization of the State, and whatever its character as an organ of the central government or of a territorial unit of the State.

An organ includes any person or entity that has that status in accordance with the internal law of the State (Article 4(2)). The human rights jurisprudence here is orthodox. Violations of the Covenant have been attributed to central government and its legislature—*Mauritian Women case*,[74] *Lovelace case*,[75] *Kitok v Sweden*[76]; federal governments—*Toonen v Australia*[77]; municipal authorities—*Waldman v Canada*[78]; courts, and administrative and judicial authorities—*Hermoza v Peru*[79]; judges—*Wright v Jamaica* 349/89[80]; court administrations—*Pinkey v Canada*[81]; police and security forces—*Guerrero v Colombia*[82]; and immigration, and extradition and deportation officials—*A v Australia*.[83] When State agents are responsible for human rights violations, such as extra-judicial executions, they should be tried and punished.[84] The obligation in Article 2(3)(a) to provide an effective remedy applies, 'notwithstanding that the violation has been

[73] Art 57 of ILC's Articles. The ILC is considering 'The Responsibility of International Organizations', see UN Doc A/58/10 (2003), pp 29–49.
[74] 1 S D (1981) p 67.
[75] A/36/40, p 166.
[76] A/43/40, p 221 (the HRC rejected the view that the case was really a dispute between Kitok and other members of the Sami community).
[77] A/49/40, Vol II, p 226.
[78] A/55/40, Vol II, p 86.
[79] A/44/40, p 200.
[80] *Glenroy Francis et al v Trinidad and Tobago*, A/57/40, Vol II, p 206, para 5.5 (in the absence of any argument by the authors that responsibility for the delay in lodging an appeal could be imputed to the State, the HRC was unable to find that there was a violation of the Covenant).
[81] A/37/40, p 101.
[82] A/37/40, p 137 See also CCPR/C/79/Add 99 (on the behaviour of Belgian soldiers in Somalia under the *aegis* of UNOSOM II).
[83] See above n 55.
[84] Concluding Observations of the HRC on Niger, CCPR/C/79/Add 17 (1993), para 7. State responsibility under the Covenant in relation to torture is wider than that under the UN Convention Against Torture (CAT) because Art 1 of CAT covers only torture etc 'by or at the instigation of or with the consent or acquiescence of a public official or other person acting in

committed by persons acting in an official capacity'.[85] The HRC has had to consider the issue of whether decrees issued by religious authorities engaged the responsibility of the State.[86]

2.4. Jurisdiction and Responsibility

For a State party to the Covenant the obligation under Article 2 applies 'to individuals within its territory and subject to its jurisdiction'. Therefore, although it is not confined to nationals of the State concerned, the scope of the obligations are limited. If the individuals concerned are not within the territory or subject to the jurisdiction of the State party then no responsibility arises under the Covenant.[87] The lack of responsibility under a particular human rights treaty does not mean that there is no State responsibility. It simply means that the responsibility can only arise where the relevant primary law applies extra-territorially, for example, international humanitarian law or the rules on the use of force between States.

2.5. Persons or Entities Exercising Governmental Authority

ILC Article 5 deals with the conduct of a person or entity which is not an organ of the State under ILC Article 4, but which is empowered by the law of that State to exercise elements of the governmental authority. That conduct is considered an act of the State under international law, provided the person or entity is acting in that capacity in the particular instance. The HRC has dealt with para-statal and private entities. States have been asked about compliance with Covenant standards where private firms run prisons and are therefore responsible for the detention of individuals.

an official capacity'. See R McCorquodale and R La Forgia, 'Taking off the blindfolds: torture by non-state actors', 1 *Human Rights Law Review* (2001), p 189.

[85] In the context of OP1, individuals must also satisfy the 'victim' requirement.
[86] On the *fatwa* against Salman Rushdie, see CCPR/SR/1196, pp 1230–31, 1251–53. The Committee on Economic Social and Cultural Rights ('CESR') had stated that in the case of a *fatwa* such as that issued by the religious authorities, State responsibility was incurred when the State did not take whatever measures were available to it to remove the clear threats to the rights applicable, see CCPR/C/SR 1253 (1993), para 25 (Herndl). The Concluding Observations of the CESR are in E/C 12/1993/17, p 7 (1993).
[87] See D McGoldrick, 'The Extra-territorial Application of the International Covenant on Civil and Political Rights', in M Kamminga and F Comans, (eds,) *The Extra-territorial Application of Human Rights Treaties* (Antwerp, 2003); *Bankovic and Others v Belgium and 16 other NATO States* (No 52207/99), ECHR 12 Dec 2001, 41 *ILM* (2002), p 517; and *US v Duarte-Acero*, 296 F 3d 1277 (11th Circuit) (The ICCPR did not regulate the extra-territorial conduct of US agents. The decision is criticised by D Sloss, 97 *American Journal of International Law* (2003), p 411.)

For example, in its Concluding Observations on New Zealand the HRC stated that it:

> remains concerned about whether the practice of privatisation, in an area where the State is responsible for protecting the rights of persons whom it has deprived of their liberty, effectively meets the obligations of a State party under the Covenant and its own accountability for any violations.[88]

The HRC has also expressed concern to States about governmental functions being exercised by paramilitary groups.[89]

The approach of the HRC is to apply the general international law rules of State responsibility. Inevitably, the HRC had to deal with questions concerning the extent of the responsibility of a State party for acts or omissions committed 'within its jurisdiction' (Article 1 OP) but committed by individuals, companies, corporations, or other bodies. A delegation of State functions to an autonomous organ does not relieve the State of its obligations. In *BdB v Netherlands*[90] the State party expressed doubts as to whether an action by an Industrial Insurance Board, composed of employers and employees, could be attributed to its State organs when the Boards operate independently and there is no way in which the State party's authorities could influence concrete decisions.[91] The HRC observed that, 'a State party is not relieved of its obligations under the Covenant when some of its functions are delegated to other autonomous organs'. This observation was repeated in *Lindgren et al v Sweden*,[92] where the education decisions being challenged had been taken at the municipal level.

In *Nahlik v Austria*,[93] N alleged discrimination as between different employees in relation to pension benefits from his former employer, the Social Insurance Board. The distinction at issue was a consequence of the implementation of a collective agreement between the Social Insurance Board and its employees. Austria submitted that such collective agreements were contracts based on private law and exclusively within the discretion of the contracting parties. The State party had no influence and there was no

[88] CCPR/CO/75/NZL, para 13. After noting that the Lebanese Government relied heavily on the private sector and NGO's for children's needs the Chairperson of the Committee on the Rights of the Child ('CRC') asked what the Government's philosophy was with regard to State responsibility, CRC/C/SR 751, para 18 (2002), reply at paras 27–28.
[89] See CCPR/C/SR 1346 (on Sri Lanka); SR 1397 (on Haiti); A/52/40, paras 278 and 294 (on Colombia); A/53/40, para 356 (on Algeria). More generally see L Zegveld, *The Accountability of Armed Opposition Groups in International Law* (Cambridge, 2002); K Altiparmak, 'Responsibility for the violation of human rights by non-state armed groups' (PhD D thesis, University of Leeds, 2002).
[90] A/44/40, p 286 (para 6.5).
[91] *Ibid*, para 4.7.
[92] A/46/40, p 253.
[93] A/51/40, p 259.

violation by a State party.[94] N disputed the State's contention and argued that the violation was attributable to the State. The HRC rejected Austria's argument in robust terms,

> The Committee observes that under articles 2 and 26 of the Covenant, the State party is under an obligation to ensure that all individuals within its territory and subject to its jurisdiction are free from discrimination, whether it occurs within the public sphere or among private parties in the quasi-public sector of, for example, employment. The Committee further notes that the collective agreement in issue in the instant case is regulated by law and does not enter into force except on confirmation by the Federal Minister for Labour and Social Affairs. Moreover, the Committee notes that the collective agreement concerns the staff of the Social Insurance Board, an institution of public law implementing public policy.[95]

This was a very significant decision. If 'employment' is in the 'quasi-public sector' then so are a number of other areas. The 'quasi-public sector' was not defined, but the criteria for inclusion appears very wide, viz that the agreement was 'regulated by law', concerned an institution of public law implementing public policy and that the agreement only entered into force on confirmation by a Government Minister.

The issue of governmental confirmation arose but was not decided in *FGG v Netherlands*[96] in which a private Dutch shipping company, in response to declining economic circumstances, dismissed 223 foreign sailors but not one Dutch sailor. In accordance with the governing employment law, the responsible State labour office approved the dismissals. The Netherlands argued that there was no violation by the State. The communication was declared inadmissible for failure to exhaust domestic remedies.

2.6. Failure to Regulate Private Relations

In *Cziklin v Canada*,[97] C argued that Article 26 was violated because his employer, Canadian Pacific Railways, could have reasonably accommodated his physical injuries and that the lack of such accommodation constituted discrimination on grounds of physical handicap. CPR was a private corporation, the capital stock of which was owned by private parties. Canada argued that CPR was not a part or agent of the Government of Canada or of any other components of the Canadian State, such as a provincial or

[94] The argument was one of inadmissibility under Art 1 OP, but the principle is the same for Art 2.
[95] A/51/40, p 259 (para 8.2).
[96] A/42/40, p 180.
[97] A/54/40, Vol II, p 348.

territorial government. Therefore, the actions of CPR could not be attributed to Canada or engage the responsibility of the Government of Canada under the Covenant.[98] The HRC did not respond to the point because the communication was inadmissible for failure to exhaust domestic remedies.

In its Concluding Observations on Hong Kong in 1995 the HRC noted the need for protection against private parties,

> that Section 7 of the Bill of Rights Ordinance provides that 'the Ordinance binds only the Government and all public authorities; and any person acting on behalf of the Government or a public authority'. The Committee emphasizes in this regard that under the Covenant a State party does not only have an obligation to protect individuals against violations by Government officials but also by private parties. It thus notes with deep concern the absence of legislation providing effective protection against violations of Covenant rights by non-governmental actors.[99]

It is important to differentiate a State's own responsibility from that of its responsibility for the acts of private bodies exercising governmental functions. A State is not generally responsible for the conduct of a legal aid lawyer 'unless it was or should have been manifest to the judge that the lawyer's behaviour was incompatible with the interests of justice'.[100] The same standard appears to be applied in relation to the actions of private legal counsel in advising and representing individuals.[101] However, State responsibility was asserted when counsel abandoned all grounds of appeal and the court did not ascertain that this was in compliance with the wishes of the accused[102] and when counsel was absent during the judge's summing up.[103] In these cases a State's own responsibility is at issue. It is not being held responsible for the failure of the private lawyer.

2.7. Conduct of Organs Placed at the Disposal of a State by Another State

Under ILC Article 6,

> The conduct of an organ placed at the disposal of a State by another State shall be considered an act of the former State under international law if the organ is acting in the exercise of elements of the governmental authority of the State at whose disposal it is placed.

[98] *Ibid*, para 4.7.
[99] A/51/40, Vol II, para 56.
[100] *Henry v Jamaica*, A/53/40, Vol II, para 7.4.
[101] See *Desmond Taylor v Jamaica*, A/53/40, Vol II, p 174 (para 6.2).
[102] See *Trevor Collins v Jamaica*, A/48/40, Vol II, p 85 (para 8.2), distinguished on the facts in *Robinson v Jamaica*, A/55/40, Vol II, p 116 (paras 10.5–10.6).
[103] *Brown v Jamaica*, A/54/40, Vol II, p 260 (para 6.8).

In accordance with this, decisions of the Privy Council on appeal from an independent Commonwealth State engage the responsibility of that State. The HRC has had to deal with a substantial number of communications from States that have retained the possibility of appeal to the Privy Council.[104]

2.8. Excess of Authority or Contravention of Instructions

Under Article 7 of the ILC's Articles,

> The conduct of an organ of a State or of a person or entity empowered to exercise elements of the governmental authority shall be considered an act of the State under international law if the organ, person or entity acts in that capacity, even if it exceeds its authority or contravenes instructions.

The HRC has dealt with a number of cases concerning alleged murder, torture and mistreatment by State officials.[105]

2.9. Conduct Directed or Controlled by a State

ILC Article 8 deals with conduct directed or controlled by a State.[106] In *Hertzberg and Others v Finland*[107] the authors argued that the Finnish authorities, including organs of the State-controlled Finnish Broadcasting Corporation (FBC), had interfered with their right to freedom of information and expression in Article 19 of the Covenant by, '[i]mposing sanctions against participants in, or censuring, radio and television programmes dealing with homosexuality'.[108] Criminal charges under the Finnish Penal Code had been brought against the editor of a programme dealing with homosexuality. In its final views the HRC stated that it started from:

> The premise that the State party is responsible for actions of the Finnish Broadcasting Company (FBC), in which the State holds a dominant stake (90 per cent) and which is placed under specific government control.[109]

[104] A new Caribbean Court of Appeal in 2002 will reduce this possibility, but presumably the decisions of that court will remain the responsibility of the relevant State.
[105] See McGoldrick, above n 14, ch. 10 on Arts 7 and 10(1) of the Covenant.
[106] See A de Hoogh, 'Articles 4 and 8 of the 2001 ILC Articles on State Responsibility, the *Tadic* Case and the Attribution of Acts of Bosnian Serb Authorities to the Federal Republic of Yugoslavia', 72 *British Yearbook of International Law* (2001), p 255.
[107] A/37/40, p 161. The decision is referenced in fn 175 of the ILC's Commentary (Crawford, above n 8, p 113.)
[108] *Ibid*, para 2.1.
[109] *Ibid*, para 9.1.

On these facts the finding of State responsibility was not too difficult a decision for the HRC. An alternative approach would have been to rest the responsibility of Finland on the legislative acts under which prosecutions had been brought. That was the approach taken by the European Court of Human Rights ('ECHR') in the *Young, James and Webster Cases.*[110] If, in a particular case, it proves impossible to hold the State party responsible for the acts concerned because it does not exercise sufficient direction or control, the possibility remains that the State party's responsibility can be based on its failure to secure the rights in the Covenant (Article 2(1) of the Covenant) or to provide an effective remedy for the violation of rights (Article 2(3) of the Covenant).

2.10. Conduct of an Insurrectional or Other Movement

ILC Article 10 provides that the conduct of insurrectional movements—which become the new government of a State or which succeeds in establishing a new State in part of the territory of a pre-existing State or in a territory under its administration—shall be considered an act of that State under international law. In both cases the conduct is considered as an act of the State under international law. In a challenging piece of jurisprudence, the HRC has strongly asserted that there is automatic succession to the human rights obligations in the Covenant when a new State is established in part of the territory of a pre-existing State. The principle of automatic succession to human rights obligations was developed and applied in the context of the dissolution of the Federal Republic of Yugoslavia and the USSR.[111] The HRC's practice was encapsulated in General Comment 26 on *'Issues relating to the continuity of obligations to the International Covenant on Civil and Political Rights'*,[112] which was, in part, a response to the purported denunciation of the Covenant by the Democratic People's Republic of Korea in July 1997. GC 26 provides:

> 1. The International Covenant on Civil and Political Rights does not contain any provision regarding its termination and does not provide for denunciation or withdrawal. Consequently, the possibility of termination, denunciation or withdrawal must be considered in the light of applicable rules of customary international law which are reflected in the Vienna

[110] *Young, James and Webster v UK*, 44 *ECHR, Series A*, (1981), paras 48–49. Accordingly, the ECHR did not examine whether, as the applicants had argued, the State might also be responsible on the ground that it was the employer or that British Rail was under its control. In *Love v Australia* (April 2003) the HRC noted that it did not have to consider the issue of whether the State was directly responsible for the actions of a State owned airline.
[111] See I Boerefijn, *The Reporting Procedure Under The Covenant on Civil and Political Rights Covenant on Civil and Political Rights*, (Antwerp, 1999), Ch XIII.
[112] A/53/40, Annex VII, adopted on 8 Dec 1997.

Convention on the Law of Treaties. On this basis, the Covenant is not subject to denunciation or withdrawal unless it is established that the parties intended to admit the possibility of denunciation or withdrawal or a right to do so is implied from the nature of the treaty.

...

3. Furthermore, it is clear that the Covenant is not the type of treaty which, by its nature, implies a right of denunciation ....
4. **The rights enshrined in the Covenant belong to the people living in the territory of the State party.** The Human Rights Committee has consistently taken the view, as evidenced by its long-standing practice, that once the people are accorded the protection of the rights under the Covenant, **such protection devolves with territory and continues to belong to them, notwithstanding change in government of the State party, including dismemberment in more than one State or State succession or any subsequent action of the State party designed to divest them of the rights guaranteed by the Covenant.**
5. The Committee is therefore firmly of the view that international law does not permit a State which has ratified or acceded or succeeded to the Covenant to denounce it or withdraw from it. (*emphases added*)

The HRC applied this approach to Hong Kong so that China succeeded to the reporting obligation under Article 40 in relation to Hong Kong.[113] It is not clear if China agreed with this view. China was not a party to the Covenant and it was not included in the list from China to the UN Secretary-General regarding treaties which China had agreed would continue to apply to the Hong Kong Special Administrative Region (HKSAR). However, Annex I, Section XIII of the UK-China Joint Declaration on the Question of Hong Kong[114] provided that the 'provisions of (the Covenant) as applied to Hong Kong shall remain in force'. China and the UK reiterated this in separate notes. The matter was still not free from doubt. The UK took the view that the 'provisions' included the reporting obligation in Article 40. A narrower interpretation would have been that the provisions referred only to the rights but not to the reporting obligations. For a long period there was a studied ambiguity as to which interpretation China accepted. The Basic Law of Hong Kong provided that the provisions of the Covenant 'shall be implemented through the laws of the HKSAR'. China signed the Covenant in October 1998 and was expected to ratify in due course. However, it did not do so (and has not done so as of 1 September 2003). Nonetheless, it reported on Hong Kong in 1999 and

[113] See CCPR/C/SR 1803–SR 1805; A/C 3/51/SR25; N Jayawickrama, 'Human Rights in Hong Kong—The Continued Applicability of the International Covenants', 25 *Hong Kong Law Journal* (1995), p 171; J Chan, 'State Succession to Human Rights Treaties: Hong Kong and the International Covenant on Civil and Political Rights', 45 *International and Comparative Law Quarterly* (1996), p 928.

[114] 33 *ILM* (1994), p 1366.

this was considered by the HRC in 1999. For the HRC the legal obligation to do this was founded in the automatic succession of the obligations from the UK to China.[115] For China it was founded in the Joint Declaration with the UK. The end result is the same but the legal basis is different.

The GA simply 'took note' of GC26. The UN Human Rights Commission was supportive of the HRC's approach, as have been the chairs of the human rights treaty bodies. The other treaty organs have followed the same practice. Some writers have supported the view of the HRC.[116] Aust considers that there is no authority for this view.[117] In contrast with the view of the HRC, he asserts that the:

> sounder view is that in so far as a human rights treaty represents rules of customary international law a successor State will be bound by those rules, but only as a matter of customary international law.

In support of this he cited the judgment of the ICJ in the *Genocide Convention (Bosnia v FRY) (Preliminary Objections)* case in which it concluded that the FRY was a party to the Genocide Convention because it had declared its intention to remain bound by the treaties to which the Socialist Federal Republic of Yugoslavia had been a party.[118] Thus it was the consent of the new State that was the basis of its obligations. If Aust's view is correct, then among the practical consequences would be that, where the new State's consent was not forthcoming, the State would not be a 'State party'—it would not be permitted to attend the meetings of States parties, nominate members of the HRC. A member of the HRC who was a national of a non-State party would arguably no longer be entitled to retain their membership of the HRC. No further communications under OP1 could be considered by the HRC from that State as they would all be inadmissible, and no further State reports could be considered under Article 40. Aust's reliance on the ICJ decision alone is not convincing. An alternative argument is that the succession declaration by the FRY simply meant that the ICJ did not have to address the issue of automatic succession to human

[115] Concluding Observations of HRC on China: Hong Kong, CCPR/C/79/Add 117, para 3.

[116] See R Mullerson, 'The Continuity and Succession of States, by Reference to the Former USSR and Yugoslavia', 42 *International and Comparative Law Quarterly* (1993), p 473; M Kamminga, 'State Succession in Respect of Human Rights Treaties', 7 *European Journal of International Law* (1996), p 469. See also the Report of the Secretary-General on 'Succession of States in Respect of Human Rights Treaties', 2 *International Human Rights Reports* (1995), pp 507–09.

[117] A Aust, *A Modern Treaty Law and Practice* (Cambridge, 2000), pp 305–31, at p 308, citing M Shaw, 'State Succession Revisited', *Finnish Yearbook of International Law* (1994), p 34; Kamminga, *ibid*.

[118] *ICJ Reports*, 1994, p 4, paras 17, 23. He also refers to the separate opinion of Judge Weeramantry on automatic succession, *ibid*, p 645 and M Wood, 'Participation by the Former Yugoslav States in the United Nations and in Multilateral Treaties', *Max Planck Yearbook of United Nations Law* (1997), pp 231–58.

rights treaties. The issue could have been directly addressed by the ICJ in its decision on Yugoslavia's request for a revision of the judgment of 1 July 1996 by which the ICJ declared that it had jurisdiction to adjudicate the case, based on Article IX of the Genocide Convention. Yugoslavia contended that a it had become clear that, before 1 November 2000 (the date on which it was admitted as a new Member of the United Nations), Yugoslavia did not continue the international legal and political personality of the Socialist Federal Republic of Yugoslavia, was not a Member of the United Nations, was not a State party to the Statute of the Court and was not a State party to the Genocide Convention. Yugoslavia requested the Court to declare that 'there is a new fact of such a character as to lay the case open to revision under Article 61 of the Statute of the Court'. In 2003 the ICJ held that that the application was inadmissible because there were no new facts on which to ground Yugoslavia's claim for a revision.[119]

2.11. Existence of a Breach of an International Obligation

Under ILC Article 12,

> There is a breach of an international obligation by a State when an act of that State is not in conformity with what is required of it by that obligation, regardless of its origin or character.

Breach of any of the obligations under the Covenant and its OPs give rise to State responsibility. This covers both the substantive obligations to respect rights and procedural obligations such as submitting reports under Article 40 or complying with interim measures orders under OP1.

2.12. International Obligations in Force for a State

Under ILC Article 13, 'An act of a State does not constitute a breach of an international obligation unless the State is bound by the obligation in question at the time the act occurs.' For the initial States parties to the Covenant the States became bound on the date of entry into force—which was three months after the date of the deposit with the Secretary-General of the UN of the thirty-fifth instrument of ratification or accession—that is, 23 March 1976.[120] Subsequent States parties become bound three months after the date of deposit of their instrument of ratification or accession.[121]

[119] Decision of 3 Feb 2003.
[120] Art 49(1) of the Covenant.
[121] Art 49(2) of the Covenant.

The relevant jurisprudence of the HRC on when international obligations under the Covenant and the Optional Protocols are in force arises under consideration of the inadmissibility ground of '*ratione temporis*' under OP1. The HRC has clearly stated that with respect to the original States parties to OP1, it is only competent to consider alleged violations occurring on or after the date of the entry into force of OP1 on 23 March 1976.[122] Similarly with respect to States which have later acceded to OP1 the HRC is only competent to consider alleged violations occurring on or after the date of the entry into force of OP1 for that State party.[123] In *ARS v Canada*[124] the HRC expressed the view that, 'No action taken before the entry into force of the Covenant for the State party concerned can, as such, be judged in the light of the obligations deriving from the Covenant'.[125] The HRC's final views in such cases commonly take the form that the facts as found by the HRC, 'In so far as they continued or occurred after the date of entry into force of the Covenant and the OP' disclose certain violations or not.[126] In *Altesor v Uruguay*[127] the HRC held that it could not establish with certainty what facts had occurred after the entry into force of the Covenant and the OP. They would, therefore, make no finding as regards those allegations.[128]

Facts occurring before the entry into force of an obligation under the Covenant may be factually relevant, for example, in cases concerning periods of detention that relate to the Covenant's obligation to ensure that accused persons are tried without delay. Germany entered a reservation *ratione temporis* to OP1, which could have the effect of excluding applications that could otherwise be admissible on the basis of a continuing violation. The reservation excluded the HRC's competence in any case, 'having its origins in events occurring prior to the entry into force of the Optional Protocol for the Federal Republic of Germany', the date of which was 25 November 1993. The 'origins of events' could be a considerable time before the entry into force of the OP, but can still produce violations after the entry into force of OP1 for Germany. In *Neremberg et al v Germany*,[129] the complaints related to delays in various court proceedings that began in 1958 and ended with a friendly settlement in 1995. After recalling the terms of the German reservation the HRC noted that the claim mainly related to proceedings that were pending prior to 15 November 1993 and that no part of the claim

[122] See *Sequeira v Uruguay*, A/35/40, p 127; *De Touron v Uruguay*, A/36/40, p 120.
[123] See *CE v Canada*, SD, p 16.
[124] *ARS v Canada*, SD, p 29.
[125] *Ibid*, para 5.1. The communication concerned certain provisions of the Parole Act 1970 and Art 15 of the Covenant.
[126] *De Bazzano v Uruguay*, SD, p 40 (para 10).
[127] A/37/40, p 122.
[128] *Ibid*, para 8(2), 9(2). See also *Acosta v Uruguay*, A/39/40, p 169 (para 14).
[129] A/56/40, Vol II, p 303.

related to events that occurred after 1995.[130] The period 1993–95 was covered by the reservation because the events at issue had their origin before 1993.

As the OP1 is a separate treaty, States can and have ratified it at a later date than they have ratified the Covenant itself. Though the obligation to respect and ensure the rights in the Covenant runs from the date of entry into force of the Covenant, the HRC have consistently held that it cannot consider alleged violations of the Covenant which occurred before entry into force of the OP1 for the State party, unless the violations complained of continued after the entry into force of the OP.[131] One member, Pocar, has taken a different view,[132] and Professor Nowak has challenged the HRC's approach,[133] but the HRC's jurisprudence has remained constant. The only exception applied by the HRC was in *Parkanyi v Hungary*[134] where the State party was considered to have waived its rights by conceding that the communication was admissible *ratione temporis*.[135] A mere failure by a State party to raise the issue of *ratione temporis* is not sufficient as the HRC can consider the issue *ex officio*, as it did in *Mukunto v Zambia*.[136]

The time that is crucial is when the alleged violation of an international obligation occurred. In *Hesse v Australia*[137] the medical experimentation on H that allegedly violated Article 7 of the Covenant took place between 1977 and 1989, which was prior to the entry into force of the OP1 for Australia in 1991. An alleged violation can occur some time after some of the factual events have occurred. In *Kim v Republic of Korea*[138] the State party argued that the violations of its national security laws in question had occurred before the entry into force of OP1 for Korea. The HRC focused on the alleged violation, namely K's conviction, which occurred after the entry into force of OP1 for Korea. A number of applications to the HRC have concerned expropriation that took place decades ago. In *Somers v Hungary*[139] the legislation dated from the 1950's. Complaints directed to that legislation were inadmissible *ratione temporis* as OP1 had entered into force for Hungary only in 1988. However, in 1991 and 1992 the Hungarian government had adopted legislation which redressed the losses of some but not all of the victims of the expropriations. That aspect of the complaint,

[130] *Ibid*, para 3.3.
[131] *E and AK v Hungary*, A/49/40, Vol II, p 336 (para 6.4).
[132] See *Aduayom v Togo*, A/51/40, Vol II, p 17.
[133] Nowak, above n 13, p 679.
[134] A/47/40, p 325.
[135] *Ibid*, para 4. Mr Wennergren dissented.
[136] A/54/40, Vol II, p 257 (para 6.3).
[137] A/57/40, Vol II, p 364.
[138] A/54/40, Vol II, p 1.
[139] A/51/40, Vol II, p 144.

namely its discriminatory nature contrary to Article 26 of the Covenant, was not inadmissible *ratione temporis*.[140] In *Inostroza v Chile*[141] the claims related to a number of deaths in 1973. These claims were inadmissible as the Covenant had only entered into force for Chile in 1976. The authors also challenged a Supreme Court decision of 1995. That decision denied their requests for the revision of earlier adverse decisions rendered by military courts. The HRC held that the 1995 decision could not be regarded as a new event that could affect the rights of a person who was killed in 1973.[142] There is a good policy reason to support this approach. Otherwise national legal systems courts would soon be faced with unlimited fruitless applications solely to form a basis for a communication to the HRC.

An affirmation by the State of a violation of the Covenant could constitute a new breach.[143] In *Paraga v Croatia*[144] the HRC had to declare part of the communication inadmissible in the light of a declaration made by the State party upon accession to the Optional Protocol. It observed:

> The Committee considered that it was precluded *ratione temporis*, in the light of the declaration made by the State party upon accession to the Optional Protocol, from considering the remainder of the communication insofar as it related to events which occurred before 12 January 1996, since the continuing effects claimed by Mr. Paraga did not appear to constitute *in themselves* a violation of the Covenant, nor could they be interpreted as *an affirmation, by act or clear implication*, of the alleged previous violations of the State party.[145]

2.13. Remedies

The same temporal principles apply in respect of an alleged violation of the right to an effective remedy under Article 2 of the Covenant. In *SE v Argentina*[146] the complaint concerned the disappearance of certain persons allegedly by agents of the State. The alleged violations occurred before the date of entry into force of OP1 for Argentina in 1986. That part of the complaint was inadmissible *ratione temporis*. Another part of the complaint related to a Due Obedience Law, enacted in 1987. It was alleged that this violated the right to an effective remedy. The HRC has repeatedly held that

[140] The complaint was dismissed on the merits.
[141] A/54/40, Vol II, p 313.
[142] See the individual opinions of Solari Yrigoyen and Chanet. See also *Vargas v Chile*, A/54/40, Vol II, p 322.
[143] *Cf* ILC's Art 11 that deals with conduct acknowledged and adopted by a State as its own.
[144] A/56/40, Vol II, p 58.
[145] *Ibid*, para 5.4. (Emphasis added.) See also *E and AK v Hungary*, above n 131.
[146] A/45/40, p 109.

the undertakings in Article 2 cannot be invoked in isolation. Thus, for example, the right to an effective remedy can only arise after a violation of a Covenant right has been established. However:

> the events which could have constituted violations of several articles of the Covenant and in respect of which remedies could have been invoked, occurred prior to entry into force of the Covenant and of the Optional Protocol for Argentina. Therefore, the matter cannot be considered by the Committee, as this aspect of the communication is inadmissible *ratione temporis.*[147]

2.14. Continuing Violations

Article 14(1) of the ILC's Articles deals with the 'Extension in time of the breach of an international obligation'. It provides that:

1. The breach of an international obligation by an act of a State not having a continuing character occurs at the moment when the act is performed, even if its effects continue.
2. The breach of an international obligation by an act of a State having a continuing character extends over the entire period during which the act continues and remains not in conformity with the international obligation.
3. The breach of an international obligation requiring a State to prevent a given event occurs when the event occurs and extends over the entire period during which the event continues and remains not in conformity with that obligation.

The HRC has an extensive jurisprudence on continuing violations. Alleged violations occurring before the date of the entry into force of the Covenant and of the OP1 for the State concerned can be considered if the violations continue or have continuing effects after that date which themselves constitute a violation of the Covenant.[148] This approach has been consistently applied in a number of cases in which the HRC has declared communications or parts of communications inadmissible *ratione temporis.*[149]

[147] *Ibid*, para 5.3. See also *RAVN v Argentina*, A/45/40, Vol II, p 191, and the accompanying individual opinion of Wennergrenote. *Cf* the decision in *Rodriguez v Uruguay*, A/49/40, Vol II, p 5.

[148] A/33/40, para 581. See *A et al v S*, SD, pp 3, 17. See J Paulewyn, 'The Concept of a "Continuing Violation" of an International Obligation: Selected Problems', 66 *British Yearbook of International Law* (1995), p 415; R Higgins, 'Time and the Law', 46 *International and Comparative Law Quarterly* (1997), p 501.

[149] See *De Bazzano v Uruguay*, SD, p 40; *LP v Canada*, SD, p 21.

What constitutes a continuation was considered in *Carballal v* Uruguay.[150] There the HRC concluded that although the date of C's arrest was prior to the entry into force of the Covenant and OP1 the alleged violations of Articles 7, 9 and 10 and 14 continued after that date.[151] In *Cabreira v Uruguay*[152] it was argued that although the alleged torture of C took place before the entry into force of the Covenant and OP1 in Uruguay, it had effects up to the date of the communication because it was on the basis of the confessions made under torture that C was sentenced to 12 years' imprisonment, which he continued to serve.[153] Unfortunately, the HRC did not reply to this argument but it would appear to have rejected it.

This question of the continuing effects of violations has been more directly considered in other cases. In *MA v Italy*[154] the communication raised various possible violations of the Covenant including the fair trial guarantee under Article 14 of the Covenant. Italy argued that the alleged violations occurred prior to the entry into force of the Covenant and OP1 in Italy on 15 December 1978 and that, therefore, the communication should be declared inadmissible *ratione temporis*.[155] MA raised the same point as in the *Cabreira* case.[156] He argued that:

> The violations did not come to an end prior to 15 December 1978, which is obvious since he is currently serving the sentence for which he was tried. Thus, the law applied is still in force and the sentence against MA is being carried out.[157] The reply of the HRC was that,
>
> It must be shown that there were consequences which could themselves have constituted a violation of the Covenant. In the opinion of the Committee there were no such consequences in the circumstances in the present case.[158]

The HRC's view seems to be a clear rejection of the argument advanced by MA. It is submitted that the HRC's view was correct. The prison sentence was clearly a consequence of the alleged violations but that is a necessary rather than a sufficient condition. The consequence itself, that is the sentence, had to constitute a violation of the Covenant and on the facts it did not.

150 A/36/40, p 125.
151 *Ibid*, para 5(a).
152 A/38/40, p 209.
153 *Ibid*, para 2.3.
154 A/39/40, p 190.
155 *Ibid*, para 7.2.
156 A/38/40, p 209.
157 A/39/40, p 190 (para 9).
158 *Ibid*, para 13.2. The decision is a good illustration of how close primary and secondary law can be.

Other consequences of a prison sentence were raised in *JK v Canada*.[159] JK was convicted of arson prior to the entry into force of the Covenant and OP1 for Canada. He argued,

> that the stigma of an allegedly unjust conviction and the social and legal consequences thereof, including the general prejudice in society against convicted persons, make him a victim today of article 14, paragraphs 1 and 3 (a) to (c), and article 25 of the Covenant—of article 14 because he was allegedly denied a fair trial and of article 25, because his conviction bars him from equal access to public service and from running for public office and because his criminal record puts him at a disadvantage, in particular in the field of employment.[160]

Again the HRC took the view, correctly it is submitted, that, 'the consequences as described by the author do not themselves raise issues under the International Covenant on Civil and Political Rights'.[161] This approach is consistent with the ILC's approach to what constitutes a continuing violation.[162]

Under Article 1 of the Optional Protocol, the Committee may only receive communications concerning alleged violations of the Covenant which occurred after the entry into force of the Covenant and the Optional Protocol for the State party concerned, unless continuing effects exist which in themselves constitute a violation of a Covenant right. In *Toala v New Zealand*[163] the HRC decided to address the issue of continuing effects when examining the merits of the case. In declaring the communication admissible it noted that:

> The authors claimed that they were, pursuant to the *Lesa* ruling, New Zealand citizens and, consequently, had the right to freely enter and reside in New Zealand territory, despite the 1982 Act which stripped them of their New Zealand citizenship. The legislation in question was enacted in 1982 after New Zealand had ratified the International Covenant on Civil and Political Rights, but before it ratified the Optional Protocol in 1989. The Committee considered, however, that the legislation in question may have continuing effects which in themselves could constitute a violation under article 12, paragraph 4, of the Covenant. The issue of whether these continuing effects were in violation of the Covenant was one which should be examined on the merits. The Committee considered therefore that it was not precluded *ratione temporis* from declaring the communication admissible.[164]

[159] A/40/40, p 215.
[160] *Ibid*, para 4.
[161] *Ibid*, para 7.3.
[162] See Commentary to Art 14 in Crawford, above n 8, pp 135–40, which cites, inter alia, the HRC's decision in *Lovelace v Canada*, A/36/40, p 166.
[163] A/56/40, Vol II, p 35.
[164] *Ibid*, para 6.3.

The ILC's Commentary to Article 14 cites the decision of the HRC in the *Lovelace Case* on the idea of a continuing breach:

> ... in *Lovelace v Canada,* it held it had jurisdiction to examine the continuing effects for the applicant of the loss of her status as a registered member of an Indian group, although the loss had occurred at the time of her marriage in 1970 and Canada only accepted the Committee's jurisdiction in 1976. The Committee noted that it was ... not competent, as a rule, to examine allegations relating to events having taken place before the entry into force of the Covenant and the Optional Protocol .... In the case of Sandra Lovelace it follows that the Committee is not competent to express any view on the original cause of her loss of Indian status ... at the time of her marriage in 1970 .... The Committee recognizes, however, that the situation may be different if the alleged violations, although relating to events occurring before 19 August 1976, continue, or have effects which themselves constitute violations, after that date.[165]

It found that the continuing impact of Canadian legislation, in preventing Lovelace from exercising her rights as a member of a minority, was sufficient to constitute a breach of Article 27 of the Covenant after that date,

> The Committee considers that the essence of the present complaint concerns the continuing effects of the Indian Act, in denying Sandra Lovelace legal status as an Indian, in particular because she cannot for this reason claim a legal right to reside where she wishes to, on the Tobique Reserve. This fact persists after the entry into force of the Covenant and its effects have to be examined, without regard for their original case ....[166]

In *E and AK* v *Hungary* the HRC stated that a continuing violation is to be interpreted, 'as an affirmation, after the entry into force of the Optional Protocol, by act or clear implication, of the previous violations of the State party'.[167] On the face of it this need for 'affirmation' is rather a severe test. Although it has been repeated in subsequent decisions,[168] it is not clear, however, whether its application will produce different outcomes than the previous approach.

[165] A/36/40, p 166.
[166] *Ibid,* para 13.1. 'Here the notion of a continuing breach was relevant not only to the Committee's jurisdiction but also to the application of Article 27 as the most directly relevant provision of the Covenant to the facts in hand', para 11 of Commentary to Art 14 in Crawford, above n 8. See also *JL v Australia*, A/47/40, p 448. Part of the communication was inadmissible *ratione temporis*, but another part was admissible because decisions of the Supreme Court had continuing effects; *Gueye v France*, text corresponding to n 54 above.
[167] A/49/40, Vol II, p 336 (para 6.4).
[168] *Aduayom et al v Togo*, A/51/40, Vol II, p 17 (previous violations were considered to be affirmed by the State party's refusal to reinstate the authors to their previous posts); *Julian and Drake v New Zealand*, A/52/40, Vol II, p 273 (State party not considered to have affirmed alleged violations resulting from the 1952 Peace Treaty between New Zealand and Japan).

2.15. Circumstances Precluding Wrongfulness

The consent (Article 20 ILC) of any one State could not excuse a breach of a human rights treaty. The obligation would be owed to all the other States parties anyway. International human rights law can take into account the consent of a corporation or a private person. The ILC Commentary notes that, 'The rights conferred by international human rights treaties cannot be waived by their beneficiaries, but the individual's free consent may be relevant to their application'.[169]

The concept of self-defence in the ILC's Article 21 would not necessarily preclude the wrongfulness of conduct violating human rights treaties. The limitation and derogation provisions of the Covenant cater for measures taken in public emergencies and this includes self-defence. *Force majeure* could in principle apply in respect of human rights obligations. The ILC Commentary cites the unforeseeability of attacks by rebels of the territorial State for damage suffered by foreigners.[170]

Article 24 of the ILC's Articles, on distress, specifically refers to a situation of saving lives. The *Rainbow Warrior Arbitration* suggested that the need for medical treatment of an individual facing a serious risk to their health could amount to a circumstance of distress precluding wrongfulness.[171] In some circumstances Articles 7 and 10 of the Covenant can oblige a State to provide medical treatment to detained persons. Article 26 of the ILC's Articles provides that:

> Nothing in this Chapter [on circumstances precluding wrongfulness] precludes the wrongfulness of any act of a State which is not in conformity with an obligation arising under a peremptory norm of general international law.

The ILC's Article 25 deals with 'Necessity'. It provides that:

> 1. Necessity may not be invoked by a State as a ground for precluding the wrongfulness of an act not in conformity with an international obligation of that State unless the act:
>   (a) Is the only way for the State to safeguard an essential interest against a grave and imminent peril; and
>   (b) Does not seriously impair an essential interest of the State or States towards which the obligation exists, or of the international community as a whole.

[169] Para 10 of the Commentary on Art 20, referring to Covenant Arts 7 (medical experimentation), 8(3) (forced or compulsory labour), 14(3)(g) (compulsion to testify against himself or confess guilt), and 23(3) (consent of intending spouses), see above n 8.
[170] Para 7 of the ILC Commentary to Art 23 in Crawford, above n 8.
[171] *RIAA*, Vol XX, (1990), p 217 (para 79).

2. In any case, necessity may not be invoked by a State as a ground for precluding wrongfulness if:
   (a) The international obligation in question excludes the possibility of invoking necessity; or
   (b) The State has contributed to the situation of necessity.

The Covenant contains a specific provision to deal with derogation measures taken in public emergencies.[172] The limitation provisions on various Articles would also cater for responses to particular kinds of emergencies. Meron has argued that, 'The language of the Covenant prohibits any derogation not explicitly permitted by Article 4, thus excluding invocation of the customary law exception of state of necessity'.[173] The HRC has rejected an argument by Israel that the humanitarian law applicable in the occupied territories displaced the operation of human rights law. The HRC's view was that Israel remained responsible where it exercised 'effective control'.[174] In some contexts necessity can form part of the legal considerations in determining the applicable substantive law. In its judgment on the *Legality of the threat or use of Nuclear Weapons*[175] the ICJ held that any violation of Article 6 in the context of an armed conflict was determined by reference to international humanitarian law.[176] That primary humanitarian law, it should be noted, could involve consideration of military necessity.[177] The HRC has made it clear that the standards in the Covenant are minimum standards that all States have agreed to observe whatever their economic or social circumstances.[178]

Article 26 of the ILC's Articles does not indicate what are the peremptory norms of general international law. The discussion on Article 26 in the ILC's Commentary refers to the following peremptory norms as clearly accepted and recognised—the prohibitions on aggression, genocide, slavery, racial discrimination, crimes against humanity, torture and the right to self-determination.[179] Five of these prohibitions find some reference in the

[172] See GC 29 on States of Emergency (Aug 2001); and D McGoldrick, 'The Interface Between Public Emergency Powers and International Law', 2 *International Journal of Constitutional Law* (2004), p 380.
[173] Meron, above n 4, p 208.
[174] Concluding Observations on Israel, CCPR/C/79/Add 3, paras 4, 10–11 (1998); reaffirmed in 2003, UN Doc CCPR/Co/78/ISR (2003). See O Ben-Naftal and Y Shany, 'Living in Denial: The Application of Human Rights in the Occupied Territories', 37 *Israel Law Review* (2004). The CERD has also rejected Israel's argument.
[175] *ICJ Reports*, 1996, p 226.
[176] *Ibid*, para 25. See L Boisson De Chazournes and P Sands (eds), *International Law, the ICJ and Nuclear Weapons* (Cambridge, 1999).
[177] See para 25 of the Commentary on Art 25.
[178] See *Lubuto v Zambia*, A/51/40, Vol II, p 11 (para 7.3); *Sextus v Trinidad and Tobago*, A/56/40, Vol II, p 111 (para 7.3); *Wanza v Trinidad and Tobago*, A/57/50, Vol II, p 55 (para 9.4).
[179] The Commentary to Art 40 also refers to the basic rules of international humanitarian law as being peremptory.

Covenant.[180] The HRC has given the prohibition of torture and arbitrary deprivation of life as examples of peremptory norms.[181]

3. THE CONTENT OF THE INTERNATIONAL RESPONSIBILITY OF A STATE

Part Two of the ILC's Articles are only concerned with obligations of reparation to States. They are without prejudice to any rights directly accruing to a person or entity other than a State.[182] The Commentary to Article 33 specifically refers to obligations under human rights treaties existing towards all other parties to the treaty, but the individuals concerned being the ultimate beneficiaries as the holders of the relevant rights. It also notes the existence of procedures like that in OP1. As Kamminga noted:

> The possible contents of an inter-state claim for reparation do not differ significantly from the contents of claims that may be submitted by individuals under international recourse procedures.[183]

Article 29 of the ILC's Articles makes it clear that the fact that a State violates any particular human rights obligations does not affect its continuing duty to perform the obligation breached.

3.1. Cessation and Non-Repetition

Under the ILC's Article 30,

> The State responsible for the internationally wrongful act is under an obligation: (a) To cease that act, if it is continuing; (b) To offer appropriate assurances and guarantees of non-repetition, if circumstances so require.

With human rights treaties, where States are not normally the beneficiaries of the specific rights protected, the obligations of cessation and non-repetition assume the greatest importance.[184] In the context of obligations

[180] See Arts 1, 2, 6, 7, 8, and 26 Covenant.
[181] GC 24, para 10.
[182] See Art 33 of the ILC's Articles.
[183] Kamminga, above n 23, p 173.
[184] A State party could be a beneficiary where the human rights of one of its nationals are violated. As the Covenant rights extend to everyone within the jurisdiction of the State (Art 2 of the Covenant) an individual from a non-State party could be a beneficiary of the treaty right, as in *Marais v Madagascar*, A/38/40, p 141, (M was South African), but the State would not have a treaty-based diplomatic claim.

of non-repetition, the ILC's Commentary notes that '[r]equests to repeal or modify legislation are frequently made by international bodies', citing three views of the HRC.[185] Where relevant the HRC has stated 'an obligation to take measures to prevent similar violations in the future'.[186]

3.2. Reparation and Restitution

Under the ILC's Article 35 a State which breaches the Covenant is under,

> an obligation to make restitution, that is, to re-establish the situation which existed before the wrongful act was committed, provided, and to the extent, that restitution: (a) is not materially impossible; (b) does not involve a burden out of all proportion to the benefit deriving from restitution instead of compensation.

The examples cited in the Commentary include the release of persons wrongly detained (for example, in breach of Article 9 of the Covenant) or the return of property wrongly seized (for example, a discriminatory taking in breach of Article 26 of the Covenant). As the ILC Commentary notes, in cases involving the application of peremptory norms, restitution may be required as an aspect of compliance with the primary obligation.[187] The Commentary to Article 35 discusses a case, the *Forests of Central Rhodope Case*,[188] where restitution was considered impossible because third parties had acquired rights to property. The HRC has had cases in which it has acknowledged that the return of property was not possible because the current owners were deserving of protection.

As there is no right to property in the Covenant,[189] the corollary of this is that there is no Covenant right, as such, to have expropriated or nationalised property restituted.[190] If a State party provides compensation for nationalisation or expropriation on equal terms, it does not discriminate against those whose property was expropriated or nationalised. *Somers v Hungary*[191] concerned the Hungarian legislation on compensation for confiscated property. S received less than full compensation for the property. The HRC considered that the legislation contained 'objective compensation criteria, which are applied equally and without discrimination to individuals in the authors situation'.[192] It then considered whether the criteria and

[185] See fn 476 of the Commentary in Crawford, above n 8.
[186] *Rawle Kennedy v Trinidad and Tobago*, A/57/40, Vol II, p 161 (para 9).
[187] Commentary to Art 35, para 3.
[188] *RIAA*, Vol III, (1933), p 1405.
[189] It was included in the Universal Declaration of Human Rights (1948).
[190] *Somers v Hungary*, A/51/40, Vol II, p 144 (para 9.6).
[191] *Ibid.*
[192] *Ibid*, para 9.4.

calculation tables for compensation were reasonable. Under the legislation the authors had received a voucher worth nominal compensation. The full value of the voucher could be set against the price of any property, shares or business shares sold during the privatisation of former State-owned property or against business shares of former State-owned companies. Only if the holder of the voucher wanted to redeem the vouchers on the open market because they were not interested in any property other than their former home would they receive less than the nominal value of the vouchers. The HRC considered these criteria to be objective and reasonable.[193] A second legislative provision gave the current tenants of former State-owned property priority in the privatisation sale of that property. The HRC did not consider this to be unreasonable because 'the interests of the 'current tenants', who might have been occupying the property for years, are deserving of protection'.[194] If the former owners were compensated on equal and non-discriminatory terms then the interplay between the two legislative provisions was compatible with Article 26.[195]

Under the ILC's Article 37 (2) 'Satisfaction' may consist in an acknowledgement of the breach, an expression of regret, a formal apology or another appropriate modality. In the *La Grand Case* the ICJ stated that an apology was not sufficient in a case where foreign nationals had not been advised of their legal rights and had been subjected to prolonged detention or sentenced to severe penalties.[196] The point might be appropriately made in relation to many violations of the Covenant that concern a foreign national.[197]

3.3. Compensation

Under the ILC's Article 36 (1) a State which breaches the Covenant is under an obligation to compensate for the damage caused thereby, insofar as such damage is not made good by restitution. Compensation is not intended as punitive or exemplary. The views of the HRC have regularly stated that compensation should be paid to victims. There has been no suggestion in HRC practice that compensation should be anything other than purely compensatory. The HRC has no specific power equivalent to that in Article 41 (formerly 50) ECHR to award damages or costs in just satisfaction.[198] Pocar, a former member of the HRC, has commented that the HRC,

[193] *Ibid,* paras 9.5–9.7.
[194] *Ibid,* para 9.8.
[195] *Ibid.*
[196] *Germany v USA, ICJ Reports*, 2001, para 123.
[197] See *Marais v Madagascar*, above n 185.
[198] On the practice of human rights bodies in awarding compensation see D Shelton, *Remedies in International Human Rights Law* (Oxford, 1999), pp 214–79.

> appears to take into account the principles that govern reparation in international law: i.e. the re-establishment, as far as possible, of the existing situation prior to the violation and, if this is not possible, compensation for the violation suffered by the victim. The measures suggested by the HRC in its views imply the termination of the violation, if an end has not yet been put to it, and consist of effective compensation and of other measures as appropriate in each case.[199]

The remedies indicated by the HRC have got more specific over time and are very specific by comparison to the European Court of Human Rights and the International Court of Justice. Examples include,

- — an effective remedy, avoiding any discrimination in the choice of their common surname. The State should further abstain from enforcing the cost order of the Supreme Court or, in case it is already enforced, to refund the respective amount of the money.[200]
- — refraining from carrying out the sentence of whipping upon the author [of the application] or providing appropriate compensation if the sentence has been carried out. The State party should ensure that similar violations do not occur in the future by repealing the legislative provisions that allow for corporal punishment.[201]
- — an effective remedy which includes consideration of early release.[202]
- — an effective remedy, consisting of modifying the applicable law so that no improper distinction is made between persons in the author's situation and EEA nationals.[203]
- — The victim would have been entitled to an effective remedy including, first and foremost, the preservation of his life. Adequate compensation must be granted to his surviving family.[204]
- — Effective measures to (a) grant compensation; (b) order an official inquiry into the death of the victim; and (c) ensure that similar violations do not occur in the future, especially by taking immediate steps to ensure that conditions of detention are

[199] F Pocar, 'Legal Value of the Committee's Views', *Canadian Human Rights Yearbook* (1991–92), p 119.
[200] *Muller and Engelhard v Namibia*, A/57/40, Vol II, p 243 (para 8).
[201] *Higginson v Jamaica*, A/57/40, Vol II, p 140 (para 6).
[202] *Wanza v Trinidad and Tobago*, A/57/40, Vol II, p 55 (para 11) (W's death sentence had been commuted to 75 years' imprisonment with hard labour).
[203] *Karakurt v Austria*, A/57/40, Vol II, p 304 (para 10).
[204] *Ashby v Trinidad and Tobago*, A/57/40, Vol II, p 12 (para 12).

compatible with the State party's obligations under Articles 6 and 10 of the Covenant.[205]

— an opportunity to file a new claim for restitution or compensation. The State party should review its legislation and administrative practices to ensure that all persons enjoy both equality before the law as well as equal protection of the law.[206]
— restitution of the property or compensation.[207]
— compensation and the opportunity to lodge a new appeal, or should this no longer be possible, to give due consideration to granting him early release. If the corporal punishment imposed on the author has not been executed, the State party is under an obligation not to execute the sentence.[208]
— refraining from removing the authors from Australia before they have had an opportunity to have their application for visas examined with due consideration given to the protection required by their child's status as a minor.[209]

If the same factual case concerning the same legal obligations were brought before the HRC, the European Court of Human Rights and the International Court of Justice, it seems impossible to argue that State responsibility can vary from forum to forum. The answer to their different responses must lie in a differing institutional conception of their roles and functions.[210]

3.4. Serious Breaches of Peremptory Obligations

Article 41 of the ILC's Articles provides:

1. States shall cooperate to bring to an end through lawful means any serious breach within the meaning of article 40.
2. No State shall recognize as lawful a situation created by a serious breach within the meaning of article 40, nor render aid or assistance in maintaining that situation.
3. This article is without prejudice to the other consequences referred to in this Part and to such further consequences that a breach to which this Chapter applies may entail under international law.

205 *Lantsova v Russian Federation*, A/57/40, Vol II, p 96 (para 11).
206 *Fabryova v Czech Republic*, A/57/40, Vol II, p 103 (para 11).
207 *Brok and Brokova v Czech Republic*, A/57/40, Vol II, p 110 (para 9).
208 Boodlal *Sooklal v Trinidad and Tobago*, A/57/40, Vol II, p 364 (para 6).
209 *Winata and So Lan Li v Australia*, A/56/40, Vol II, p 199 (para 9).
210 *Cf* R Higgins in ch 1 of this Volume on the *Cameroon v Nigeria* case (2002), paras 308–24, where the ICJ did not decide on the claims in relation to State responsibility for various reasons.

In relation to Article 1(3) of the Covenant on the promotion of the right of self-determination, the practice of individual members of the HRC has been to inquire as to the situations of the Palestinians and peoples in South West Africa (now Namibia).[211]

3.5. Invocation of Responsibility

In the context of a multilateral human rights treaty like the Covenant a State will rarely be an injured State for the purpose of Article 42 of the ILC's Articles.[212] Its invocation of responsibility will more usually be in terms of Article 48. Under Article 48(1), any State, other than an injured State, is entitled to invoke the responsibility of another State in accordance with Article 48(2) if:

> The obligation breached is owed to a group of States including that State, and is established for the protection of a collective interest of the group; or (b) The obligation breached is owed to the international community as a whole.

The Commentary to Article 48(1)(a) gives a regional system for the protection of human rights as an example of collective obligations. There seems to be no reason why a universal human rights treaty like the Covenant cannot similarly establish collective obligations. The HRC has stated that the Covenant is not a 'web of inter-State exchanges of mutual obligations'. Rather it concerns, 'the endowment of individuals with rights'.[213] In any event, some of the obligations in such a treaty reflect the 'basic rights of the human person' (to use the language of the *Barcelona Traction Case*)[214] and would clearly seem to be covered by paragraph (b). Under Article 48(2), a State invoking responsibility under Article 48(1) may only claim cession, assurances and guarantees of non-repetition in accordance with Article 30; and performance of the obligation of reparation in the interest of the injured State or of the beneficiaries of the obligation breached. The Commentary to Article 48 notes that provisions in some human rights treaties [which includes Articles 41–42 of the Covenant] allow the invocation of State responsibility by any State party.[215] The Commentary goes on to note that:

> In those cases where they have been resorted to, a clear distinction has been drawn between the capacity of the applicant State to raise the matter and the interests of the beneficiaries of the obligation.

[211] GC 12 on Art 1 and CERD Recommendation 21; K Knop, *Diversity and Self-Determination in International Law* (Cambridge, 2002).
[212] It could be an injured State when one of its nationals is concerned.
[213] GC 24, para 17. The fact that States object to reservations by other States suggests that they have a legal interest in the observance of the Covenant.
[214] See above n 2.
[215] Commentary to Art 48, para 12 in Crawford, above n 8, p 279.

The requirements for the invocation of responsibility by an injured State under Articles 43, 44 and 45 apply to an invocation of responsibility by a State entitled to do so under paragraph 1. This appears to mean that the State, which is not an injured State, would have to satisfy the nationality of claims rule in Article 44. This seems odd given that Article 48 is concerned with collective interests or obligations owed to the international community as a whole. The ILC commentary provides no clarification or explanation.

3.6. Countermeasures

In its discussion of the idea of reciprocal countermeasures the ILC Commentary states that:

> for some obligations, for example those concerning the protection of human rights, reciprocal countermeasures are inconceivable. The obligations in question have a non-reciprocal character and are not due to the other State but to the individuals themselves.[216]

One of the general limitations on countermeasures is that, inter alia, they must not involve any departure from 'obligations for the protection of fundamental human rights' (Article 50(1)(c). Would this extend to all of the rights in the Covenant or only those considered as being fundamental? The Commentary suggests the latter by noting that, 'the relevant human rights treaties identify certain human rights which may not be derogated from even in time of war or other public emergency'.[217] It also notes that Article 1(2) of the Covenant provides that, 'In no case may a people be deprived of its means of subsistence'. Article 1 is not a non-derogable article in terms of Article 4 of the Covenant, but the HRC has stated that in its view a reservation to Article 1 denying peoples the right to determine their own political status and to pursue their economic, social and cultural development, would be incompatible with the object and purpose of the Covenant.[218] In any event, Article 50 (1)(d) provides that countermeasures shall not affect 'obligations under peremptory norms of general international law'. Self-determination is often considered to be a peremptory norm.[219]

The ILC's articles on countermeasures are limited to measures taken by an injured State. However, the articles are without prejudice to the right of

[216] Commentary to Art 48, para 5, referring to the decision of the European Court of Human Rights in *Ireland v UK*, Series A, No 25 (1978).
[217] Commentary to Art 50, para 6. See also *ibid,* para 10.
[218] GC 24, para 9.
[219] See the General Recommendation 21 of the CERD on self-determination, A/51/18 (23 Aug 1996).

any State, entitled under Article 48 (1) to invoke the responsibility of another State, to take lawful measures against that State to ensure cessation of the breach and reparation in the interest of the injured State or of the beneficiaries of the obligation breached.[220] The Commentary states that such cases are 'controversial and the practice is embryonic'.[221]

3.7. Measures Taken by States Other Than an Injured State

Article 54 of the ILC's Articles deals with measures taken by States other than an injured State. It provides that:

> This Chapter does not prejudice the right of any State, entitled under Article 48, paragraph 1 to invoke the responsibility of another State, to take lawful measures against that State to ensure cessation of the breach and reparation in the interest of the injured State or of the beneficiaries of the obligation breached'.[222]

Among the small number of examples in the ILC Commentary are two which concern States parties to the Covenant and where the substance of the issue was human rights violations. First, the measures taken by certain Western countries against Poland and the Soviet Union in 1981 in response to the imposition of martial law in Poland and the suppression of demonstrations and the internment of dissidents.[223] Secondly, collective measures against Yugoslavia in 1998 in response to the humanitarian crisis in Kosovo.[224]

4. CONCLUSION

This essay began with Professor Meron's description of the principles of state responsibility as *terra incognita* for human rights lawyers. He concluded his book with the comment that:

> ... generalist international lawyers should not regard human rights and humanitarian norms as merely theoretical principles or moral desiderata, but as norms of international law the breach of which has objective consequences

[220] See Art 54 in Crawford, above n 8, p 302.
[221] Commentary to Part Three Ch II, para 8 in Crawford, above n 8, p 283. See Meron, above n 4, pp 229–45.
[222] On the public order dimension of this provision see M Koskenniemi, 'Solidarity Measures: State Responsibility As A New International Order?', 72 *British Yearbook of International Law* (2001), p 337.
[223] 86 *RGDIP* (1982), p 603.
[224] See 69 *British Yearbook of International Law* (1998), p 580.

> which can and should be analysed by reference to the general law of state responsibility. By clarifying the relationship of human rights and humanitarian norms to state responsibility we can contribute to their effectiveness, create remedies for their violations, more effectively protect human dignity, and generally enhance their import and standing in the international community.[225]

It is submitted that the empirical evidence relating to the Covenant considered in this essay reveals that the classic principles of State responsibility are alive and well. Indeed, international human rights law has in fact given them a new lease of life. The Covenant provides a modern text, and the HRC a modern institutional forum, in which the principles of State responsibility are applied in an empirical fashion. The human rights jurisprudence that has emerged has developed those principles to respond to the extensive interpretation of the primary obligations imposed on States. International human rights lawyers have been focused on the primary obligations but they have really been operationalising the principles of State responsibility all of the time. International human rights lawyers are rather like Molière's Monsieur Jourdain who was delighted to discover he had been talking prose all the time without realising it.[226] The '*terra*' of State responsibility is not, it seems, quite so '*incognita*' to international human rights lawyers after all.

[225] Meron, above n 4, p 248.
[226] Molière (Jean-Baptiste Poquelin), *The Bourgeois Gentleman*, Act 1, Scene III.

11

Environmental Law and Non-Compliance Procedures: Issues of State Responsibility

GERHARD LOIBL*

ENVIRONMENTAL ISSUES HAVE gained world wide public attention in the last three decades. The United Nations Conference on a Human Environment, held in Stockholm 1972, may be seen as the starting point for the evolution of legal provisions in municipal and international law addressing environmental problems. In the last decades the number of international legal norms that deal with environmental concerns has grown rapidly. In particular, a large number of treaties have been adopted and entered into force.[1] Moreover, customary international law has evolved, eg Principle 21 of the Stockholm Declaration[2] or the obligation to notify possibly affected States in case of natural or man-made emergencies. Furthermore, in the last decades numerous resolutions and declarations addressing environmental matters have been adopted within international organisations and at international conferences.

The development of international law has also led to the establishment of new institutions dealing with environmental issues, such as the United Nations Environment Programme or the Commission for Sustainable Development and institutions under multilateral environmental agreements.[3]

* Professor of Public International Law, Diplomatic Academy and University of Vienna.

1 Cf eg United Nations Treaty Series (UNTS) and the register of the United Nations Environment Programme (UNEP) of international treaties.

2 Principle 21 of the Stockholm Declaration has been restated in Principle 2 of the Rio Declaration on Environment and Development and may also be found in a number of treaties (eg Art 3 of the Convention on Biological Diversity, 1992).

3 See R Churchill and G Ulfstein, 'Autonomous Institutional Arrangements in Multilateral Environmental Agreements: A Little-noticed Phenomenon in International Law,' 94 *American Journal of International Law* (2000), p 623; G Loibl, 'The Proliferation of international institutions dealing with International Environmental Matters', in N Blokker and H Schermers (eds), *Proliferation of International Organisations* (The Hague, 2001), p 151.

Thus, since 1972 a large set of environmental legal rules as well as institutions have been established. In particular the United Nations Conference on Environment and Development 1992, held in Rio de Janeiro, and the United Nations Summit on Sustainable Development 2002, held in Johannesburg, have underlined the focus of the world community on environmental matters.[4]

The following questions may be posed: whether this focus on environmental issues and the growth of international environmental law during the last several decades has resulted in an increased number of cases before international courts and arbitral tribunals dealing with environmental issues; whether other ways have been explored to address violations of international environmental law; and to what extent specific rules developed in international environmental law may affect the law of State responsibility.

Although already in the 1940's the Trail Smelter Arbitration addressed transboundary environmental damages, the number of cases that have been brought to international adjudication has been limited. This is underlined by the fact that since the ICJ established a special Chamber for Environmental Matters in 1993, no case was referred to this Chamber.[5] Furthermore, environmental issues have hardly been at the heart of disputes before other international courts or arbitral tribunals between States. The only international court that has experienced a significant increase in its case-load concerning environmental issues in recent years has been the European Court of Human Rights.[6] These cases concerned environmental pollution that led to the infringement of individual's rights, but none of these cases dealt with transboundary environmental issues.[7]

International environmental rules cannot be seen as a homogenous set. The nature of the obligations in international environmental law varies depending on the subject matter the rules regulate. Rules in international environmental law might oblige States to take certain measures for the protection of their own environment (eg natural habitats), to reduce or prevent transboundary significant harm (protection of transboundary watercourses) or to protect resources of a global or regional concern (eg the ozone layer or the global climate). These provisions might establish bilateral obligations (ie owed towards another State) or multilateral obligations (ie owed towards a group of States or the international community as a whole).

[4] See the Johannesburg Plan of Action and Johannesburg Ministerial Declaration on Sustainable Development.

[5] Cf M Fitzmaurice, 'International Protection of the Environment', 293 *Recueil des Cours* (2001), p 363; Sir Robert Jennings, 'Need for an Environmental Court', *European Policy and Law* 22/56 (1992), pp 312–14.

[6] See M Fitzmaurice, *International Protection of the Environment, ibid*, p 315.

[7] Cf eg *Hatton and others v UK*. This case concerned noise emissions from night flights to Heathrow airport (Judgment of 2 Oct 2001, application number 00036022/97; Judgment by the Grand Chamber of 8 July 2002).

This differentiation of types of legal norms in international environmental law is decisive for the question which State or States may invoke immediate remedial consequences against a breach or are entitled to invoke merely the responsibility. In order to invoke responsibility the following elements have to be established: a breach of a legal duty has to have occurred, a subject to which the act is attributable is to be found, and—as has been argued by some academic writers—the damage has to be determined and the causality between the act or omission and the damage has to be established.[8] In the environmental area to establish these elements in a particular case raises a number of questions, eg it will be impossible to establish that a particular damage has been caused by a specific activity within the territory of another State. For instance, persistent organic pollutants (POPs), such as DDT which is used to combat malaria in a number of countries, tend to concentrate in colder parts of the globe, ie in higher mountain areas such as the Alps or around the South and North pole, notwithstanding in which part of the globe they are used. POPs have a negative impact on human health, flora and fauna. Yet, due to the specific nature of POPs it is not possible to determine their origin. Thus, an affected State will not be able to invoke successfully the responsibility of a specific State for the damage suffered as, *inter alia*, it will not be possible to establish causality. Similarly, damages suffered by a particular country due to the depletion of the ozone layer will not be attributable to the activities within a specific other State.

This essay will be mostly devoted to the new developments in environmental law relating to issues of State responsibility, ie non-compliance procedures. The 'new generation' of procedures such as the one adopted in the Kyoto Protocol—discussed below—are characterised by more stringent measures towards the fulfilment of States' obligations. The imposition of such measures may raise issues involving general problems of State responsibility.

1. CASES BEFORE INTERNATIONAL COURTS AND ARBITRAL TRIBUNALS CONCERNING RESPONSIBILITY IN THE ENVIRONMENTAL AREA

As mentioned above the number of cases referred to international courts or arbitral tribunals concerning responsibility for damages to the environment is limited. Cases relevant in this context are the *Trail Smelter Case*,[9]

[8] The ILC's Draft Articles on State Responsibility of States for Internationally Wrongful Acts determine, in Art 2, that the two constituent elements of an international wrongful act are: the conduct attributable to a State and the inconsistency with the State's international obligations. Neither damage nor fault are constituent elements. (See J Crawford, *The International Law Commission's Articles on State Responsibility* (Cambridge, 2002), p 81.)

[9] *United States v Canada, RIAA*, Vol III, (1938–39), p 1905.

the *Lac Lannoux Case,*[10] the *Gabcikovo-Nagymaros Case*[11], the *Nuclear Test Cases*[12] and—most recently—the *OSPAR Case*[13] and the *MOX Case.*[14] These cases concerned damage to the environment suffered by a State due to activities within the territory of another State.[15]

They, thus, concerned situations of a 'bilateral' nature. None of the cases addressed situations where the alleged breach of international law concerned an obligation towards a group of States or the international community as a whole. Situations as described above concerning POPs or the depletion of the ozone layer, let alone the global climate, have not yet been considered before international courts or arbitral tribunals.

The ILC Articles on State Responsibility foresee rules on the violation of international law relevant in international environmental law. Articles 42 and 48 of the ILC Articles on State Responsibility—by analogy to Article 60 of the Vienna Convention on the Law of Treaties 1969—address a number of different situations of an 'injured' or 'interested' State in case of a breach of an international obligation.[16] Article 42 envisages three situations that entitle a State as 'injured State' to invoke the responsibility of another State: either the obligation breached is owed to,

— The injured State individually (Article 42 (a)),[17]
— A State 'specially' affected by a violation of an obligation owed to a group of States or the international community as a whole (Article 42 (b) (i)),[18] or

[10] *Spain v France*, 24 *ILR* (1957), p 101.
[11] *Gabčíkovo-Nagymaros Project (Hungary/Slovakia)* case, *ICJ Reports*, 1997, p 7: see on that case: R Lefeber, 'The *Gabčíkovo-Nagymaros Project (Hungary/Slovakia)* and the Law of State Responsibility', 11 *Leiden Journal of International Law* (1998), pp 609–23.
[12] *Australia v France; New Zealand v France*, *ICJ Reports*, 1973, p 99; *ICJ Reports, 1974*, p 253: *New Zealand v France*, Order, *ICJ Reports*, 1995, p 288.
[13] *Ireland v United Kingdom*, Final Award of 2 July 2003 (available at: www.pca-cpa.org).
[14] Order of 3 Dec 2001 issued by the International Tribunal of the Law of the Sea (available at: www.itlos.org); Order of 24 June 2003 on the 'Suspension of Proceedings on Jurisdiction and Merits and Request for Further Provisional Measures' issued by the Arbitral Tribunal (available at: www.pca-cpa.org).
[15] Eg in the *Trail Smelter* case the arbitral tribunal found that Canada was responsible for the damage caused within the territory of the USA. It held that Canada was responsible in international law for the conduct of the Trail Smelter and the damage caused. In the *Gabčíkovo-Nagymaros Project (Hungary/Slovakia)* case Hungary argued that it had suffered damages due to the operation of the 'Gabčíkovo-dam-system' on Slovak territory.
[16] J Crawford, *The International Law Commission's Articles on State Responsibility* (Cambridge, 2002), p 255; S Wittich, 'The International Law Commission's Articles on the Responsibility of States for Internationally Wrongful Acts Adopted on Second Reading', 15 *Leiden Journal of International Law* (2002), p 891, at p 906.
[17] Eg in case of a bilateral treaty or if under a multilateral treaty a specific obligation is owed to a particular State.
[18] A multilateral treaty establishes certain obligations for all parties, eg to prohibit the emission of certain toxic substances into an international watercourse. In case of a breach of this obligation a party that suffers damage on its territory is to be considered a specially affected State. All other parties are to be considered to be affected in their legal interest pursuant to Art 48.

— All States or a group of States and the breach of the obligation changes radically the position of all the parties (Article 42 (b) (ii)).[19]

Furthermore, Article 48 envisages that responsibility may be invoked by a State other than the injured State in case of breach of a collective obligation.

These possible situations relate to the three-fold nature of international environmental obligations as described above. But it remains to be seen whether these provisions will lead to a change in State practice in the environmental area and increase the number of cases of breaches of obligations invoked by other States.

The *Gabčíkovo-Nagymaros Project (Hungary/Slovakia)* case, although focused on traditional issues of State responsibility within the bilateral context, does, however, merit a brief reminder of the issues involved, since it was the first case in which the ICJ reviewed in a comprehensive manner the classical law of State responsibility in relation to environmental issues. This case also brought to the attention of the Court the issue of the controversial link between the material breach of a treaty (Article 60 of the 1969 Vienna Convention on the Law of Treaties) and the law of State responsibility (countermeasures). This issue came about in this case in connection with the unilateral termination of the 1977 Treaty by Hungary. The Court, however, was very adamant that the law of treaties and the law of State responsibility belong to different domains.[20] This approach was also adopted by the International Commission in its work on the law of State Responsibility. Special Rapporteur Crawford said as follows:

> ... article 60 is concerned exclusively with the right of a State party to a treaty to invoke a material breach by another party as grounds for its suspension or termination. It is not concerned with the question of responsibility for breach of a treaty. This is why article 60 is restricted to 'material' breaches of treaties. Only material breach justifies termination or suspension of the treaty, whereas in the context of State responsibility any breach of a treaty gives rise to responsibility irrespective of its gravity.[21]

[19] This provision envisages a breach of a collective obligation owed to a group of States or to the international community as a whole that 'is of such a character as radically to change the position of all the other States to which the obligation is owed with respect to the further performance of the obligation'. An example of such a treaty would be the Antarctic Treaty.

[20] The Court states: 'a determination of whether a convention is or is not in force, and whether it has or has not been properly susepended or denounced, is to be made pursuant to the law of treaties. On the other hand, an evaluation of the extent to which the suspension or denouncation of the convention, seen as incompatible with the law of treaties, involves the responsibility of State which proceeded to it, is to be made under the law of treaties.' (*Gabčíkovo-Nagymaros Project (Hungary/Slovakia)* case, above n 11, para 47).

[21] Third Report on State Responsibility, Fifty-second session, Geneva, 1 May-9 June. 10 July-18 August 2000, A/CN.4/507, p 296. See also, Report of the Intenational Law Commission, Fifty-third session, 23 April-1 June and 2 July–10 August 2001, General Asembly, Official Records, Supplement N 10 (A/56/10), p 326.

This case gave rise to other questions of State responsibility as well, such as a plea of a state of necessity, countermeasures, the cessation of the wrongful acts and their legal consequences. Hungary has invoked the existence of a state of 'ecological' necessity as a circumstance precluding wrongfulness of its acts. It related to the abandonment of the project in 1989 and the termination of the 1977 Treaty in 1992. The Court agreed that a state of necessity precludes wrongfulness and acknowledged that the 1996 ILC Draft reflected existing international customary law. The Court has identified the conditions that have to be fulfilled in order to invoke such a circumstance. The state of necessity must relate to 'essential interest' of the State that has not acted in conformity with its international obligations; the interest must have been threatened by 'grave and imminent peril'; the act that was challenged must have been the 'only means' to safeguard the interest; the challenged act must not have seriously impaired an essential interest of a State towards which the obligation existed; and the State that did not act in conformity with its international obligations must not have contributed to the occurrence of a state of necessity. The Court agreed that Hungary's concerns with respect to its natural environment relate to an 'essential interest' within the context of Draft Article 33. Therefore, a state of ecological necessity could be a valid reason for a State not to act in conformity with its international obligations. However, the Court decided that the peril was not imminent and, moreover, that the suspension and abandonment of the project was not the only choice of means available as a response to the peril. Slovakia pleaded countermeasures as a circumstance precluding wrongfulness of the unilateral damning of the Danube by it. In connection with this, the Court listed the conditions that justify the application of countermeasures. As Lefeber observes:

> it is noteworthy that the Court did not state that Draft Article 30 of the 1996 ILC Draft Articles on State Responsibility reflects customary international law, but only referred to Draft Articles 47–50 as one of the sources of the conditions which a countermeasure must meet for it to be justifiable.[22]

These are the conditions specified by the Court in relation to countermeasures: it must be taken in response to a previous wrongdoing of another State and must be directed against that State; the injured State must have asked that State to no effect to cease its wrongful act or to provide reparation for it; and the effects of counter-measures must be commensurate to the injury suffered, taking into consideration the requirement of proportionality. The Court found that Slovakia had failed to meet the condition of proportionality, based on the observation that Slovakia had assumed unilateral control over the shared resource, and therefore deprived Hungary

[22] Lefeber, above n 11, p 617.

of its right to an equitable and reasonable share of the natural resources of the Danube. Hungary also pleaded counter-measures.[23] Hungary, in its pleading before the Court, mixed arguments deriving from the law of treaties and those from the law of counter-measures. To justify the termination of the 1977 Treaty, it did not only rely on the material breach of that Treaty by Slovakia but also invoked the violation of environmental obligations under general international law. As Lefeber comments:

> Hungary, thus confused its right to terminate the 1977 Treaty in response to a material breach of Slovakia with its right to resort to countermeasures in response to the internationally wrongful act of Slovakia.[24]

The Court segregated the arguments made by Hungary based on the law of treaties and on the law of State responsibility but it did not examine whether the violation of the provisions of the 1977 Treaty or any rules of general international law justified the termination of the 1977 Treaty under the law of countermeasures.[25] As to the consequences of an internationally wrongful act, the Court relied on a principle enunciated in the *Chorzow Factory case* namely that

> reparation must, as far as possible wipe out all the consequences of the illegal act and re-establish the situation which would, in all probability, have existed if that act had not been committed.[26]

In this case, the Court adopted, as a means of reparation, the solution that provides for mutual obliteration of intersecting wrongs, a means that was not provided for in the 1996 ILC Draft Articles on State Responsibility on which the Court relied in this case. The Court stated that Hungary and Slovakia

> ... resume their co-operation in the utilisation of the shared water resource of the Danube, and if the multi-purpose programme, in the form of a co-ordinated single unit, for the use, development and protection of the watercourse is implemented in an equitable and reasonable manner.[27]

[23] *Gabčíkovo-Nagymaros Project (Hungary/Slovakia)* case, above n 11, para 106.
[24] Lefeber, above n 11, p 618.
[25] The Court said as follows: 'As to that part of Hungary's argument which was based on other treaties and general rules of international law, the Court is of the view that it is only a material breach of treaty itself, by a State party to that treaty, which entitles the other party to rely on it as a ground for terminating the treaty. The violation of other treaty rules or rules of general international law may justify the taking of certain measures, including countermeasures, by the injured State, but it does not constitute a ground for termination under the law of treaties.' (Above n 11, para 106).
[26] *The Factory at Chorzow (Claim for Indemnity) (Germany v Poland), Merits,* Judgment No 13 of 13 September 1928, *PCIJ, (SerA), No 17* (1928), p 47.
[27] *Gabčíkovo-Nagymaros Project (Hungary/Slovakia)* case, above n 11, para 150.

2. COMPLIANCE PROCEDURES

These practical difficulties in invoking responsibility for environmental damage as well as the reluctance of States to do so has led to the creation of new (alternative) mechanisms for dealing with breaches of international obligations. In particular, this has given rise to discussion as to how best to ensure that States live up to their commitments in the case of damage to the environment that not only has a negative impact on a particular State, but on a group of States or on the international community as a whole.

Although almost all international environmental agreements that were concluded in recent years contain provisions for dispute settlement by arbitral tribunals and/or the International Court of Justice[28] that may be used by States to invoke violations of international obligations under these agreements, until now they have not been employed by any party to an international environmental agreement. This lack of practice does not mean that violations of international environmental agreements do not occur. In recent years such breaches occurred eg under the Montreal Protocol on Substances that Deplete the Ozone Layer 1987 where a number of States did not meet their obligations.[29] In none of these cases did a party to the Montreal Protocol invoke the responsibility of the party in breach of its obligations. The reason for that is that only a limited number of parties to international environmental agreements have made declarations accepting arbitration or the jurisdiction of the International Court of Justice. Furthermore, States willing to invoke responsibility for damage to the environment face difficulties in, for example, proving the causality between a certain activity and damage suffered, as mentioned above.

These elements contributed to the establishment of so-called 'compliance' or 'non-compliance procedures and/or mechanisms'. The first of these procedures has been established under the Montreal Protocol, and since then most international environmental agreements have included such procedures or they are currently under negotiation for inclusion. The compliance mechanisms under the Montreal Protocol on Substances that Deplete the Ozone Layer and the compliance system under the ECE Convention on Long-range Transboundary Air Pollution are the best-known examples of such mechanisms, already in operation. But compliance mechanisms have also been set up under the Kyoto Protocol, the Basel Convention on the Transboundary

[28] See eg Art 14 of the United Nations Framework Convention on Climate Change, 1992 and Art 19 of the Kyoto Protocol, 1997; Art 27 of the Convention on Biodiversity, 1992 and Art 32 of the Cartagena Protocol on Biological Safety, 2000 (which provides that Art 27 of the Convention on Biodiversity applies to the Cartagena Protocol); Art 18 of the Stockholm Convention on Persistent Organic Pollutants, 2001.

[29] Cf the reports of the meeting of State parties of the Montreal Protocol. States parties that have found to be in non-compliance are, for example, the Russian Federation and the Ukraine.

Movement of Hazardous Waste and their Disposal, the Aarhus Convention on Access to Information, Public Participation in Decision-Making and Access to Justice in Environmental Matters[30] and the Convention on the Protection of the Alps and its Protocols.[31] Furthermore, the establishment of compliance procedures are discussed under the Convention on Persistent Organic Pollutants, the Convention on Prior Informed Consent for Certain Chemicals and Pesticides and the Cartagena Protocol on Biological Security.

The main elements of compliance procedures—as they were seen at the beginning of the 1990's—were described in the ECE Lucerne Declaration Concerning the Environment 1993.[32] It described the main elements of such mechanisms as to:

— avoid complexity,
— be non-confrontational,
— be transparent,
— leave the competence for taking decisions to be determined by the Contracting Parties,
— leave to the Contracting Parties to each Convention to consider what technical and financial decisions may be required, within the context of the specific agreement.
— include a transparent and revealing reporting system and procedure, as agreed by the Contracting Parties.[33]

The compliance procedures that have been established share these basic features, however they differ to a certain extent depending on the character of the commitments under the international environmental agreement in question.[34] On the one hand so-called 'multilateral consultative procedures' which aim to facilitate compliance have been created, such as the MCP procedure under the United Nations Framework Convention on

[30] The compliance procedure under the Aarhus Convention is unique as it—unlike other international environmental agreements—aims to ensure that parties live up to their commitments to establish specific internal legal procedures for environmental decision-making.

[31] Under the Convention for the Protection of the Alps the first compliance procedure has been established on a sub-regional level. Cf M Reiterer, 'The Alpine Convention and Beyond: Recent Development Concerning Mountainous Regions', 6 *Austrian Review on International and European Law* (2002).

[32] Para 23.1 of the Luzerne Declaration Concerning the Environment, 1993.

[33] Cf G Loibl, 'Dispute Avoidance and Dispute Settlement in International Environmental Law—Some Reflections on Recent Developments', in *Organización de los Estados Americanos, Comité Juridicio Interamericano, XXIV Curso de Derecho Internacional* (1997), p 101, at p 120.

[34] During the negotiations it has been stated that compliance procedures need be 'tailor-made', ie that although there are certain common elements to be found in all of them, they have been found to be adjusted to the specific circumstances of the international environmental agreement in question.

Climate Change,[35] on the other hand 'compliance procedures' which might even include 'sanctions' for breaches of the respective obligations, such as the compliance procedures under the Kyoto Protocol. At the centre of these procedures is the establishment of a committee consisting of a limited number of parties—in the case of the Montreal Protocol 10 parties selected on the basis of equitable geographic distribution—or individuals elected in their individual capacity, as in the case of the Kyoto Protocol.

The different functions of compliance procedures today may be clearly seen when comparing the objectives of the different procedures: on the one hand procedures aim to facilitate and promote compliance with the international environmental agreements (eg under the UNECE Convention on Long-range Transboundary Air Pollution); and on the other hand, some of them also have the 'enforcement' objective as regards compliance (eg under the Kyoto Protocol).

With the creation of the 'enforcement' procedure, a new element has been added to the functions of the compliance procedures. A question may be asked whether the evolution of compliance procedures within the last decade has changed their legal nature. To answer this question the compliance procedures under the Montreal Protocol, the first such procedure to become operative, and under the Kyoto Protocol, so far the most far reaching compliance procedure in relation to 'sanctions for non-compliance', will be compared.

2.1. Non-Compliance Procedure under the Montreal Protocol

The compliance procedure under the Montreal Protocol is conducted by a committee—the so-called Implementation Committee—consisting of a limited number of 10 States representatives. It is entrusted with the task of dealing with cases of non-compliance or potential non-compliance by States parties to the Montreal Protocol.[36] The procedure may be initiated by the party itself, another party or on information provided to the Implementation Committee. In dealing with the case the committee may suggest ways and means to improve the implementation of and compliance with the internationally agreed rules of a specific State. They may suggest measures to be taken to the Conference of the States parties—the organ that comprises all States parties to the Montreal Protocol—ranging from

[35] Art 13 states that an MCP shall be established 'for the resolution of questions regarding the implementation of the Convention'. Although the main elements of the MCP have been agreed, no consensus has been reached on the size of the committee and its composition.

[36] The Implementation Committee is not only mandated to deal with cases where a party has failed to meet its commitments, but also with cases where a party is not likely to meet its commitments in the future.

incentives and assistance, to suspension of certain rights and privileges under the Protocol. The measures that might be suggested by the Implementation Committee to the meeting of the States parties are contained in an 'indicative list of measures':

> A. Appropriate assistance, including assistance for the collection and reporting of data, technical assistance, technology transfer and financial assistance, information transfer and training.
> B. Issuing caution.
> C. Suspension, in accordance with the applicable rules of international law concerning the suspension of the operation of a treaty, of specific rights and privileges under the Protocol, whether or not subject to time limits, including those concerned with industrial rationalisation, production, consumption, trade, transfer of technology, financial mechanism and institutional arrangements.[37]

2.2. Procedures and Mechanisms Relating to Compliance under the Kyoto Protocol

The compliance procedure under the Kyoto Protocol is more complex than the one under the Montreal Protocol. This might be explained by the difference in the obligations undertaken under the Kyoto Protocol and the means available to the parties to achieve their commitments. The central obligation under the Kyoto Protocol is the commitment of industrialised countries to reduce or limit their 'carbon dioxide equivalent emissions of the greenhouse gases' in the commitment period 2008 to 2012.[38] These commitments might either be reached by policies and measures on the national level[39] or by use of the 'economic' mechanisms (joint implementation, clean development mechanism and emissions trading).[40] The general idea underlying these mechanisms is to help to achieve emission reduction and limitation obligations at lower costs for the countries concerned than if they were

[37] Annex V, UNEP/OzL.Pro4/15. For a detailed analysis of the non-compliance procedure under the Montreal Protocol see M Koskenniemi, 'Breach of Treaty or Non-Compliance? Reflections on the Enforcement of the Montreal Protocol', 3 *Yearbook of International Environmental Law* (1992), p 125.
[38] Annex A lists six gases for which these commitments apply: carbon dioxide, methane, nitrous oxide, hydrofluorocarbons, perfluorocarbons and sulphur hexafluoride. Annex B lists the qualified emission limitation and reduction commitments undertaken by each industrialised State, ranging from a reduction of 8% to a limitation of emission increase by 10%.
[39] Art 2 of the Kyoto Protocol.
[40] Art 6 (joint implementation), Art 12 (clean development mechanism) and Art 17 (emissions trading) of the Kyoto Protocol.

to have to take all necessary measures within their territory. But in order to allow these economic mechanisms to operate successfully a strong monitoring and controlling mechanism was regarded as essential by the negotiators to ensure that industrialised parties would not be able to escape their obligations.

Other provisions contained in the Kyoto Protocol are formulated in a manner that commits countries merely to undertake efforts, eg, to co-operate in scientific and technical research.[41] That differentiation of commitments under the Kyoto Protocol is reflected in the structure of the 'procedures and mechanisms relating to compliance under the Kyoto Protocol'.[42] A comprehensive compliance system has been created addressing all obligations under the Kyoto Protocol, but its operation is divided into two branches: the facilitative and the enforcement branch. The facilitative branch, which follows the example of the Montreal Protocol, is responsible for providing advice and facilitation to States parties in implementing the Protocol and promoting compliance, unless the issues at stake fall within the mandate of the enforcement branch. The enforcement branch is responsible for dealing with the provisions of the Kyoto Protocol that relate to the commitments of the industrialised States to reduce or limit their emissions. The mandate of the enforcement branch comprises the following obligations: under Article 3 paragraph 1 (and Annex B) on quantified emission limitation and reduction commitments; Article 5 paragraphs 1 and 2, and Article 7, paragraphs 1 and 4 on methodological and reporting requirements; and eligibility requirements to make use of the mechanisms under Articles 6, 12 and 18.

Common to both branches is that their members are elected in their individual capacities. The procedural aspects of both branches are regulated in great detail.[43] This particularly holds true for the enforcement branch that provides for specific procedural rights for parties under consideration.[44] These procedural rules resemble to a large extent procedures before judicial bodies, ie courts and tribunals. Furthermore, an appeal procedure—against a decision of the enforcement branch—is permitted to the Conference of the States parties in case the party concerned argues that it has been denied due process.

The 'consequences' that might be applied by the two branches, if a party is found to be in non-compliance with its obligations, differ. Whereas the

[41] See Art 10 (d) of the Kyoto Protocol.

[42] By Decision 24/CP.7 COPVII adopted the text containing the compliance procedure under the Kyoto Protocol and recommended it for adoption to COP/MOP1.

[43] Eg if a question concerning compliance is brought before a branch, the relevant branch has to ensure, that it '(a) is supported by sufficient information; (b) is not *de minimis* or ill-founded; and (c) is based on the requirements of the Protocol.'

[44] It should be noted that the procedural requirements for the enforcement branch are stricter than those for the facilitative branch. For the beginning of the negotiations it was understood that the consequences to be applied by the enforcement branch will have a more severe impact on the party concerned. Thus, a number of parties requested that the principle of due process has to be a central element of the enforcement branch procedure.

facilitative branch might provide advice and facilitate assistance as well as make recommendations to the party concerned, the consequences under the enforcement branch are more serious.

If a party is found in non-compliance with its obligations under Article 3 paragraph 1 and Annex B the enforcement branch shall apply the following consequences:

> (a) deduction from the Party's assigned amount for the second commitment period a number of tonnes equal to 1.3 times the amount in tonnes of excess emissions;
> (b) development of a compliance action plan in accordance with paragraphs 6 and 7;[45] and
> (c) suspension of the eligibility to make transfers under Article 17 of the Protocol until the Party is reinstated in accordance with section X, paragraph 3 or paragraph 4.

Moreover, if a party is found in non-compliance with their reporting obligations,[46] the enforcement branch

> shall apply the following consequences, taking into account the cause, type, degree and frequency of the non-compliance of that party: (a) Declaration of non-compliance; and (b) Development of a plan in accordance with paragraphs 2 and 3.[47] Where a party is found not to meet the eligibility requirements for the mechanisms, the party's eligibility is to be suspended.

By creating the enforcement branch the compliance procedures have been elaborated further. Although the Kyoto Protocol has not yet entered into force,[48] it deserves a more detailed scrutiny as regards issues raised by these new developments.

3. QUESTIONS RAISED BY THE ESTABLISHMENT OF COMPLIANCE PROCEDURES

Already the establishment of the first compliance procedure has given rise to a number of questions concerning the legal nature of compliance procedures and on the relationship between compliance procedures and general rules of public international law, in particular the law of State responsibility, the law

[45] These paragraphs set out the elements of a compliance action plan.
[46] These obligations are set out in Article 5 paras 1 and 2 and Art 7 paras 1 and 4.
[47] These paragraphs set out the elements of such a plan.
[48] The Kyoto Protocol will enter into force when the number of States that ratify the agreement represents 55% of the level of emissions of industrialised countries. Until now more than 100 States have ratified the Kyoto Protocol, but the 55% requirement has not yet been reached.

of treaties—especially Article 60 of the Vienna Convention on the Law of Treaties 1969—and provisions on the settlement of disputes.

With regard to the relationship between compliance procedures and dispute settlement systems all compliance systems that have been created contain a provision stating, 'compliance systems shall operate without prejudice to dispute settlement procedures'.

Although this statement seems to clarify the relationship, it leaves a number of questions open, such as what would be the legal consequence if a compliance procedure and a dispute settlement procedure take place at the same time involving a particular party and the same subject matter. As regards the traditional type of compliance procedure—as established under the Montreal Protocol—the different objectives of the two procedures have to be borne in mind. The dispute settlement procedure aims at determining whether a breach of an international obligation has occurred and if so, what are its legal consequences. The compliance procedure's objective is to ensure that a party fulfils its obligations. Furthermore, the measures taken under a 'traditional' compliance system focus on 'soft consequences'—give advice and facilitate assistance to the party concerned.[49] Even the Montreal Protocol's compliance system envisages in case of a violation of the obligations by a party that the committee may propose—in addition to 'soft consequences'—that the Conference of the States parties suspend the rights and privileges of a party 'in accordance with the applicable rules of international law concerning the suspension of the operation of a treaty'. This consequence may be seen as a reaction to the 'material breach' of a multilateral treaty by the other parties as provided for in Article 60 of the Vienna Convention of the Law of Treaties 1969 and does not address questions of State responsibility.[50] Thus, in light of the judgment in the *Gabčíkovo-Nagymaros Project (Hungary/Slovakia)* case,[51] the suspension of rights and privileges under the Montreal Protocol in accordance with the law of treaties would not affect the international responsibility of the party in breach of its obligations.[52]

[49] For a detailed discussion of the relationship between dispute settlement and compliance procedures see M Fitzmaurice and C Redgwell, 'Environmental Non-Compliance Procedures and International Law', XXXI *Netherlands Yearbook of International Law* (2000), p 35, at p 43.

[50] Art 73 of the Vienna Convention of the Law of Treaties, 1969 explicitly states that the provisions of the Vienna Convention on the Law of Treaties do not prejudge questions of State responsibility relating to treaties.

[51] *ICJ Reports*, 1997, para 47. The Court held: 'Thus the Vienna Convention of 1969 on the Law of Treaties confines itself to defining—in a limitative manner—the conditions in which a treaty may lawfully be denounced or suspended; while the effects of a denunciation or suspension seen as not meeting those conditions are, on the contrary, expressly excluded from the scope of the Convention by operation of Article 73. It is moreover well established that, when a State has committed an internationally wrongful act, its international responsibility is likely to be involved whatever the nature of the obligation it has failed to respect.'

[52] The reference in the MP to 'the applicable rules of international law concerning the suspension of the operation of a treaty' could also be read as including the law of State responsibility.

Does this distinction really hold true when looking at the enforcement branch that has been created under the compliance system of the Kyoto Protocol? The procedure under the enforcement branch has added new flavour to the debate on the legal nature of compliance procedures. As has been described above, the compliance committee consists of individuals who act in their own capacity, the procedure to be applied is laid down in detail (including safeguards for the party concerned), and the consequences to be applied are not limited to 'soft sanctions' and suspension, but include specific activities of the party concerned. Thus, one could argue that the compliance system under the Kyoto Protocol has come very close to a judicial procedure, albeit not a traditional procedure that is based on the contradictory interest of the parties to the procedure, but rather an administrative procedure—as known in most municipal legal systems—where the authority is to monitor and ensure that the administrative law is complied with by individuals. The enforcement branch could be seen as an international authority that has been entrusted by the parties to the Kyoto Protocol to monitor the individual countries performance and take 'sanctions' if necessary to ensure that the treaty obligations are complied with. Thus, the enforcement branch could be seen as an international authority to ensure the application of an objective legal regime.

Another new element under the Kyoto Protocol is that in contrast to 'traditional' compliance procedures, whose objective is to bring the party into compliance with its obligations in the future, ie although these systems are forward looking, facts and situations are addressed that have occurred in the past,[53] the enforcement branch procedures will deal with situations which have happened in the past. Whether a party has met its obligations under Article 3 paragraph 1 in conjunction with Annex B can only be established once the first commitment period (2008 to 2012) is over.[54] Thus 'sanctions' do not have the objective here of bringing a party back into compliance, but to determine 'consequences' for its failures in the past. At the same time they aim to ameliorate the environmental situation, such as the consequences to be applied by the enforcement branch if a party is found in breach of its commitments under Article 3 paragraph 1 to deduct 'from the

During the negotiations no reference was made to State responsibility and the wording clearly points to suspension of the operation of a treaty as envisaged in Art 60 of the Vienna Convention of the Law of Treaties 1969.

[53] 'Traditional' compliance procedures are entrusted to take measures to advise a party how to come back into compliance (ie the party is currently not meeting its commitments) or how to avoid not being able to meet its commitments in the future.

[54] The 'procedures and mechanisms relating to compliance under the Kyoto Protocol' even provide for an 'additional period for fulfilling commitments' under Art 3 para 1 after the end of the first commitment period. During this additional period countries may acquire emission reduction units which bring them into compliance with their commitments.

Party's assigned amount for the second commitment period of a number of tonnes equal to 1.3 times the amount in tonnes of excess emissions' and to establish a compliance action plan.[55]

The difficulty that the enforcement branch might face when determining whether a party is in breach of its obligations under the Kyoto Protocol and applying consequences is that the compliance procedures do not provide—in contrast to the law of State responsibility—for 'circumstances precluding wrongfulness'.[56] Thus it remains to be seen how, for example, the enforcement branch would deal with a party's argument that due to say an earthquake—that led to heavy damage to its infrastructure—it could not meet its emissions targets.

The question also arises whether international environmental agreements setting up compliance systems that are to determine breaches of commitments and apply consequences can be regarded as 'lex specialis' in the sense of Article 55 of the ILC articles on State responsibility. Before the establishment of the enforcement branch of the Kyoto Protocol, 'traditional' compliance systems could be seen as limited regarding the measures they could apply. With the enforcement branch of the Kyoto Protocol a new stage has been reached, that, it can be argued, involves elements that belong to the sphere of the law of State responsibility. The creation of such compliance procedures—and their further evolution—could mean that general rules of State responsibility would no longer apply but would be replaced by special rules under the treaty regime, bearing in mind that all compliance procedures operate without prejudice to dispute settlement. But how would the dispute settlement provisions of international environmental agreements fit into such a framework? As the consequences set out in the compliance procedures are only to be applied by the institutions set up within these systems, it seems obvious that if a dispute is referred by the parties to an international court or an arbitral tribunal the consequences as contained in the law of State responsibility are to be applied. The decision which establishes the compliance procedures under the Kyoto Protocol also lists the consequences to be applied by the two branches. Thus, if an international court or an arbitral tribunal is called upon to determine whether a party is in breach of its obligations under the Kyoto Protocol it will have to apply the law of State responsibility.[57]

Examples that have been used to demonstrate the issues raised by the emergence of compliance procedures in recent years are procedures under

[55] During the negotiations it was argued by a number of parties that the factor 1.3 is to be seen as an 'interest to the environment' and the excess amount of emissions has to be made up in the second commitment period (the treaty provisions for the second commitment period still remain to be agreed upon by the parties).

[56] Cf Arts 20 to 27 of the ILC Articles on State Responsibility.

[57] See Part II of the ILC Articles on State Responsibility.

international environmental agreements dealing with natural resources that are in the interest of the international community and therefore it is very unlikely that a 'bilateral dispute' might arise. It must be noted, however, that in recent years compliance procedures have been established or are also under negotiation for multilateral environmental treaties where it is most likely that 'bilateral disputes' will arise.

An example of such an international environmental agreement is the Cartagena Protocol on Biosafety. One of the central provisions of this treaty is the 'Advanced Informed Agreement Procedure' for 'Living Modified Organisms' concerning their transboundary movements. The procedure sets out a strict time frame for the country of import to decide whether to permit or prohibit the import of a living modified organism. Thus if a party to the Cartagena Protocol does not take a decision within the time frame set it is to be seen as being in breach of its obligations under the Protocol and a bilateral dispute may arise between the importing and the exporting country.

The Cartagena Protocol provides traditional dispute settlement mechanisms—including recourse to arbitration and the International Court of Justice—and envisages the establishment of a compliance procedure. If the compliance procedure is to apply 'consequences' that exceed those envisaged under the law of treaties, the question of the legal nature of the compliance regime will become more urgent, as both dispute settlement mechanisms and compliance procedures under the Cartagena Protocol may be used to deal with a 'bilateral dispute.' Considering, however, that the Cartagena Protocol deals with transboundary movement of goods, a dispute might also be referred to dispute settlement procedures under the World Trade Organisation.

4. CONCLUSION

The evolution of new mechanisms over the last years in the environmental field addressing issues of non-compliance has been criticised as softening the obligations of States by providing a mechanism that allows them to escape responsibility. Thus far, available practice has not confirmed this prediction. Rather, these mechanisms have helped to ensure that parties live up to their obligations. The success of the Montreal Protocol's compliance procedure has proved this. The enforcement branch of the Kyoto Protocol has added a new dimension to compliance procedures. It contains many elements that have only been known from judicial procedures before, such as the principle of due process and 'sanctions'. Increasing overlap between such compliance procedures and the law of State responsibility seems likely to occur, and, as observed above, the question might even be raised whether they may constitute *lex specialis*.

12

The UN Compensation Commission and Liability for the Costs of Monitoring and Assessment of Environmental Damage

OLUFEMI ELIAS*

1. INTRODUCTION

IN ITS RESOLUTION 687 (1991), the United Nations (UN) Security Council reaffirmed Iraq's liability for 'any direct loss, including environmental damage and the depletion of natural resources' arising as a result of Iraq's unlawful invasion and occupation of Kuwait (August 1990–March 1991), and decided to create both a fund to pay compensation for eligible losses and a commission to review claims for compensation and to administer the fund.[1] On the basis of recommendations made to the Security Council by the UN Secretary-General, the Council established the UN Compensation Commission ('the Commission') and the UN Compensation Fund.[2]

As will be described in more detail hereafter, the Governing Council of the Commission determined, in sub-paragraphs 35(c) and (d) of its Decision 7,[3] that 'direct environmental damage and depletion of natural resources' include losses or expenses resulting from (i) the reasonable monitoring and assessment of environmental damage undertaken for the purpose of evaluating and abating the harm, and (ii) the monitoring of public health

* Legal Adviser, Governing Council Secretariat, United Nations Compensation Commission.
The author is grateful to Elisabeth Bowes for her comments on a draft of this paper. The views expressed here are the author's alone, and this paper is not to be considered as an expression of the views of the Commission.

1 Security Council resolution 687 (1991), section E, paras 16–19.

2 See Security Council resolution 692 (1991), and the *Report of the Secretary-General Pursuant to Paragraph 19 of Resolution 687* (1991), S/22559, 2 May 1991.

3 See Governing Council Decision 7 (S/AC 26/1991/7/Rev 1), para 35.

for the purposes of investigation and combating increased health risks arising as a result of the environmental damage. These two heads of damage are included in a non-exhaustive list, in paragraph 35, of 'substantive' (in the sense that they are not merely incidental or ancillary) heads of compensable environmental damage, alongside other heads of loss such as liability for expenses arising from measures taken to abate and prevent environmental damage and to clean and restore the environment, as well as the depletion of natural resources.

The aim of this paper is to examine briefly the nature and status of the two heads of loss mentioned in sub-paragraphs 35(c) and (d), namely the costs of monitoring and assessment of environmental damage and the public health impacts thereof. These are independent substantive heads of liability for environmental damage in their own right, separate and distinct from liability for the actual damage caused to the environment. The examination will be based on considerations of principle and some international practice, which, it is hoped, will place in context the possible contribution of the Commission to the issue of liability for environmental damage in international law in this regard.

2. OVERVIEW OF THE COMMISSION AND CLAIMS SUBMITTED FOR ENVIRONMENTAL DAMAGE

2.1. The Institutional Structure of the Commission

The Commission is composed of three bodies, namely the Governing Council, the commissioners and the secretariat. The Governing Council, whose membership is the same as that of the Security Council, is the main policy-making organ of the Commission. It is responsible for the establishment of the criteria for the compensability of claims, the rules and procedures for processing the claims, the guidelines for the administration and financing of the Compensation Fund and the procedures for the payment of compensation. It is also responsible for taking decisions, which are final and not subject to appeal or review, on recommendations made by the panels of commissioners concerning claims reviewed by the latter. The commissioners are responsible for the review and processing of claims submitted to the Commission. They are required to determine whether the alleged losses or injury arose as a direct result of Iraq's invasion and occupation of Kuwait. They are also required to assess the value of losses considered to be direct and to make written recommendations as to compensation to the Governing Council.[4]

[4] See section III, Arts 18–27, and section IV, Arts 28–43, of the Commission's Provisional Rules for Claims Procedure ('The Rules', annexed to Governing Council Decision 10, S/AC 26/1992/10).

Funds to pay the awards of compensation are drawn from the United Nations Compensation Fund which currently receives 5 per cent of the revenue generated from the export of Iraqi petroleum and petroleum products, pursuant to Security Council resolution 1483 (2003).[5]

2.2. Claims for Environmental Damage[6]

More than 2.6 million claims seeking compensation with an asserted value in excess of US$300 billion were submitted to the Commission. These claims were grouped into six categories (A–F) for the purposes of processing. Category F claims are claims filed by Governments and international organisations, and claims for environmental damage and the depletion of natural resources form a sub-category, namely category F4.[7] Most of these claims were submitted by States in the Persian Gulf region on whose territory environmental damage and depletion of natural resources are alleged to have occurred (the 'regional Governments', namely Iran, Jordan, Kuwait, Saudi Arabia and Syria). Claims were also submitted by non-regional claimants for expenses incurred in the provision of assistance in responding to the environmental damage caused as a result of the invasion and occupation of Kuwait. The claimants seek compensation for alleged losses connected to, inter alia, the release and transport, into their territories, of airborne pollutants caused by oil fires resulting from the ignition of hundreds of oil wells in Kuwait by Iraqi forces during Iraq's invasion and occupation of Kuwait; numerous oil rivers and lakes formed by oil from the destroyed oil wells that did not ignite; the release, by Iraqi forces, of millions of barrels of oil into the Persian Gulf from oil pipelines, offshore terminals and oil tankers; disruption of fragile desert and coastal terrain caused by the movement of military vehicles and personnel, coupled with the construction of thousands of kilometres of military trenches and

[5] Security Council resolution 1483 (2003), para 21. Prior to that, 25% of the revenue derived from Iraqi oil sales was paid into the Compensation Fund pursuant to Security Council resolution 1330 (2000), within the framework of the 'oil-for-food' mechanism set up pursuant to resolution 986 (1995).

[6] See, generally, M Kazazi, 'Environmental Damage in the Practice of the UNCC', in M Bowman and A Boyle (eds), *Environmental Damage in International and Comparative Law* (Oxford, 2002).

[7] The State-owned Kuwait Oil Company filed the Well Blowout Control Claim in category E (claims of corporations and other entities) on behalf of the Kuwaiti oil sector. This claim was filed as a corporate claim and not as an environmental claim (see S/AC.26/1996/5/Annex generally, especially paras 47–61). The claim concerned the work performed to extinguish the wellhead fires that were burning upon the withdrawal of Iraqi forces from Kuwait, the initial sealing of the wells to stop the flow of oil and gas, and the making safe of the wellheads so that work on the reinstatement of production of oil could be started. The same panel also reviewed the claims by the Kuwait Petroleum Corporation that could be considered as claims for depletion of natural resources (see S/AC 26/2000/16, paras 89 *et seq*).

the emplacement of mines, weapons caches and other fortifications; and adverse impacts on the environment resulting from the transit and settlement of thousands of persons who departed Iraq and Kuwait as a result of Iraq's invasion and occupation of Kuwait. The claimants also seek compensation for the expenses resulting from monitoring and assessment activities undertaken or to be undertaken to identify and evaluate the environmental damage or loss suffered by them.

2.3. Procedure[8]

Given that Iraq's liability under international law for environmental damage resulting from its invasion and occupation of Kuwait has been affirmed by the Security Council,[9] the role of the Commission—in particular, the panels of commissioners—is essentially administrative in nature. This is reflected in the recommendation made by the Secretary-General in his report to the Security Council concerning the nature of the Commission, to the effect that:

> The Commission is not a court or an arbitral tribunal before which the parties appear; it is a political organ that performs an essentially fact-finding function of examining claims, verifying their validity, evaluating losses, assessing payments and resolving disputed claims. It is only in this last respect that a quasi-judicial function may be involved.[10]

This recommendation is reflected in the functioning of the Commission, and the compensation process established by Security Council resolution 692 (1991) is distinct from previous mechanisms established for the resolution of international claims.[11] Proceedings before the Commission are inquisitorial rather than adversarial in nature, given the need to avoid excessive delays in the processing of the claims, and the Rules generally allow for more limited participation in the proceedings by claimants and Iraq than is the case in traditional courts and tribunals.[12] The panels of

[8] See M Raboin, 'The Provisional Rules for Claims Procedure of the United Nations Compensation Commission: A Practical Approach to Mass Claims Processing', in R Lillich (ed), *The United Nations Compensation Commission* (Thirteenth Sokol Colloquium) (New York, 1995), p 119.
[9] See Security Council Resolution 687, paragraph 16: text corresponding to n 1 above.
[10] See Report of the Secretary-General Pursuant to Paragraph 19 of Security Council resolution 687 (1991) (S/22559), para 20.
[11] See, eg, BG Affaki, 'The United Nations Compensation Commission: A New Era in Claims Settlement?' 10 *Journal of International Arbitration* (1993), p 21.
[12] See Arts 16 and 36–39 of the Rules, above n 4. See, eg, Report and Recommendations made by the Panel of Commissioners Concerning the Fourth Instalment of E3 Claims (S/AC 26/1999/14), paras 40, 61–62.

commissioners operate within strict time-limits, and it is left to their discretion to decide whether additional information and documentation, or oral proceedings, are required.[13]

Between 2000 and mid-2001, the Governing Council undertook a review of the claims review process and adopted a number of significant procedural changes,[14] with a view to increasing the level of Iraq's participation in the claims review process, and many of these changes are applicable to category F4 claims. First, the Governing Council called for the convening of oral proceedings in certain circumstances, including 'where the claims under review are substantive "F4" environmental claims',[15] and this has been reflected in the practice of the F4 Panel thus far. Secondly, and perhaps more significantly, the Governing Council established an exceptional arrangement for the provision of 'technical assistance' to Iraq,[16] the aim of which is:

> to facilitate the promotion of the legitimate interests of Iraq with respect to 'F4' claims, which give rise to particular questions due to their complexity and the limited amount of relevant international practice, and is also aimed at assisting the 'F4' panel of commissioners in the conduct of its tasks, through ensuring the full development of the facts and relevant technical issues, and in obtaining the full range of views including those of Iraq.[17]

The role of the experts is to assist Iraq in preparing written submissions and any other communication with the Commission on F4 claims, and participating in oral proceedings before the panel. These procedural modifications are intended to ensure the full participation of Iraq in the review of F4 claims.

3. CLAIMS FOR THE MONITORING AND ASSESSMENT OF ENVIRONMENTAL DAMAGE BEFORE THE COMMISSION

As mentioned earlier, paragraph 35 of Governing Council Decision 7[18] sets out a non-exhaustive list of the kinds of environmental damage and the

[13] Rules, above n 4, Art 36.
[14] See generally, C Lim, 'On the Law, Procedures and Politics of United Nations Gulf War Reparations', *Singapore Journal of International and Comparative Law* (2000), p 435.
[15] Governing Council Decision 114 (S/AC 26/Dec 114 (2000)), para 21.
[16] Governing Council Decision 124 (S/AC 26/Dec 124 (2001)).
[17] *Ibid*, at para 2.
[18] See n 3 above.

depletion of natural resources for which compensation would be available. It provides that compensable environmental damage losses

> will include losses or expenses resulting from:
> (a) Abatement and prevention of environmental damage, including expenses directly relating to fighting oil fires and stemming the flow of oil in coastal and international waters;
> (b) Reasonable measures already taken to clean and restore the environment or future measures which can be documented as reasonably necessary to clean and restore the environment;
> (c) Reasonable monitoring and assessment of the environmental damage for the purposes of evaluating and abating the harm and restoring the environment;
> (d) Reasonable monitoring of public health and performing medical screenings for the purposes of investigation and combating increased health risks as a result of the environmental damage; and
> (e) Depletion of or damage to natural resources.

It will be apparent that sub-paragraphs (c) and (d) could be distinguished from the other heads of loss listed in paragraph 35. Such a distinction could be made on the basis that sub-paragraphs (a), (b) and (e) all relate more directly to compensation for damage actually caused to the environment, as they deal with the actual measures taken to abate and prevent environmental damage (such as fighting oil fires and stemming the flow of oil in coastal and international waters) and to clean and restore the environment, and with compensation for the depletion of natural resources. Sub-paragraphs (c) and (d), in contrast, might then be considered to relate to matters that in a certain sense are ancillary to those listed in the other sub-paragraphs, in the sense that the activities listed in those sub-paragraphs could provide information upon which claims for those other heads of loss could based. In response to such an argument, however, it should be noted that the fact that the costs of monitoring and assessment are included in the same list of compensable environmental damage losses as the other substantive heads of damage indicates that they are not merely ancillary or subsidiary losses. The following sub-sections will attempt to substantiate further the view that liability for monitoring and assessment costs is independent of related claims for environmental damage.

3.1. The Priority Accorded to the Treatment of Claims for Monitoring and Assessment

The Governing Council, at the request of claimants, decided to treat the claims for monitoring and assessment differently from the other claims for environmental damage. It decided to accord priority of processing and payment of compensation to the claims for monitoring and assessment. In 1998, the claimants based in the Persian Gulf region (Saudi Arabia, Iran, Jordan, Kuwait and Syria) requested that the Governing Council establish a procedure under which awards of compensation, based on recommendations made by the panel of commissioners, for the monitoring and assessment of claims would be made in advance of the review of the related substantive claims. After due consideration, the Governing Council requested the Executive Secretary of the Commission to invite the claimants (including Turkey, the other claimant that submitted claims for the costs of monitoring and assessment), to identify and to file separately within a specified time-limit, those portions of their claims already filed with the Commission that pertained to the monitoring and assessment of environmental damage. The Governing Council also decided that appropriate priority should be accorded to the processing of such claims, so that the claims could be resolved in advance of the other claims for environmental damage.[19] It is clear that the priority accorded to these claims shows their importance to the overall environmental claims review process. The question is whether this decision of the Governing Council provides a basis for considering the claims for monitoring and assessment as being of a different, less substantive nature than the other claims for environmental damage, or whether it affirms these claims as substantive claims in their own right.

The F4 panel of commissioners, in its first report[20] (which, pursuant to the same decision of the Governing Council, was concerned exclusively with monitoring and assessment claims), provided some explanation for the Governing Council's decision to accord priority to the claims based on paragraphs 35(c) and (d). It stated as follows, in the context of its discussion of the relationship between these claims and other claims for environmental damage:

> Most of the monitoring and assessment claims are related to substantive claims for environmental damage and depletion of natural resources *because the Claimants expect to use information obtained from the monitoring and assessment activities to support their substantive claims.* The Panel stresses that its recommendations on monitoring and assessment claims do not in any way prejudge its findings on related substantive claims that it may review subsequently. Each substantive claim will be reviewed on its own merits on the basis of the evidence presented to support it.

[19] See Documents of the United Nations Compensation Commission (S/AC.26/SER.A/1, 2001), p 186.

[20] Report and Recommendations made by the Panel of Commissioners concerning the First Instalment of F4 Claims (S/AC.26/2001/16, approved by the Governing Council in Decision 132 (S/AC 26/Dec 132 (2001)), paras 15–17.

> However, *the Panel anticipates that the results of some monitoring and assessment activities will assist its review of related substantive claims.* It recalls that the Governing Council's decision to authorize expedited review of monitoring and assessment claims was, in large part, *intended to make funds available to claimants to finance activities that might produce information to support their substantive 'F4' claims.* The Panel, therefore, emphasizes the importance of early submission of the results of monitoring and assessment activities for which compensation is awarded.[21]

This contains two reasons for the decision of the Governing Council. The first is the utility to the Panel of the information to be provided for the review of the other claims for environmental damage. The availability of such information is essential for the Panel's proper discharge of its duties. The second is the provision of funds to the claimants to finance activities that might produce information to support their other claims for environmental damage. Given the nature of the Commission, this second reason is best seen as being but a variation on the first, because the Commission is primarily a fact-finding institution rather than an essentially judicial and/or adversarial one; while the claimants may be considered to benefit from this arrangement, the provision of the information is again ultimately necessary for the fulfilment of the Panel's mandate.[22] In any event, the point is that the priority accorded to claims for monitoring and assessment was based on these reasons, and does not affect the status of these claims as claims for heads of damage on an equal footing with the other heads of environmental damage. This is borne out further in the following section.

3.2. The Absence of a Link between Recovery of the Costs of Monitoring and Assessment and the Success of the Claims for Environmental Damage

In its report and recommendations, the Panel was mindful of the fact that the monitoring and assessment claims were being reviewed at a point where it may not have been established that environmental damage or depletion of natural resources occurred as a result of Iraq's invasion and occupation of Kuwait. The Panel made three rulings in connection to this issue, which, taken together, indicate that the monitoring and assessment claims stood on their own and were not contingent or parasitic on other types of claim for environmental damage.

[21] *Ibid*, paras 38–39. Emphasis added.
[22] We will return to this issue in section 5. At this stage, it should be noted that concerns relating to equality of treatment between the claimants and Iraq are met by the Governing Council's Decision 124 to provide financial assistance to Iraq in the presentation of its 'F4' claims, and the provisions of para 21 of Decision 114; see section 2.3 above.

First, the Panel considered that since the results of the monitoring and assessment activities could be critical in enabling claimants to establish the existence of damage and to evaluate the quantum of compensation to be claimed:

> it would be both illogical and inequitable to reject a claim for reasonable monitoring and assessment on the sole ground that the claimant did not establish beforehand that environmental damage occurred. To reject a claim for that reason would, in effect, deprive the claimant of the opportunity to generate the very evidence that it needs to demonstrate the nature and extent of damage that may have occurred.

Accordingly, the Panel did not require conclusive proof of environmental damage as a prerequisite for a monitoring and assessment activity to be compensable under sub-paragraphs 35(c) and (d); the purpose of monitoring and assessment is 'to enable a claimant to develop evidence to establish whether environmental damage has occurred and to quantify the extent of the resulting loss.'[23]

Secondly, the Panel did not consider it necessary that the monitoring and assessment activities should establish conclusively that environmental damage had in fact been caused. It stated that:

> In the view of the Panel, a monitoring and assessment activity could be of benefit even if the results generated by the activity establish that no damage has been caused. The same may be the case where the results indicate that damage has occurred but that it is not feasible or advisable to undertake measures of remediation or restoration. Confirmation that no damage has been caused or that measures of remediation or restoration are not possible or advisable in the circumstances could assist the Panel in reviewing related substantive claims. It could also be beneficial in alleviating the concerns of Claimants regarding potential risks of damage, and help to avoid unnecessary and wasteful measures to deal with non-existent or negligible risks.[24]

Thirdly, the Panel considered the possibility that natural and other phenomena could have caused environmental damage of the kinds that were the subject of the claims submitted to the Commission, with the result that the monitoring and assessment activities could end up demonstrating that the damage had been caused either by factors unrelated to Iraq's invasion of Kuwait or by a combination of such factors and the invasion. The Panel also noted the possibility of a lack of adequately documented baseline information on the state of the environment and conditions regarding natural resources prior to the invasion and occupation of Kuwait, which would

[23] See Report, above n 20, at paras 29–30.
[24] *Ibid*, para 32.

make it difficult to distinguish between losses caused by the invasion and losses caused by other factors. The Panel ruled that although damage revealed by the monitoring and assessment activities to have been caused by factors unrelated to the invasion would not be compensable, the possibility, however, that such damage could have been wholly or partly caused by factors unrelated to the invasion did not of itself exclude compensation for the costs of those activities. The Panel also decided that claims for monitoring and assessment activities would not be unreasonable merely because it might be difficult for the claimant to distinguish between damage caused by the invasion and damage caused by other factors.[25]

These three rulings clearly indicate that the costs of monitoring and assessment were independent heads of loss that did not require the submission of successful claims for actual environmental damage. The success of claims for monitoring and assessment depended on other criteria, namely:

> whether there was evidence that the activity proposed or undertaken could produce information that might be helpful in identifying environmental damage and depletion of natural resources, or that could offer a useful basis for taking preventive or remedial measures.[26]

Accordingly, the minimum requirement is that '[t]here should be a sufficient nexus between the activity and environmental damage or risk of damage that may be attributed directly to Iraq's invasion and occupation of Kuwait.'[27]

3.3. The Review of Claims for the Costs of Monitoring and Assessment

In evaluating the scientific and technical appropriateness of monitoring and assessment activities and assessing the reasonableness of the expenses claimed, the Panel was assisted by a multi-disciplinary team of expert consultants retained by the Commission,[28] in fields such as chemistry; toxicology; biology (including microbiology, marine biology, biological oceanography, marine zoology and plant pathology); medicine; epidemiology; environmental, ecological and natural resource economics; geology (including geochemistry, hydrology, geo-ecology); atmospheric sciences; oil spill assessment and response; rangeland management and accounting. The expert consultants prepared professional judgement reports on all the monitoring and assessment activities for which compensation was sought,

[25] *Ibid*, paras 33–34.
[26] *Ibid*, para 35.
[27] *Ibid*, para 31.
[28] Pursuant to Art 36 and 38 of the Rules; see n 4 above.

including their opinion regarding the appropriateness of the activity by reference to generally accepted scientific criteria, standards and methodologies, as well as their evaluation of the reasonableness of the costs claimed, having regard to the results likely to be produced. Where appropriate, the expert consultants suggested modifications to the proposed activities or adjustments to the cost estimates made by the claimant.[29] In addition, the Panel requested information from a number of international organisations on issues relevant to the claims, including compensation for oil pollution damage; air quality monitoring and modelling; hydrogeology and groundwater pollution; soil remediation techniques; public health and epidemiology; and environmental and ecological economics.[30]

The panel's report is replete with examples of claims for monitoring and assessment that it rejected for various reasons. In one claim,[31] the claimant sought compensation for a study to determine damage that may have been caused to unexcavated archaeological sites in the southern part of its territory by pollutants from the oil fires in Kuwait. The Panel found that the study did not constitute reasonable monitoring and assessment because, in its opinion, the unexcavated sites were likely to have had significantly less, if any, exposure to airborne pollutants from the oil fires than outdoor or indoor cultural heritage materials. The claimant had also developed neither a methodology for the study nor a procedure for selecting sites for damage assessment and unaffected control sites. In another claim,[32] the claimant sought compensation for a project to assess the susceptibility of museums and archaeological sites to sudden increases of pollutants and to develop strategies for air pollution control in museums and repositories on its territory, stating that the purpose of the project was to prepare a blueprint for measures to protect and preserve historic cultural objects from future pollution. The Panel considered that the project was intended to establish a system to prevent future damage, rather than to evaluate or abate harm that may have been caused as a result of Iraq's invasion and occupation of Kuwait. Similarly, the Panel rejected a claim for the costs of a study that would isolate a number of bacteria from the Persian Gulf, genetically modify them and release them into its marine environment to assist biodegradation of any remaining hydrocarbons and tarballs, because, in addition to concerns based on the precautionary principle about the effects of releasing such organisms into the environment, the relevant scientific literature demonstrated that bacterial biodegradation of oil would be of lesser or limited effect

[29] Where the Panel found that modifications to monitoring and assessment activities were necessary or desirable, it provided details of those modifications, which are set out in the report and in the technical annexes thereto; see pages 128–80 of the Report, above n 20.
[30] *Ibid*, paras 42–48.
[31] *Ibid*, paras 99–101.
[32] *Ibid*, paras 103–5.

given the period of time that had elapsed since the oil spill that resulted from Iraq's invasion and occupation of Kuwait a decade earlier.[33] Other claims were rejected because the scientific literature suggested that the activities that were the subject of the claims would not produce the desired results,[34] or where the information sought by the activity was already available in the scientific literature.[35] The Panel also declined to recommend compensation for the costs of studies to assess the loss of recreational use of parts of the claimants' territory such as beaches,[36] sport fishing[37] and desert camping opportunities[38] on the basis that the potential usefulness of such studies had not been demonstrated and because the passage of time and high turnover rates of the expatriate communities in the relevant areas would make it difficult to obtain reliable data from the interviews proposed by the claimants more than 10 years after the invasion and occupation of Kuwait. Furthermore, the possibility that changes in recreational beach use patterns might be due to other factors would raise questions about the validity of any results obtained from the study. Costs of projects that would duplicate the work to be undertaken in other monitoring and assessment claims of the same claimant were also rejected, as the Panel required that projects be cost-effective.[39] Finally, the Panel determined that costs relating to damage caused by claims that are not admissible are not compensable.[40]

4. OTHER INTERNATIONAL PRACTICE ON THE RECOVERY OF THE COSTS OF MONITORING AND ASSESSMENT

A cursory overview of international and national practice, mainly in the context of civil rather than State liability, indicates that the provision of

[33] *Ibid*, 169–72. See also paras 266–71.
[34] *Ibid*, paras 174–77 (study on the use of Persian Gulf algae and cyanobacteria as a tool for bioremediation of marine ecosystems where the available evidence suggested that photosynthetic organisms do not have any significant ability to degrade petroleum hydrocarbons); paras 205–8 (study on the use of aquatic fungi for biodegradation of oil in wetland and coastal regions where the literature showed that the contribution of fungi to petroleum degradation in marine ecosystems was 'virtually zero').
[35] *Ibid*, paras 234–37.
[36] *Ibid*, paras 444–47.
[37] *Ibid*, paras 448–50.
[38] *Ibid*, paras 488–93. Iraq had argued in response to this claim that camping activities are a 'personal matter', and that, although they may affect some people economically, they have no relation to environmental problems. Iraq further pointed out that camping itself is an activity that usually results in deterioration of the environment.
[39] *Ibid*, paras 580–83.
[40] *Ibid*, para 346. However, expenses to determine the areas affected by operations of Jordanian military personnel and equipment are not eligible for compensation because, pursuant to para 34(a) of Governing Council decision 7, damage caused by military activities is only compensable if it results from 'military operations or threat of military action by either side'.

compensation for the costs of monitoring and assessment of environmental damage as a separate independent head of loss in international law is not unique. It has been written that:

> in order to claim for the costs of measures of reinstatement it will usually be necessary to determine whether an injury has been caused to natural resources and whether it is possible and necessary to take measures to reinstate the damaged environment. The costs of these often expensive and time-consuming studies are recoverable on the condition that the studies are necessary and useful for establishing the precise nature and extent of the damage and the need for restoration.[41]

As has been demonstrated in the preceding section, these are much the same considerations upon which the F4 panel of commissioners proceeded when dealing with sub-paragraphs 35(c) and (d) of Decision 7.

One treaty regime that provides for such recovery is that set up by the 1969 International Convention on Civil Liability for Oil Pollution Damage, the 1971 International Convention on the Establishment of an International Fund for Compensation of Oil Pollution Damage and the 1992 Protocols to both Conventions.[42] The 1969 Convention establishes a system of strict liability for shipowners with respect to pollution resulting from oil escaping from laden tankers, and provides for a system of compulsory insurance,[43] while the 1971 Convention sets up a system to indemnify victims of oil pollution damage if they are unable to obtain full compensation under the 1969 Convention, with payments made out of the International Oil Pollution Compensation Fund (the IOPC Fund). Under this regime, claims for the costs of monitoring and assessment are compensable.[44] The studies must be necessary and useful for determining the nature and extent of the damage, must be a direct consequence of the relevant oil spill, must

The E2 Panel found that, 'to find a threat of military action by Iraq outside Iraq or Kuwait for the purpose of establishing the Commission's jurisdiction over a claim based on that threat ... a specific threat by Iraq must have been directed at that location ... [and] ... the target of that threat, if any, must have been within the range of Iraq's military reach' (S/AC.26/1996/6, para 68). The F2 Panel noted that 'military operations did not take place within the land territory of Jordan. Nor was that land territory the subject of an Iraqi threat of military action, even though it was within the range of Iraqi military reach' (Report and Recommendations Made by the Panel of Commissioners Concerning the First Instalment of F2 Claims, S/AC.26/1999/23, para 25). Moreover, Jordan has provided no evidence that its territory was the subject of military action or the threat of military action from Iraq. Accordingly, this portion of the claim was not compensable.

41 E H P Brans, *Liability for Damage to Public Natural Resources* (The Hague, 2001), p 354.

42 For the 1969 and 1971 Conventions, see *International Legal Materials*, vol 9 (1970), p 45 and vol 11, p 284; for the Protocols, see *International Transport Treaties, Supplement* 17 (1993), I–459 and I–476. See also, generally, the discussion in Brans, *ibid*, pp 354–55.

43 See the 1969 Convention, Arts III and VII.

44 FUND/WGR.7/10, p 7 (1994).

not be speculative or general and must contribute to the submission of admissible claims.[45] As seen above, all these requirements exist in the case of the Commission.[46] Similarly, the voluntary regime set up by the Contract Regarding a Supplement to Tanker Liability for Oil Pollution[47]—which was adopted by tanker owners and the oil industry following the *Torre Canyon* incident in 1967 and which came to an end in 1997—compensated the costs of environmental studies, provided that these studies were authorised by, and were designed to assist in, the quantification or the verification of oil pollution damage.[48] Similarly, Annex III to the EC White Paper on Environmental Liability (2000) concludes that:

> the measure of damages under the proposed EU liability regime as regards natural resource damage should be the cost of restoring, rehabilitating, replacing, or acquiring the equivalent of the damaged natural resources, including compensation of interim losses and reasonable costs of assessing damage.[49]

Evidence of recognition of liability for the costs of monitoring and assessment also exists at the domestic level. Under US law, the Oil Pollution Act[50] and the Comprehensive Environmental Response, Compensation and Liability Act[51] make provision for the recovery by trustees of the reasonable costs of monitoring and assessment and of devising appropriate remediation measures. It is also noteworthy that the party responsible for the damage is liable for these costs even where the trustees decide not to proceed with restoration measures.[52] However, in order for these claims to be

[45] FUND/A.17/23 (1994).
[46] See above section 3. Unlike the Commission, however, the position taken under the oil pollution regime was not to compensate where environmental impact assessment studies showed no evidence of environmental impact, or where they showed environmental impact that could not be repaired for technical or financial reasons. This was the case even where, as in the Sea Empress incident, the results of the study were considered by the relevant Evaluation Committee to be important. Following the objections raised by some States, based inter alia on the consideration that the polluter, rather than the taxpayer, should pay for such studies where they are 'properly designed and co-ordinated' and are 'in proportion to the severity of the pollution and the predictable effects', the Fund decided to modify its position and consider each claim on its own merits rather than automatically reject them where no evidence of recoverable damage is revealed (92 FUND/A.2/27 (1998). As Brans (above n 41) points out, the decision is not a model of clarity; but it brings the practice under this regime closer to that of the Commission in not making compensability conditional upon the outcome of the study, and suggests independent status for monitoring and assessment claims.
[47] See *International Legal Materials*, vol 10 (1971), p 137.
[48] See further J Bates and C Benson, *Marine Environmental Law* (New York, 1993), sections 4.90–4.111, esp 4.108.
[49] COM(2000) 66 FINAL, 9 Feb 2000, Annex 3, p 48.
[50] 33 USC ss 2701–61, at s 2706(C).
[51] 42 USC ss 9601–75, at s 9607 (C).
[52] 61 Fed Reg 1996, p 447.

compensable, the US Department of the Interior's regulations on Natural Resource Damage Assessment require that (1):

> the anticipated increment of extra benefits in terms of the precision or accuracy of estimates obtained by using a more costly ... methodology are greater than the anticipated increment of extra costs of that methodology

and (2) the anticipated cost of the assessment is expected to be less than the anticipated damage amount.[53] In the Netherlands, Article 6:96(2) BW of the Dutch Civil Code allows recovery for the reasonable costs of monitoring and assessment, which may include the cost of hiring experts to investigate the extent of the damage and, significantly for present purposes, to collect evidence to substantiate the plaintiff's case, as well as to cover the plaintiff's own administrative costs.[54] Perhaps more interesting than this handful of illustrative rules is the basis for treating claims for monitoring and assessment as independent heads of loss, and it is to this that we now turn.

5. THE RATIONALE FOR CLASSIFICATION OF CLAIMS FOR MONITORING AND ASSESSMENT AS AN INDEPENDENT HEAD OF LOSS

It is important to remember that the Commission is primarily a political organ that performs an essentially fact-finding function.[55] As mentioned above, the 'F4' panel of commissioners has found monitoring and assessment activities to be important and useful for the discharge of its duties;[56] in fact it could be argued that without these studies, the ability of the Commission to fulfil its mandate under paragraph 16 of Security Council resolution 687—to provide compensation for environmental damage and the depletion of natural resources—would be impaired. It was also mentioned earlier that it will always be necessary to conduct injury assessment studies in order to determine the nature and extent of the injury, to establish causation and to determine the necessity of restoration measures and thus the quantum of damages (given that the cost of restoration measures is often essential for assessment of the quantum of damages).[57]

[53] In *Ohio v US Department of the Interior*, 880 F 2d 432 (1999), some States, environmental groups and industry bodies challenged, unsuccessfully, the requirement that the anticipated damage amount be greater than the anticipated cost of the assessment. See the Report of the Working Group of Experts on Liability and Compensation for Environmental Damage arising from Military Activities, UNEP/Env.Law/3/Inf.1, 15 Oct 1996, esp the Introductory note by the Rapporteur, pp 1–32.
[54] Discussed in Brans, above n 41, p 259.
[55] See above section 2.3.
[56] See above section 3.
[57] See, eg, above section 3.

In order to shed more light on the nature of monitoring and assessment costs, it is worth comparing them with other related costs, namely (i) technical fact-finding missions and (ii) costs awarded to a successful party in litigation or arbitration. With regard to the former, such missions are often sent, at the instruction of the panels of commissioners, to conduct on-site inspections at relevant sites when considered necessary or useful for the panel's review of the claims.[58] The costs of such inspections, which are important for the fulfilment of the Commission's mandate, are met from the Compensation Fund, as are the costs of the successful claims for monitoring and assessment of environmental damage, and these two kinds of fact-finding expenses are similar in that they are intended to assist the *panel* in its review of the claims. However, it could be argued that there is a significant difference between them, in that fact-finding missions are undertaken by the Commission at the instruction of the *panel*, while the monitoring and assessment activities are undertaken by the *claimants*. So can it be said that the real reason for compensating claimants for monitoring and assessment costs is to assist the claimants in presenting and preparing their claims? It will be recalled that the F4 panel referred to the benefits to the claimants of providing funds for monitoring and assessment,[59] which would suggest an affirmative answer to this question. If so, it could then be argued that (i) the real similarity is not between fact-finding missions on the one hand, and monitoring and assessment costs on the other; rather (ii) it is between the liability for the costs of monitoring and assessment and the liability for the costs of a claimant in preparing and presenting its claim, and that (iii) the justification for compensating claimants for the costs of monitoring and assessment is the same as that for the award of the costs to a successful party in normal litigation or arbitral proceedings.[60]

However, this similarity is superficial. In the first place, the Commission does not conceive of compensation for the costs of monitoring and assessment as being akin to costs awarded to the successful party in third-party proceedings. While the costs of monitoring and assessment are provided for as separate heads of loss in paragraph 35 of Decision 7,[61] the costs of claim presentation and preparation will be the subject of a specific decision of the

[58] Pursuant to Art 36 of the Rules (above n 4). See, eg, Report and Recommendations made by the Panels of Commissioners Concerning the Sixth Instalment of E1 Claims (S/AC.26/2001/16; oil sector corporate claims), para 13; Report and Recommendations made by the Panels of Commissioners Concerning the First Instalment of F3 Claims (S/AC.26/1999/24; Kuwaiti Government claims), para 15; Report and Recommendations made by the Panels of Commissioners Concerning the Third Instalment of F2 Claims (S/AC.26/2002/7; Saudi Arabian Government Claims), para 12.

[59] See above nn 21–22 and accompanying text.

[60] See, eg, A Redfern and M Hunter, *Law and Practice of International Commercial Arbitration*, 3rd edn (London, 1999), pp 405–9.

[61] See n 3 above.

Governing Council of the Commission. For example, the Governments of Kuwait and Saudi Arabia—which submitted monitoring and assessment claims and have been awarded some of the amounts they claimed therefor—have not been awarded compensation for claims relating to preparation costs for their other non-environmental claims.[62] This accords with the argument made in this paper as to the independent nature of liability for the costs of monitoring and assessment. Also, unlike the position in different fora regarding the award of costs, the final outcome of the claim for actual environmental damage does not determine the compensability of monitoring and assessment costs.[63]

It appears that the better view is to consider liability for the costs of monitoring and assessment as a *sui generis* head of loss, one that is peculiar to claims for environmental damage, regardless of any similarities that may exist with other kinds of compensation. Particularly in the case of a fact-finding body such as the Commission, where the liability of the polluter in principle has been established, the identity of the party that presents the necessary information upon which the review of the claims is to be based is of less significance. It is more important, and in many cases more cost-effective, to have the affected States play a central role in this regard; the information they provide is still subject to assessment by the panel of commissioners assisted by experts.[64]

But perhaps the ultimate justification for having the costs of monitoring and assessment as an independent head of liability is, then, that it facilitates the task of reinstating the environment where the prime concern is its restoration in the public interest, rather than the mere settling of a dispute or series of disputes in a bilateral/adversarial context. The aim is not merely to compensate the claimants for injury suffered, but rather to restore the environment. This is further borne out by the Governing Council's establishment of a procedure to ensure that the awards made to successful claimants for the costs of monitoring and assessment activities are spent solely on the monitoring and assessment of environmental damage. Paragraph 6 of Governing Council Decision 132 provides that:

> to ensure that funds are spent on conducting the environmental monitoring and assessment activities in a transparent and appropriate manner and that the funded projects remain reasonable monitoring and assessment activities, the 'F4' panel of commissioners is requested to issue procedural orders directing claimant Governments to submit periodic progress reports concerning the environmental monitoring and assessment projects to the panel. The panel,

[62] See, eg, S/AC.26/1999/24, above n 58, paras 497–500; S/AC.26/2002/7, above n 58, paras 176–77.
[63] See section 3.2 above.
[64] See n 21 above.

> through the Executive Secretary, will therefore keep the Governing Council informed of such progress reports for any appropriate action that may be required.[65]

Such an approach, which is concerned primarily with the restoration of the environment, goes some way to avoiding some of the often-noted inadequacies of traditional State responsibility, which is for the most part bilateral in nature, in dealing with environmental matters. This approach would seem to place the environment first by attaching such importance to the availability of relevant information that—as stated clearly in sub-paragraphs 35(c) and (d) of Governing Council Decision 7—is aimed at both 'evaluating and abating the harm and restoring the environment' and 'the investigation and combating [of] increased health risks as a result of the environmental damage'.[66] In this respect, the Commission can be considered to have made a contribution to the progressive development of the law regarding liability for environmental damage by recognising such costs as an independent head of liability.

[65] See n 20 above.
[66] See Brans, above n 41, p 414, noting the welcome trend from litigation to co-operation in US law, and the benefits that come with such an approach. He also proposes that 'given the complexity of the issues involved, it should be considered to set up regional damage assessment centres with experts that are able to support the claimants—public authorities and non-governmental organisations—in filing their claims'.

www.ingramcontent.com/pod-product-compliance
Ingram Content Group UK Ltd.
Pitfield, Milton Keynes, MK11 3LW, UK
UKHW020808290926
15470UKWH00003B/1020